CAUGHT IN THE MIDDLE

Reading and Writing in the Transition Years

DAVID BOOTH

TEACHER COORDINATORS:

Jane Paterson, Tania Sterling,
Amy Robinson, John Myers

Pembroke Publishers Limited

In memory of Cathy Costello, teacher extraordinaire

© 2011 Pembroke Publishers
538 Hood Road
Markham, Ontario, Canada L3R 3K9
www.pembrokepublishers.com

Distributed in the U.S. by Stenhouse Publishers
480 Congress Street
Portland, ME 04101
www.stenhouse.com

We acknowledge the financial support of the Government of Canada through the Book Publishing Industry Development Program (BPIDP) for our publishing activities.

We acknowledge the assistance of the Government of Ontario through the Ontario Media Development Corporation's Ontario Book Initiative.

Library and Archives Canada Cataloguing in Publication

Booth, David
    Caught in the middle : reading and writing in the transition years / David Booth. — 2nd ed.

Includes bibliographical references and index.
Issued also in electronic format.
ISBN 978-1-55138-265-4

    1. Reading (Middle school). 2. English language — Composition and exercises — Study and teaching (Middle school). I. Title.

LB1632.B66 2011   428.4071'2   C2011-904791-8

eBook format ISBN 978-1-55138-830-4

Editor: Kate Revington
Cover Design: John Zehethofer
Typesetting: JayTee Graphics Ltd.

Printed and bound in Canada
9 8 7 6 5 4 3 2 1

MIX
Paper from
responsible sources
FSC® C004071

Contents

Preface

Welcome to our project *Caught in the Middle: Reading and Writing in the Transition Years.*

It has been over 10 years since my earlier book on the subject, *Reading and Writing in the Middle Years*, was published, and much has changed both inside and outside school, especially in the field of literacy — reading, writing, media, and speaking and listening. Just consider the impact of technology on the literacy practices of everybody — students, teachers, and parents. More books are sold online by Amazon.com than in paperback. Many schools are full of computer labs and/or laptops, SMART Boards, digital cameras, blogs, and glogs. The world is now one globe educationally, and students can have access through the Internet to people, places, and information from international sources.

A teacher in New York once asked me, "How do you get to be good?" Her eyes were full of tears, and all I could answer was, "Hang around good people." That is what I have done throughout my professional life, which includes teaching in a senior elementary school system for 10 years. I can remember the names of the team of teachers working with the middle-years students during those years, and, from my memories of and my experiences working with them, I know they were all excellent professionals who had the interests of the students at heart. At our team meetings held every other week, we worked out common themes to be explored with the students, we shared curriculum ideas and student information, and we ate lunch together, still a viable mode of building a collaborative team of professionals.

While we developed a solid program for 640 middle-school students, we benefited from having Wayne Heacock as librarian. Wayne built and stocked an amazing library in one year. (Imagine what he would have done with today's technology.) Hurray for those teachers from 50 years ago: John, Robert, Bob, Barbara, Audrey, Arlene, Bill, Esther, Don, Bea, Roy, Bruce, Dawn, and Ted.

Then, working for three decades at a faculty of education kept me inside the teaching circle, with new teachers and associate teachers in the schools sharing strategies and resources, as schools changed and morphed into the new world.

We need to ask ourselves, How will all this change the literacy goals for schools educating students for the 21st century? The teachers who have contributed to this book offer many insightful suggestions for preparing middle-school students for the future, and we can explore with them the new information, strategies, and tools that can help transform our classrooms into spaces for learning about and participating in the world of literacy, with all the modes and forms and functions our students will confront as they build their literate lives.

This book, then, grew alongside a group of teachers who work with young adolescents. These teachers took the time to discuss and demonstrate their teaching with me, and to brainstorm, rethink, reflect on, and articulate their programs, their dreams for their students, their continuing growth as professionals, and the challenges they face in helping youngsters who are caught in the middle of developing into literate citizens. The contributors to this collective text have shared examples of their teaching philosophies and practice that reveal the excitement and satisfaction of growing as professionals in teaching. Several worked in small teams to outline their ways of being with young adolescents as they engage and encourage them into deeper literacy learning.

As you read through this book, you will meet fine educators and their students, and you may find yourself rethinking your own practice, recognizing events and experiences that resonate with your own teaching life, and surprising yourself into changing and modifying your classroom behaviors and perhaps, intentions. The voices of these educators are found in Part B of this book, where you will discover authentic classroom experiences that bring to life the thoughts about literacy that I discuss in Part A.

All of us will continue to grow professionally by being together in the conversation, freed from judgmental fears, open to finding out what seems to work best with youngsters, listening to our colleagues down the hall and on screen, ready to try out new strategies, and fascinated by the assessing processes that occur all the time and that influence and direct the next phases of our work. Never a dull moment in a middle-school classroom, and aren't we lucky to be in the middle of the whirlwind?

Acknowledgments

I want to thank the teachers who contributed their insights and suggestions to this book. I know that their colleagues teaching students caught in the middle will be grateful.

My special thanks go to Maria Martella of TINLIDS, to Shelley Stagg Peterson of the Ontario Institute for Studies in Education, and to Janice Reynolds, the Lead teacher for Library in the Elementary Schools for the Near North Board of Education, for their help with suggestions for classroom resources.

PART A

Towards a Literate Future

1

In the Classroom: Student Engagement, Teacher Support

For the purposes of this book, the *middle years* include pre-adolescent and young adolescent students who are developing their own interests as readers and expanding their personal abilities as writers. They may be in schools that are organized in a variety of ways: Kindergarten to Grade 8, Grades 6 to 8, Grades 7 and 8, or Grades 7 to 9. Of course, these students will be in different stages of development while placed in one classroom, caught between childhood and adolescence. Some are avid voluntary readers while others are struggling; some write easily with a good command of transcription skills while others lack confidence to put pencil to paper or cursor to screen. Some speak up in discussions about novels, eager to share their responses, while others draw back and remain silent. Most want to work independently, manage their own learning, and follow their own interests. As they try to find their own voices, they are discovering the complexities of relationships and the tentative nature of their roles in a middle-school community.

We are right in the middle of things and eager to find our voices.

Tina Benevides teaches Literacy and Psychology at Nipissing University. She is completing her Ph.D., examining the role of technology on the literacy development of middle-years students.

According to Tina Benevides, of Nipissing University, we can observe many of the following features and qualities in these young adolescents.

Qualities of Adolescents

The lives of middle-years students are changing every day, something that is reflected in their *literacy* lives, both their manners and attitudes, and in the content of what they say, read, and write. Family patterns are altering. Young people are becoming more critical of parents, adults in authority, and siblings; they depend more and more on peer groups, and have celebrities, sport heroes, and friends as role models. Establishing an identity becomes the most significant task of adolescences, and they begin to integrate the opinions of influential people in their lives — parents, friends, and teachers — into their own beliefs.

Future careers are talked about, and they start to look forward to their own independence, testing their own positions at every stage.

Many are developing a sense of history and of their place in society; they are becoming concerned with justice and the unfair treatment of minority groups. They may have a justice orientation and tend to see issues in "black and white," allowing little room for error, evidencing extreme idealism, becoming very cause oriented. Some believe that they are invincible — "It can't happen to me."

Their physical development is a central factor influencing their lives, relationships, and identities. Boys experience growth spurts about two years later than girls, something that may encourage separation between boys and girls. Neurological changes allow young adolescents to begin to develop metacognition — the ability to think about their thinking; they also allow them to increase their ability to examine symbolic or abstract ideas or concepts, and advanced reasoning skills. Middle-years students are able to think about multiple options, possibilities, and hypothetical situations, and are able to consider concepts such as faith and spirituality. They generally prefer active over passive learning activities and enjoy working with their peers.

Middle-years students may experience increased sensitivity to popularity and appearance, becoming more sensitive about weight, gender changes, or about their skin (acne), hair, or teeth (braces). They experience increased identification with peers and have an increased need for their acceptance and approval. Therefore, adolescents spend more time with friends than their families.

So, what will we develop as an excellent literacy education for all of these students in our schools right now? How will we ensure that they will be ready to make their way successfully into secondary school and beyond? A tall order, so let's begin by exploring what is expected of these students and how teachers can work with them to achieve these expectations.

Great Expectations

Students in the middle years are expected to read and write independently and more often, to read longer and more difficult texts in a variety of curriculum areas, to read faster and more selectively, to write coherently with their own voices, to remember more information, to make integrated connections with the curriculum, and to explore the various modes and uses of technology.

Yet there are new words, terms, and content to learn in all of the different subject areas, and some of the texts teachers are using may be outdated, inaccessible, or unclear. Readers of widely differing abilities may be expected to read the same resources with few support structures. There may be little technological support, such as computers or adaptive technology; still, schools and districts are finding ways of transitioning into the 21st century, and more and more teachers are incorporating the New Literacies into the daily work of the classroom.

Fortunately, all of us can build our programs around our students' voices, so that they are engaged in and contributing to their own learning through talking, responding to reading, writing about their lives, researching significant inquiries, and presenting their discoveries to one another. We want to encourage students in these middle-years classrooms to work responsibly together as a community. If we negotiate with them how to explore the curriculum as language learners, we can observe from the inside out how each student learns best and select our strategies carefully, so that young people do not waste their time attending to what they already know or pretending they understand what they do not.

Voice is an important component in the formation of an individual's identity or self-image, and efforts to focus learners on developing their own authentic voice can help them to develop confidence in their own capacities, to realize their own potential, to maximize their abilities, and to take a self-determined path of personal growth. We can listen to them, value their contributions, and prompt them into discovering more about themselves and their world.

When accompanied by effective social and emotional learning that creates a safe space where all participants are respected, student voice increases student engagement and promotes a willingness to take part in classroom activities or school activities as a whole. This welcoming atmosphere is especially important when dealing with the relatively sensitive issues that powerful and relevant texts tend to elicit. Students may not feel that they can move on to discuss their thoughts and feelings, or to question texts, until trust in the relationship with the teacher has been built and a welcoming climate created. Building a sense of membership in a community helps students overcome anxiety and gain positive self-efficacy; it also enhances learning and understanding. Perhaps then students can sustain their involvement in all types of learning activities, demonstrate positive attitudes towards school life, and become enthusiastic, optimistic, curious, and interested participants in their own growth. As teachers, we dream big, and we do our best to honor each of our students.

A dynamic interplay

Young people develop their thinking abilities and social dispositions by interacting with peers, other youngsters, adults, and their environment. The relationship between the teacher, the student, and the other learners becomes an integral part of the interplay in the classroom. This dynamic interaction helps our students develop an awareness of other viewpoints as they examine their own beliefs, standards, and values, increasing their ability to reflect on their own attitudes and behaviors and perhaps, alter their own thoughts about life. Students construct understandings together that would not be possible alone and, we hope, are better able to learn about and respect the uniqueness of others.

Relationships with friends, classmates, and teachers help students to cope with the sometimes rigorous demands of a mainstream literacy classroom. Collaboration among learners takes advantage of Vygotsky's zone of proximal development, where learners are challenged to achieve challenges slightly above their current level of development. Through working with other students who have different strengths and experiences, learners can extend their learning. Students with different skills and backgrounds collaborate in tasks and discussions and thereby arrive at a shared understanding. Through working with peers and building a sense of belonging, students are more likely to be able to bridge the distance between their developmental and experiential levels.

Learning needs to become an active process, where students make discoveries, developing their skills at prediction and intuitive thinking; where they can select tasks that are challenging, initiate activities, exert intense concentration, and expend great effort. Teacher development advocates encourage teachers to actively acknowledge student voice in decision-making power. Students can gain access to information and resources for making effective decisions, have a range of choices, develop an ability to exercise assertiveness in collective decision-making, increase positive thinking on the ability to make change, learn skills for improving personal or group power, change others' perceptions by democratic means and involvement in the growth process, increase their positive self-image, and begin to understand how to sort out right and wrong, important processes in the middle years.

More and more researchers, institutions, and support organizations worldwide advocate for the inclusion of students in school reform efforts. They see the

---

I liked the slogan on the T-shirts of the student helpers at a conference I attended: *How can I help you*? Not a bad mission statement for this book.

Community Building Through Drumming

Peter Stratford supports community building through his physical education program for all divisions at Hawthorne Village Public School. He incorporates literacy and physical activity through Drum2BFit. His interactive and engaging program uses upbeat music as the students drum on fitness balls for a great workout for both the body and the mind. By linking expectations from music, language, and physical education, Peter feels that teachers can provide students with multiple opportunities to reinforce and demonstrate their knowledge and skills in a range of settings. For example, students can act out favorite fairy tales such as "Snow White and the Seven Dwarfs." Each dwarf has a different sound, and students, through their drumming, can help tell the story as it is read aloud.

inclusion of voices of youth as a vital element, an essential component of effective school change. It is not enough for young people to simply listen; we have an obligation to include students in meaningful, interactive practice.

When students feel the liberation that comes from having a say in what they read and write, and what they interpret and construct, they have a stake in creating and maintaining a classroom that stimulates and supports deep learning. At the same time, the teacher is freed to concentrate on how to best guide, inform, and strengthen their abilities. Students can gain a sense of ownership of their school lives and, of course, of the responsibility that accompanies it.

A Grade 9 student expresses his thoughts about learning.

The Most Important Thing I Have Learned About Learning

I have learned a lot over the past few years about what makes school a successful experience for students, especially those who struggle academically. I have learned that teachers need to be explicit in teaching students what works and what does not work for them. I have learned that giving students' choice in the ways in which they demonstrate their understanding is important. Integrating Ministry-provided technology into lessons and ensuring that students use it daily can be the difference between an engaged student and a disengaged one. In Grades 7 and 8, teachers expect us to be able to advocate for ourselves — this skill needs to be taught.

But the most important thing that I have learned is that every student needs to feel part of the class. Education has and will continue to move forward, technology will advance, and expectations will change, but one thing will remain the same: students' engagement and success depend on a teacher's ability to see them for who they are.

— *Matthew Cote*

We work together in our class, supporting one another as literacy partners.

In this complicated world, you as teacher have never been more necessary. You know about the reading and writing processes; you have knowledge about how language works, what elements of craft authors use, and what pitfalls young students face. You know how to locate books that can lead to deeper thought, how technology supports reading and writing, researching and presenting. Sometimes, you will tell your students things they need to know, but balance those times by working alongside them, encouraging them in their beginning efforts, nudging them into richer meaning making, dialoguing with them about their ideas and their research, reflecting on and possibly illuminating their expanding worlds.

We need to engage our students in both intensive and extensive literacy activities. Doing so will enable them to expand and refine their ability to use language appropriately and effectively, and increase their knowledge about how oral and written communication works. In *When Writers Read*, Jane Hansen says that students must read as writers and write as readers, going beyond the doing of the activity to a reflective awareness of all the different aspects of making meaning.

Literacy teaching is about honoring each student's potential as a developing speaker, reader, and writer.

In *The Courage to Teach,* Parker Palmer sums up this approach to teaching with these principles:

> A desire to help my students build a bridge between the academic text and their own lives and a strategic approach for doing so;
>
> A respect for my students' stories that is no more or less than my respect for the scholarly texts I assigned to them;
>
> An aptitude for asking good questions and listening carefully to my students' responses — not only to what they say but also to what they leave unsaid. (p. 82)

More than 40 years ago, noted educator James Moffett said that we need to make the solitary acts of reading and writing *socially constructed events* if we want to promote literacy development in young people. The "peer group imperative" demonstrated every day by our students may be our greatest classroom asset. There is such satisfaction in watching developing readers enter a discussion with a group about a shared selection, as they begin to notice how they create meaning, to wrestle with ideas, to prove a point by reading a portion of the text, to ask questions about the comments of group members, to draw inferences from the discussion and the words on the page, and to gain insights from their own experiences with print. They are constructing meaning together, making sense of their responses to what they have read and heard, mediated by the ideas and feelings of group members. Suddenly, reading has become an interactive process, a socially constructed learning experience. All members of the class, including us as teachers, are part of the classroom community of readers and writers.

Strengthening a Community of Literacy Partners

One way to strengthen the literacy community is to gather the students together each day to share in different literacy events, explore common units, demonstrate strategies, and support one another's work. We often read independently, but our power as literate humans is acquired from the connections we make to the responses and comments of other members of the larger community.

We want to build a classroom community that encourages the development of an atmosphere of co-operation and respect. Language arts offer a context for these classroom sessions, as we need a forum for sharing the many facets of literacy.

Effective teachers have always supported students with individual needs, abilities, and interests, but there is much that is good about working with the whole class some of the time. I think a viable classroom program includes the following:
- discussions of the issues that arise from reading and research, planning of the week's schedule, modelling of strategy use (e.g., how to question a text or to explore differing perceptions)
- introduction and exploration of whole-class units built around themes and genres that offer unique chances to observe students in a large-group setting (their level of participation, their ability to follow a discussion, their ability to raise relevant issues, and their use of strategies for understanding), as well as their participation in reading and writing workshops that expand and deepen a unit

Modelling Our Own Literacy

As teachers, we are wise to model our own literacy with our students as often as possible. We all remember a teacher who read us a letter she had received or a newspaper editorial about an issue he cared deeply about, who showed us the novel she was reading or the information books he had found about his hobby. My high-school algebra teacher would try to solve the math puzzle from the morning newspaper on the chalkboard before our class began. He loved his discipline and told stories of how he used it as a fighter pilot during the Second World War. I remember him 50 years later.

- mini-lessons and demonstrations by the teacher; seminars with the teacher and students who are sharing information and ideas; and book talks featuring new resources
- drama lessons built around significant themes and issues, presentations by students who have important work to share
- films and guests in the room and on Skype
- time for reflecting in notebooks or journals

We need to incorporate all kinds of physical and timetable arrangements that benefit as many students as possible and as often as possible.

As teachers, we participate in the literacy events of the classroom, sometimes reading to the whole class, or leading them in song, showing videos, and using the SMART Board to demonstrate and share strategies. But even during those collaborative events, we observe the students — their behaviors, their attitudes, their individual focusing abilities — so that we can assess and organize future literacy events that will support them into learning.

Reading Aloud to Students

One of the most enjoyable tasks in my career has been to read aloud to students all over the world, in classrooms, libraries, auditoriums, cafeterias, wherever we can gather together. It is a time-honored activity, and watching the faces of those young people, having again and again the value and power of story affirmed, gives me courage to continue.

I am always on the lookout for sources that will hold young audiences from the beginning page. When we read aloud to our students,
- we model our own respect for and satisfaction in texts
- we demonstrate how proficient readers read, the strategies we use, and our fix-up techniques
- we can choose texts that differ from those our students select, opening up their worlds of cultures and global understanding, and increasing their options for future independent reading, research, and writing
- we provide models of writing so that student writers can borrow and absorb the components of the writer's craft
- we let students consider and respond to the issues and ideas, the characters and conflicts in the text, freed from their print struggles so that they can focus on deep and engrossing higher-level thought
- we provide real reasons for careful, engaged listening

Today, reading aloud to students while they read the same text silently seems a contradiction in teaching outcomes. How can they gain reading strength if they are not meeting reading challenges on their own? Yet many authorities, such as Janet Allen, present insightful reasons for hearing and reading the words silently at the same time, especially for readers having difficulties.

Eliciting responses to a read-aloud

I know that reading is a complex process that requires modelling, and when I engage students in a text that lifts the words from the pages in front of their eyes, the students make connections that might not have happened otherwise. I can use the experience as a source for all kinds of literacy learning, with all types and genres of texts.

Out of the Silence

When I read Mary Rose O'Reilley's book *Radical Presence: Teaching as Contemplative Practice*, I wished I could begin my career in teaching all over again.

O'Reilley presents her process for drawing a class to a close: "Write a moment and gather your thoughts on today's discussion; come to some experience of closure."

Then, after 15 minutes, she asks: "Does anyone wish to speak out of the silence? Share any final thoughts?"

And time and time again, students thank each other, and the room fills with respect because of this gentle closing.

She reminds us that school may be a sacred space for many students, perhaps the only site of reflection in their multimedia-filled culture.

The first time student teachers read aloud to a class, it is a daunting, if not terrifying, experience for them, especially for the young men. But their elation when they discover the children listening and learning moves them on to seek other occasions for sharing texts.

For more information, read *Yellow Brick Roads* by Janet Allen.

Throughout the year, I use my read-aloud time for requiring students to respond by talking together as a community and in small groups. This activity helps them understand how to think and talk about the text we have heard or read. I carefully select the text. It might be a picture book with many layered meanings, a short story or poem, or nonfiction, many samples of which I have clipped from magazines or newspapers, or downloaded from the Internet. I read the selection with as much ability as I can muster and organize different response activities. I structure the response questions the first time or at least set a context for the discussion.

Sometimes I have each group discuss a different aspect of the text, creating a real reason for sharing afterwards. Since students used to ask to see my copy after they had listened to it, in order to confirm or argue different points, I began to make copies of the text available to them, either printing the text or projecting it on a data projector or SMART Board. I recommend working with one group in a Fishbowl demonstration to help students see how text conversations work and what roles should be filled if we are to benefit from a community event.

I often choose a picture book to read aloud, and middle-years students are sometimes uncomfortable with my choices. But today, there are so many fine picture books that work on every level that student ages seem almost irrelevant. The words and images in picture books work together to synthesize a new creation, likely to appeal to today's visually oriented students. The pictures draw the eye and the text catches the imagination. The words can offer powerful language input for students, new and unusual vocabulary, varied syntactic patterns, strong contextual clues for exploring meaning, and characters that struggle with life's problems — sometimes symbolic, sometimes real. Illustrations in picture books run the gamut of styles and techniques — watercolors, woodcuts, lithography, photography, and collage. They illuminate the text; they extend the words into possibilities of meaning; they shock the reader or listener with new interpretations, lifting the student's own experience into different conceptual realms. The old is made new; the new is made relevant.

Demonstrating Literacy Strategies with the Class

When we think out loud during the act of reading, we make the processing of ideas visible to our students, so that they see how we handle a piece of text either as a reader or as a writer. During these brief "think-aloud and show" sessions, we can reveal what we think before we read, while we read, and after we read. When students have opportunities to see our thinking processes in action, they may be able to apply similar strategies in their own work.

You can model and demonstrate your own reading strategies using a think-aloud technique whenever the class needs to understand how a reader handles meaning making with a particular type of text. If once a week you present a 5 to 10 minute demonstration of how you handle a text, at the end of the year, your students would have a repertoire of more than 30 types of texts that can reveal the different strategies proficient readers employ in making meaning. You could also ask students to conduct a think-aloud demonstration once they are aware of the reading strategies they can model.

Only by asking questions that have no ready answers will we ever move forward in any field, including education. If you open your mind to possibilities, this openness will give rise to queries, as we would hope. To make sense of a

. . . We Just Knew That We Were Learning

Years ago, my English consultant Bill Moore would come into my classroom with poems he had prepared and, before he read, he would distribute copies to the students. I can still recall the absolute joy I felt with this ritual: my Grade 8 students would hear powerful words by authors they hadn't met yet, read aloud in a marvellous voice as they followed along with their own copies. Afterwards, Bill would involve them in choral speaking or poetry writing, and when he left, we still had his poems to return to and our own writings to share.

No one ever thought that he was teaching; we just knew that we were learning. He had complete attention from those kids. What greater gifts could there be for a new teacher?

particular text in a demonstration with our students, we must continue to puzzle our way through the literacy maze right in front of their eyes.

Teaching with Explicit Focus

While a demonstration can highlight your own use of strategies as a reader and writer, a mini-lesson can be a brief, focused instructional session that allows you to teach a specific skill or idea in a short, purposeful way.

You can select a topic for a mini-lesson based on your observation of student needs and interests, or by considering the curriculum goals. Different aspects of reading, writing, and thinking strategies as well as tools can be demonstrated using mini-lessons. Mini-lessons focus on topics that are essential for students to learn, such as the routines and procedures for independent reading, or suggestions for revising or editing a composition. They present a frame of reference for what the expectations will be during reading and writing workshops.

Conferring with Student Readers and Writers

Students tell us that one-on-one conferences — times when the teacher focuses on their concerns — have great impact on their school lives. Conferences are essential in developing a community of readers and writers, and should be a part of each school day. Some may last two minutes; others, 20. They should take place in a relaxed atmosphere, where students feel secure and comfortable in expressing their feelings or concerns about what they are reading or writing.

During a conference, we can encourage students to extend their exploration of a text or we can assess and evaluate their writing progress. In addition, our support helps to promote the sharing aspect of reading and writing, and encourages students to feel they are members of a literacy community.

How we participate in these conversations with a student or with a small group of students will often determine the conference's success. We want to engage the students in dialogue, so that we can acquire information about them as readers and writers. We also need to determine whether we should offer specific help or just be supportive of their efforts and accomplishments. We need to confer with each of our students as frequently as possible, either making a brief check-in or having an in-depth conference.

It is important that we encourage students to reflect on their own development as readers and writers, to guide them into becoming aware of their own successes and challenges, so that they can move towards independence as literacy learners.

Differentiating Our Teaching

We differentiate our teaching so that students can differentiate their learning. I hope we can recognize the value in teaching the whole community of students at times *and* the professional satisfaction in varying the interactive formats that effective organization and management can offer us as we support growth in each of our students.

Dichotomies of Teaching

Here are ideas for us as teachers to keep in mind.

My role as a teacher is complex and changing:

I need to lead, but I need to respond.
I need to inform, but I need to listen.
I need to instruct, but I need to collaborate.
I need to evaluate, but I need to teach.
I need to demonstrate, but I need to participate.
I need to organize, but I need to become involved.
I need to manage, but I need to support.
I need to model, but I need to assist.
I need to confer, but I need to observe.
I need to criticize, but I need to appreciate.

I think of all the teachers who find time, opportunities, and ways of supporting those students who need us most, and I celebrate their lives as professionals: they care for all the students in their classrooms, as best they can, with the knowledge they have.

"Mindful teachers learn to yield in the classroom — slow down to pay attention to what is arising, proceed with awareness, and renew the intention to *be with* their students on a daily basis. To enact this professionalism, mindful teachers take up a practice of calming their mind and opening their heart to let go of preconceptions of who students should be, to more readily see students as they are. Teachers learning to stand in their wholeness with compassion may be one of the powerful gifts to students, because it is presence that enables secure relationships in the classroom that in turn nurture students' social and emotional growth, and inspire engagement and learning."
— Dr. Geoffrey Soloway

Twelve things teachers need to do

- to know each of our students: their abilities, their skills, their fears, and their talents
- to assess their individual strengths and challenges, so that we can support and strengthen their learning
- to adapt our lessons, our models of instruction, and our activities to respond to their needs, interests, and learning styles
- to locate resources that offer opportunities for choice by our students
- to find and develop strategies for including all of our students in the teaching/ learning situations, providing choices where possible
- to incorporate new adaptive technologies so that students can find support for their literacy tasks: computers for reading, writing, and researching, and programs that read the print text aloud, that read our writing back to us, that highlight inconsistencies, and that note spelling difficulties
- to scaffold instruction, to make small achievements possible, and to take time to work with those students with different levels of experience
- to organize opportunities for whole-class community building, for small, flexible groups based on need and/or interest, and for individuals to work at their own pace and competence level
- to become reflective teachers, unafraid to change our habits, our behaviors, prepared to search for new ways and different resources to reach our students
- to engage in professional conversations with our colleagues, to participate in workshops, to take courses, to read journals and books, in print and online, about education and young people
- to involve our students in our planning and listen to their voices as we build a sense of ownership for them in their program — they may then be more likely to reveal their concerns and ask for assistance, learning to take charge of their own progress.
- to incorporate assessment into our planning and teaching, through formative and summative assessments, using objectives and/or outcomes, rubrics, benchmarks, and exemplars
  Carol Ann Tomlinson says, "Differentiated instruction is 'response' teaching, . . . and the opportunity to learn in ways that make learning more efficient is also likely to make learning more effective."

We know what we have to achieve, and we are learning how to make it happen.

While evaluation is used when communicating with parents and other educators, assessment, which informs our daily teaching, involves observing students on an ongoing basis, having conferences, making anecdotal records, giving formal and informal tests, and providing opportunities for self-assessment. The outcomes of our assessment procedures allow us to plan programs that reflect each student's current learning and that capitalize on individual strengths in order to develop other areas of growth. We assess so that we can teach more effectively.

Evaluation is made up of the judgments (marks and grades) we make on the basis of our assessment practices. Since the quality of our evaluation reflects our assessment procedures, we need to assess all the different areas of a student's development. For example, we can observe a student read for a period of five minutes and note the book, the strategies used, aspects of the text that appeared to be challenging, and what the student does when difficulties are encountered. Or, we can watch the student for a similar time as she or he selects a book, noting how long the student can read independently and how much movement the student exhibits during the activity.

We need to remember that observation guides and checklists are only indicators of a student's progress. They are most helpful when used several times throughout the year so that trends and progress over the year can be noted. Their value is in the information they can contribute to the overall analysis of a student's growth. Beyond that, observations arising from the checklists can be shared with the students, in order to help them focus on areas that require change.

Formal and informal tests are helpful when they assess learning that is measurable and when they reflect program content. You and the students should view test results as a way to check the effectiveness of the program. If, however, information gleaned from tests does not reflect your ongoing assessment, the testing device may need to be amended or — in a less likely scenario — your ongoing assessment may need to be altered.

Keep in mind that if both the test and the instruction are sound, there are still reasons a student may not perform well on an isolated test. Whether it's a bad night's rest or a problem at home, these factors must be taken into account when discussing test results. We also need to consider that one test for all may not be the most effective measure.

Mock Literacy Test Results

Lynda Marshall, the literacy resource teacher at Widdefield High School, runs a "mock" literacy test each fall with the incoming Grade 9 students. The purpose is to assess their levels of proficiency in reading and writing before the following year's mandatory Grade 10 government test. The information gleaned can help teachers design appropriate programs for the students. By working in partnership with the Grade 8 feeder schools, which are doing an excellent job with the students in different aspects of literacy, teachers can promote literacy growth in the middle years and beyond. Lynda writes:

"The test this year revealed some challenges. The amount of writing the students completed on the Mock test was impressive, but topic development and use of conventions were definitely below level. Some difficulties we can accommodate with extra time, computers, scribes, and so on. The feeder schools do not have a Language Arts class or an English class; therefore, the writing takes place across the curriculum and must be considered literacy in all areas across these disciplines. There is no dedicated time for language, so that language needs to be addressed at all times.

"If the assignment is a reading response, a book report, or chapter questions in geography or history, it is considered a reading event and the piece is not assessed for written conventions — problems for the students' development in literacy can result.

"While the feeder schools do have a Literacy Coach, all teachers must be addressing writing conventions in all grades. At the high-school level, though, this remains a problem. We continue to work with all the staff, but promoting literacy across the curriculum is an ongoing challenge. Some students entering high school have written personal responses, but few language conventions have been addressed. In the

In *Supporting and Sustaining Differentiated Instruction*, Karen Hume offers three guiding principles of differentiation:

1. All activities must address the same learning goals or expectations.
2. All tasks must be marked using the same success criteria, evaluation standards, or rubric.
3. All tasks must be equitable and respectful of all the learners (not limiting one student to always creating a poster because he or she is a weak writer, but finding opportunities to support that student into writing in carefully structured ways).

"If we expect to recruit and retain good principals and teachers in hard-to-staff schools, stop judging them inappropriately by test scores and start listening to educators. Most oppose the current test-based thrust of North American educational policy. Educators want safe working environments, reasonable class sizes, and adequate resources."
— Diane Ravitch, education historian, *New York Times*

middle years, narrative is the text of choice, but when students move from fiction to non-fiction, they need to negotiate and interpret text forms and cues, since informational and graphic texts are the main forms of reading in secondary school.

"As well, students manipulate and negotiate computer pages efficiently, but often do not translate those screen literacy skills to the printed page. We must make that connection with them.

"Opportunities to differentiate are also a growing concern. Differentiated opportunities must include writing in some form, and often when the 'choices' for responding are given, some students seldom choose writing from the list of suggestions.

"The issue of homework needs to be thought through carefully, with guidance provided for spending an hour or so with thoughtful activity."

Self-assessment — for all of us

Knowing that self-assessment will form a part of their overall assessment helps students develop a sense of ownership and an understanding that they can shape the course of their own learning. Their contributions in conferences, journals, portfolios, and discussions are all part of the self-assessment process. Sharing in their assessment helps students recognize what they know, what they need to know, and ways in which they can learn.

In addition to assessing and evaluating students, we also need to assess our teaching programs so that we can check on their ability to meet the goals we set for them. In part, program assessment arises from the progress students make. Given that, we need to ensure that what we do in class, from selecting texts through assessing a student's responses, is sound and valid, and contributes to our students' overall development.

All of us — students and teachers — need to consider our effectiveness, our progress, our sense of satisfaction, personal and professional. We grow from considering our interactions with our students, reflecting on possible changes, talking to others about our shared concerns, and connecting other aspects of our lives to what is going on in our work and our learning. We can become what we dream we can become.

Planning a Language Arts Program for the Year

So many factors play a role in determining how each teacher could organize a language arts or English program for a school year. The school administration may have an organizational framework, required texts, formal assessments, and institutional expectations that determine how many semesters, days, or hours a student will spend in a language arts class. Specialist subjects on a rotary timetable may mean different teachers for different components, and students with special needs may be withdrawn or have support teachers working with them. What we hope for all students is a learning year, filled with literacy events that support them in their journey towards becoming literate, informed, engaged, and participating citizens.

On page 20 there is a list of all the components that could be explored throughout the year in classes in the middle years. How the components are implemented depends on the teaching style of the teacher, the resources, including space, books, library, and technology, the teaching team, and the dispositions and backgrounds of the students.

Students grow in literacy through continued and recurring practice: speaking in discussions and presentations so that each student's voice will be heard; reading a variety of text forms individually, in a group, or as a class; responding and altering opinions as the community converses together; writing to be read for different reasons and developing a personal style; researching inquiries through interviews, in print forms, and from the Internet; developing specific tools and strategies for reading and writing; learning about language and how language works; moving deeply into concepts and issues of social justice with tools that promote thought and reflection; becoming familiar with e-learning; monitoring and managing — indeed, co-constructing — their own independent literacy lives.

Teachers approach the teaching of literacy differently. Some teachers will organize daily reading workshops and writing workshops; some will combine reading and writing events through their genre and theme units; some will use technology as the construct for their literacy components, with each child having a personal laptop or iPad; others will divide the year into semestered units of study.

Students need structure. Structure allows them to understand the expectations for the year and find ways to be successful literacy learners. It gives them a sense that they have a say in what is to be explored and investigated, something that is achieved or supported through best literacy practices. All teachers will want to discover the strengths and resources that each student brings and where differentiated instruction can support a student's progress.

All of our program components will build capacity in our students' literacy lives. What matters for the students is how they will come to see themselves developing control over their lives as literate humans, how they are learning to handle different text requirements, to write with both the self and the reader in mind, to inquire about issues that matter, to find their own voice through drama and communication activities.

Each component is a vital piece of the Lego-like building blocks that affect and develop literacy strengths in our students. No piece should be left over; instead, pieces may be snapped together to create unusual shapes and designs — different but significant designs in the lives of the students and teachers in the place called school.

Resources for literacy experiences

"Habits of reading, of thoughtful study, of commitment to projects, are built upon moments in which a student comes to believe there is something interesting for them in literate activity. English class should be about making more such moments possible. We, as literacy educators, should take a deep interest in what people do when they read, write, design, attend and create. We need to create our English classroom as a container for exactly that interest."
— Randy Bomer, *Building Adolescent Literacy in Today's English Classrooms*

Think of all the diverse and language-rich resources we could find to fill our classrooms: some we can use as read-aloud material; some will work well for demonstrating a particular point; some will be part of the language play that brightens our community time; some will be effective as the shared text for our small-group time; some will support independent reading; some will act as models for the students' own writing; and some will be there just to strengthen our own resolve as literacy teachers. Such resources are the impetus for our literacy events, all of the organized activities that promote and celebrate reading and writing.

There is such a wide array of different kinds of resources that can enrich our classrooms:
• novels, contemporary, graphic, and classic, at different reading levels, with new titles added throughout the year

The Necessary Components of a Literacy Program

Creating a Literate Community
- ☐ Organizing community meetings
- ☐ Promoting whole-class conversations
- ☐ Supplying daily newspapers
- ☐ Requiring personal notebooks
- ☐ Connecting outside reading and writing to school
- ☐ Incorporating technology as medium and message
- ☐ Recording and celebrating the year's work
- ☐ Treating the whole-class novel or non-fiction text as a teaching/learning unit
- ☐ Organizing in-depth author, genre, and theme units
- ☐ Building thematic or genre literacy events
- ☐ Offering adaptive technology for some students

Conducting Teacher Demonstrations
- ☐ Demonstrating your own literacy life as a reader/writer
- ☐ Sharing read- or think-aloud strategies
- ☐ Noting how students can monitor personal understanding of texts
- ☐ Making global connections
- ☐ Learning about technology

Presenting Mini-lessons
- ☐ Continuing to explore the conventions of print
- ☐ Expanding on specific literacy strategies
- ☐ Solving language puzzlements
- ☐ Giving instructions on how technology works

Planning for Students to Read in Groups
- ☐ Incorporating e-readers and laptops
- ☐ Giving students options and choices
- ☐ Exploring group dynamics and collaborative activities
- ☐ Engaging students in thoughtful and grand conversations
- ☐ Encouraging both teacher and student-led discussions
- ☐ Promoting interpretive, creative, and critical thought
- ☐ Planning opportunities for reflecting and sharing

Structuring Opportunities for Independent Reading
- ☐ Locating resources for differentiated levels and interests
- ☐ Helping students implement strategies for reading
- ☐ Mentoring students in ways to self-monitor reading progress
- ☐ Encouraging authentic and relevant responses to books in print and online
- ☐ Giving opportunities for students to share books

Supporting Students as Authors
- ☐ Incorporating writers' notebooks
- ☐ Supporting independent writing projects
- ☐ Encouraging the use of "mentor" texts (writing from reading)
- ☐ Building students' ownership of and stamina for their writing
- ☐ Conducting regular individual conferences
- ☐ Supporting revision towards a "personal best" product
- ☐ Offering revision and editing techniques
- ☐ Teaching elements of style and craft
- ☐ Publishing each student's writing during the year

Developing Inquiry Projects
- ☐ Incorporating a variety of research modes
- ☐ Solving problems as group members
- ☐ Using graphic organizers
- ☐ Involving issues of social action
- ☐ Integrating curriculum connections
- ☐ Investigating and understanding media
- ☐ Promoting digital research

Arranging for Student Presentations
- ☐ Using technology: Image, sound, and movement
- ☐ Sharing results of individual research projects
- ☐ Presenting data from group inquiries
- ☐ Participating in seminars, panels, and debates
- ☐ Sharing personal writing that has been published

Engaging in Drama
- ☐ Developing situations for role playing
- ☐ Encouraging embodied thinking through movement
- ☐ Organizing Readers Theatre presentations
- ☐ Building documentaries through research and role playing

Developing Linguistic Awareness
- ☐ Using inquiry as a model for language growth
- ☐ Recognizing language and power
- ☐ Expanding writing conventions
- ☐ Developing abilities with spelling and grammar
- ☐ Comparing Standard English usage and colloquialisms
- ☐ Recognizing different sentence structures
- ☐ Playing with words through games, puzzles, and online activities

Conducting Informal and Formal Assessment
- ☐ Conducting daily assessments
- ☐ Practising for various modes of tests

- non-fiction by authors who craft their writing
- publishers' anthologies — full of useful, short selections for working in small groups
- picture books that offer students in the middle years an aesthetic experience with words and visuals
- magazines, in print and online, both to be read and to be used as resources for responding, researching, and creating
- audio versions of books of all kinds, for readers in difficulty and for gifted readers
- interactive computer software
- website content in different curriculum areas
- poetry anthologies to be read and listened to: that would be undiscovered unless we introduce them
- letters, emails, blogs, memos, and advertisements to use in our demonstrations
- student writing and media modes that highlight and represent intellectual and/or emotional power
- teacher writing, bits and pieces saved from the texts of our lives
- book talks, discussions, Voicethreads, Skype interviews, guest speakers, video clips — voices from outside the walls that resonate within
- jokes, riddles, puns, funny anecdotes, riddles, tongue-twisters, rhymes — all representing the play of language
- selections from newspapers that students may not find in their homes, along with articles and reviews from free community newspapers and magazines
- references, in print and online, such as dictionaries, thesauruses, writing handbooks, and books of quotations

Each day, if we jot down the language resources we have used in our lives at school, we should be surprised at the amount, the quality, and the variety. Those literacy experiences enrich our programs while nourishing our students.

Timetabling for the literacy program

Every teacher will need to design a literacy timetable for the reading workshop and the writing workshop that suits the particular needs of that classroom. In some cases, the teacher will combine the two areas and create an integrated literacy program.

In designing your program, you will need to consider all the different factors you have to deal with in your school setting.
- What types of activities will best suit the concepts that will be learned in the time period?
- What are the timing and resource requirements for activities in each workshop?
- How much time will be needed for preparation, completion of activities, cleanup, follow-up activities and discussions, reflection, and evaluation?
- Will students have the opportunity to work as a whole class, as members of a small group, and on their own in order to engage in literacy activities?
- Is there a good balance between activities that are mandatory and those that allow choice?
- Which aspects of the curriculum could be integrated?
- Have appropriate amounts of time and effort been allocated to activities?

- Have timing, transitions, and pacing been considered from the students' perspective?
- Do activities address a range of learning styles, needs, and interests?
- Will all students be challenged by the activities?
- Will all students be included in the teaching and activities?
- Does the program allow students to take responsibility for their learning, or is it primarily teacher driven?
- How will reflective assessment be carried out?

Literacy Program in Practice: iPad Literacy

A school in Timmins, a mining community in Northern Ontario, is part of a research project conducted by Tina Benevides of Nipissing University exploring literacy development through the incorporation of iPads into the daily reading and writing events of an all-boys classroom. With each student being supplied with an iPad for the year, I became a partner in the project, helping to set up the e-resources that would act as a library of novels for small-group and whole-class reading, organizing some of the units the students would explore, and visiting the class as a guest teacher, where I could demonstrate literacy strategies that the iPad could support. These relate to promoting both the reading of texts and the enriching and expansion of the big ideas that fiction explores.

I wasn't prepared for the power that technology puts in the hands of young-sters, and I became part of the learning process with the boys and their teacher, Suzanne Chartrand, caught up in the ease and accessibility of the world of information that this wireless tool can offer. The boys were given some hands-on workshops by the technology consultant, and within moments, they had found the games that connect them to the pop culture of the techno generation, and swiped their way across the screens into more text forms than I knew existed.

Suzanne Chartrand teaches a Grade 7 class of boys at O'Gorman Inter-mediate Catholic School in Timmins, Ontario. With the support of Principal Ted Weltz, Suzanne has incorporated the use of iPads into her classroom and welcomed me into the literacy community there.

Independent reading

The boys had read several of the e-novels that we had purchased and expressed their delight with one in particular: *The Hunger Games*. Indeed, many had asked for the sequel for Christmas, and now I see that this book is an international best seller, with a film adaptation to be released.

The satisfaction these boys felt with this novel reminds us of the importance of recognizing student choice and popular culture in the lives of our students, and the connections to be made inside school from their outside interests. Quantity reading is one precursor of literacy success. Throughout the year, the iPad seemed to release these boys from some of the blocks to reading novels they had formerly experienced, and along with earbuds and audio, they read away.

Reading an assigned text as a class

I decided to work with a whole-class text experience, and had purchased an e-anthology of short stories to begin my unit. I asked the boys to read the selection and to think about the literary genre it represented. Four boys used audio versions, and some increased the font size. After the story had been read, I asked the boys to classify the genre. One or two said it was a folk tale, and when I questioned them about a couple of anachronisms I had noticed, they began to recognize the parody that the author had intended. On the SMART Board, a student recorded the examples the boys found of all the contemporary references the writer had incorporated in his story — 35 in all.

When we reflected on their reasons for missing the story mode, the boys said they had been fooled by the initial setup and the vocabulary that seemed to indicate knights of old; they had raced through the text because that was their past experience of most school reading — to read as fast as they could in order to get to the questions. Valuing and appreciating the literary qualities were not part of the game when the teacher selected the story and prepared the response questions.

I questioned a boy at the back of the room about his thoughts on the story, only to find out he hadn't located it on his iPad yet. He had gone unnoticed in my classroom dynamics, and with his buddy's help, he found the text and began reading. Limited readers, these students lost in the shadows often need as much support with ebooks as with printed books.

Electronic heroes

For the next demonstration, I wanted to explore research strategies using the Internet with the iPads. I asked the boys to find information on the Internet about a hero who interested them. I wrote their responses on the SMART Board. Their heroes ranged from Batman to Terry Fox to J. F. K. As the list grew longer, I asked the boys to classify their responses, and they came up with these categories: political heroes, celebrities, artists, sports heroes, war heroes, people who demonstrated courage, and when one boy shouted out "Jesus," we added religious heroes. The lists they had discovered on the Internet could not have been found in any one reference book.

As they dug deeper into what defines a hero, a student called out, "Nellie McClung." I asked him to tell us why she should be included, and he read something about her in a halting voice. Then he shared other names from his list, suddenly stating, "Dr. Booth, these are all women, and they are Canadian." This was the same lad who had not found the story the rest of us had read. His discovery represented for me the value of this kind of freewheeling research, like years ago when I would walk among the stacks in a library and discover books I had not known about, that I would not search for in the card catalogue, backpacking in "idea countries" and surprising myself into new discoveries.

These boys had stumbled upon Greek myths, athletes who had passed on, comic heroes, law makers, and ordinary folk who had behaved in extraordinary ways. They tried dozens of websites, used hundreds of cue words, and argued and debated the qualities of heroic action.

Then, the moment arrived that we as teachers hope for in every teaching situation: a student asked whether Leonardo da Vinci could be classified as a hero. There were comments back and forth, until one boy informed us that the artist had painted the Mona Lisa, and that alone should classify him as a hero. There was consensus, and his name was added to the list. I asked the class to find a picture of the painting on their iPads, and 22 boys held up images of the Mona Lisa in a classroom in Northern Ontario, far from the Louvre in Paris — I felt that I was in a Fellini film.

When one student said, "I heard that there is a secret code in her left eyebrow," 22 left eyebrows appeared on their screens, and a new inquiry was born.

Reading images

In my next meeting with the class, I began by asking the boys to tell me interesting facts about their city and community. Two of them mentioned monuments, and I directed them to find pictures of them on their iPads, along with relevant information. The students were surprised at how many statues and monuments could be located in their environment and shared their findings with partners.

I read aloud an excerpt from *The Monument* by Gary Paulsen, where, in the story, an artist is commissioned by the town to create a memorial to the fallen soldiers killed in the Vietnam War. The novel deals with the complexities of representing the different viewpoints and perceptions in a memorial of those citizens who had lost family members and friends.

The students then went on a web search, looking for statues and memorials generated by the losses incurred in different wars, and we began to develop a list of them as a class. The images they located were drawn from over centuries: Iwo Jima, the Holocaust, the American Civil War, cenotaphs, Waterloo, General Isaac Brock, and many more. Each student was asked to select one statue that incorporated three or more humans in its design, and the image and necessary background information were captured by each boy on his iPad.

The boys now had to plan how they would use their classmates in re-creating both the statue and the emotion in a frozen picture: How would people be placed? What levels could be used? What symbols would be necessary? The class and I went outside onto a grassy part of the playground, and the boys took turns moulding their statues with the help of the others. I photographed the results, and later these were transferred electronically to their iPads. Now each student had the image of the monument located through the Internet, alongside the photograph of his attempt at representing the statue through drama.

Back inside, and as a class, we shared the different creations, and students read aloud some of the background information they had found about their memorials. Many boys left their seats to cluster around others who had selected particular monuments. Building on this interest, I decided to ask each boy to write a brief poem that captured the essence of the statue they had sculpted with the bodies of their friends. These bits of writing turned out to be powerful mementos of their work, and with a little coaching, the work morphed into authentic poems, as they borrowed words and phrases from the information they had researched, as they revised the writing into shorter lines, using some repetition, and as they included an emotional truth that grew from their exploration.

A poem can be an icon of the distilled energy of the work.

Front and centre

I was only a visitor in this classroom throughout the year, but my time with these boys in their special classroom and their gifted teacher, Suzanne Chartrand, allowed me to see into the future, to tap into the virtual library that is infinite, to enable the students to own the work, to make and defend their choices, to support their finding significant information that they had discovered to share with others, to leave the confines of the building called school and surf the globe for knowledge.

I watched the one lad with muscular dystrophy participate fully in the activities of the class. He swiped the pages of his iPad, shared his researched picture of the statue, joined the groups of boys building their frozen images, as his classmates lifted him from his wheelchair and placed him in their designs, and wrote his poem scribed by his assistant. In the picture of the boys holding up their images of the Mona Lisa, he is front and centre.

Wave hello.

Three Perspectives, One Student

Because I thought that was what I was supposed to do, I said, "Only those students with their homework complete in the morning will be going on the trip."

He came in with homework that was incomplete. I wasn't clear about why. He made an attempt at an explanation. He said his mother was going to call me. He sat with his workbook in his hands and looked at the book and then at me. He looked heartbroken but resigned, like this was a familiar situation. He said he really wanted to go to the art gallery and promised to do the homework that night.

I said rules were rules.

The Teacher

The office buzzed the classroom. There was a phone call for me. His mother pleaded. She said the art gallery was a perfect match for her son's interests: that he struggled at school, academically and socially, but that he loved my class and he loved art, and couldn't there be some other consequence for the homework issue? I said I was sorry, but no, there would be no other consequence.

The students gathered their things. He walked slowly down the hall to spend the day in a classroom of younger students. The principal stopped me outside of the office. She had spoken to the mom. Was I sure? I asked for her opinion. She said it was my decision and she would support me either way. I turned towards the bus.

The Mother

We'd had a late start to our morning. He said it was pointless to go to school. He wouldn't be going on the trip because his homework wasn't done. I said that was ridiculous; no one stays back from a trip to the art gallery because of homework.

The evening before had been a struggle — most school nights were. I got home from work late and we were both tired. When I asked about homework, he said he'd get to it, and when I asked later on, he said he was too tired and went to bed. Homework hangs in our house like a dark cloud. It sours perfectly good evenings, and I don't know what to do about it. It was easier when he was younger.

When I arrived at work, I called the teacher just to make sure that the trip was on and to apologize about the homework and promise to double my efforts on that front. I had a hard time with her response. I was so disappointed for him. I told her that he had said that she was different, that she did the things she promised she'd do and he was so much more positive about school this year. I said if it was any other trip I'd understand, but the art gallery held a special place for him. He knew the paintings and the sculpture, even the floor plans of the building, and his favorite spot was the bench behind the stairwell on the second floor.

The principal said she, too, understood how much the art gallery meant to my son, but that homework was important too. She agreed to talk to the teacher but in the end, it would be the teacher's call.

The Student

My homework wasn't done. It's hardly ever done; she just doesn't know most of the time. I have ways of making it seem done. I sit at the table after dinner and stare at the pages, the writing, the math. I start in, but I never finish. I get distracted, I goof

Jane Paterson is the coordinator of resource development in the Curriculum & Instructional Services Department of the York Region District School Board. In that role, she is responsible both for developing multimedia resources for teacher professional learning and for the instructional design of learning resources offered in the online environment.

around, I draw, listen to music. At school, when the homework is assigned, I think it will be okay and then I'm alone with it in the kitchen, at night.

I was the only Grade 7 student not going to the art gallery. I was angry and frustrated. I couldn't even speak. I just looked at my homework book and silently kicked myself for not trying harder.

I knew my mom was going to call. I asked her not to because most of the time that only made things worse. I was embarrassed about what I knew she'd say: that I loved the art gallery and that people couldn't see that about me because all they saw were the low marks on tests but that she knew me differently. I wish she'd just stay out of it.

I'll sit with the grade sixes all day; I'll do the work I've been assigned and this will all go away.

— *Jane Paterson*

2

Inside, Outside, and All Through the Text

In my son's Kindergarten classroom of more than 25 years ago, the teacher had one computer, and each child was assigned to that centre once a week. My son waited his turn with great anticipation and reported to me on his success with the activity. No five-year-old in that class felt they lacked computer resources; it was a significant part of the program.

Compare this situation to my graduate class in the summer of 2011: there were 30 teachers enrolled in the course New Literacies, many of whom carried their laptops to class each day and took notes on them while I taught. As part of the program, we spent time each day in the computer lab, participating in interactive workshops on a variety of programs, searching for specific research papers that featured information on the topics, sharing YouTube films that explored similar issues and preparing their final course projects, which had to include a component from the multiliteracies world now available to them. The experience with technology varied in the group, from newcomers to wireless experts, but everyone grew in both the medium and the content they were exploring, especially me. I had developed this particular course so that I could connect to the world my graduate students inhabit more and more, and they carried me along with them.

We read screens, books, newspapers, and even our projects in our school.

The New Literacies describe multiple linguistic systems within literacy. There is not one definition of literacy since literacy practices are multiple and shift, based on context, speaker, text, and function of the literacy event (e.g., doing a Google search versus reading your grandmother's holiday letter).

Even our definition of the term *text* has gone beyond the traditional acts of reading and writing using an alphabetic code or symbol system, to include digital technology, images, sounds, and oral discourse. Now we refer to a text as a *medium* with which we make meaning through a variety of *modes* that are written, visual, tactile, or oral (e.g., an audiobook, a magazine, a painting, a film, a computer screen, a tweet, a narrative, new information, a list, an opinion, an editorial, poetry, songs, a script, instructions and procedures, a graphic text).

Changing Definitions of Reading

Our definitions of *reading* and *reading instruction* are changing, and as a result, the way we see the world is changing. The New Literacies are profoundly shaping the ways in which we view and use language. Just as the telephone altered communication strategies, our students will encounter a wide and perhaps unthought-of variety of information and communication technologies. Just think of video cameras, web editors, spreadsheets, listservs, blogs, PowerPoint, virtual worlds, avatars, and dozens more. Our traditional way of thinking about and defining literacy will be insufficient if we hope to provide young people with what they will need to be full participants in the world of the future. Students will require technological expertise in their home, work, and civic lives. They will need to be plugged in (or wireless) for survival.

The disparities between the plugged-in or wireless electronic home and the traditional school contribute to the alienation many students feel about what goes on in the classroom. We need to find a way to build on their digital literacies as we reconceptualize how to teach reading and writing in ways that would help them to value the *intertextuality*, or the connections made by many different literacy texts in their lives. We can be "plugged in" at times, and still gather together and sit in a circle to listen to a tale 2000 years old.

Our choice of texts in the classroom needs to reflect the multimodalities seen on the Web and in CD-ROMs to appeal to students' reading behaviors. Yet computer use can be balanced by programs involving print resources that connect the students to the worlds they inhabit, while stretching their abilities and interests. We can include novels, biographies, poems, columns, and articles that represent the best writers we can find who will enrich the lives of our students. Resources that touch the emotions and the intellect have a much greater opportunity for moving readers into deeper frames of understanding. Aesthetic knowledge lets us see further and sense the "as if, the hallmark of thoughtful, mindful citizens," as the education philosopher Maxine Greene puts it.

Since literacy is now defined as more than a matter of words on a page, the exploration of the media, computers, television, film, magazines, and so on has been seen as an integral part of the learning continuum. Students of all ages need opportunities to be critical viewers to ensure that they become media literate. We have to consider the effect of these media and their influence on the thinking, reading, and writing proficiencies of our students as we develop our school curriculum.

Consider the literacy opportunities for collaborating and creating that technology makes possible. We need to be aware that computer use may affect development in areas that boys and girls should and need to cultivate, such as collaborative learning and having a meta-awareness of texts they read. We also need to help all students become active and critical in their use of multimedia, and vigilant that they do not get lost in cyberspace or incorporate inaccurate or incorrect information into their written work.

In the feature below a student reflects on her time online in middle school.

All in an Email

Basic knowledge is used to address an email, comprehension is necessary to read the message, a reader applies knowledge when acting on the information from the email, analysis is used to discriminate between essential and non-essential parts of the message, synthesis is used to collectively interpret multiple messages, and evaluation is used to interpret the sender's intended tone.

Adapted from *Digital Literacies: Concepts, Policies and Practices*, edited by Colin Lankshear and Michele Knobel

Who Knew? I'm a Computer Geek!

Before I went to middle school, I thought that the computers in our computer lab were boring, hard to use, and the graphics were blurry. I thought computers were just for people interested in technology, **people who were wasting their time**. I never thought we would be able to use them to read, write, make art, or create anything worthwhile.

Well, it's a few years later, and my opinion of everything involving computers has completely changed. As well as using computers to store data and calculate big numbers, we now use them to communicate, teach classes, and we can be as creative as we want. I now use drawing and photo editing programs, and make movies, music, and websites. I never thought computers could be this exciting.

Stuck on a Password

In my middle school, we have a computer lab full of Mac computers. I have only been going to my school, Swansea P.S., since Grade 7, but I have learned more about technology in our lab, than all my years of primary school combined. In Grades 2 to 6, I went to an alternative school. We had a computer lab with about 15 PCs. We always had to share computers. There was a computer lab teacher, but she was also the librarian, so we never really saw her in either place.

This is how a lesson would go:

Our teacher would take forever figuring out where we were supposed to sit, because if she didn't, we would all rush for the two computers that actually worked. Then, when we were all seated, our teacher would realize that our passwords expired because we hardly ever went to the computer lab, unless we really needed to. She'd have to call the librarian/computer lab teacher to come and change all our passwords. When she finally arrived, she'd take forever setting the passwords.

The system was set up so that the librarian set everyone's password the same. When someone typed in the password, there would be an option on the screen to change it. That was a big mistake. Most kids typed the passwords incorrectly, didn't press the "change password" button, or changed their passwords but promptly forgot them.

If we had any time left after the passwords were set, we would fool around, or do nothing. By the end of Grade 6, I was convinced I would never like computers. I thought they sounded terribly slow and boring. How wrong I was . . .

Exploring I.T.

That was when I moved to the middle school. We have computer lab time — we call it information technology or I.T. class — five times every 10 days. Our teacher creates fun but challenging assignments, he is not the librarian, and no one forgets their passwords. I.T. periods are for everyone except Kindergartners, and there are 31 Macintosh computers, all fairly new and in good shape, except one. Our teacher, Mr. Higgins, always helps us when we need it — I can't say it wasn't a relief when I came to the I.T. program. We make movies, explore websites, and make our own websites to blog about them. It seems like we're exploring every artistic program there is.

In the space of a few months, I got a Mac computer at home, learned all sorts of things about Macs at school, and changed my whole opinion of technology. I went from avoiding technology to becoming, well, a computer nerd. I now want to get a job related to computers. To put it simply, it has changed my life forever. (For the better I hope.)

Being as Creative as You Want

There are many reasons why I like I.T. classes. One is definitely that I can learn about a program at school and then use the program at home. Also, when our teacher tells us about a project, he never tells us exactly what to do, so that we can personalize our projects, such as the time we did a unit on PowerPoints. Mr. Higgins told us to put any topic we wanted in them, as long as every slide was about that one topic and the topic was appropriate. He explained how to import pictures and make links, but he doesn't tell us what color to make it, or what topic to use. I guess what I'm trying to say is that all the projects and the software can let you be as creative as you want. Another great thing about I.T. classes is that Mr. Higgins runs a media club on Mondays at lunch. We film kids, teachers, and parents participating in events, or just fooling around.

Mr. Higgins answers all our questions and organizes the projects well. Whenever we are using a new type of software, he will show us how to use it on his SMART Board. I wish he'd give us more time to work on our projects, but at least he lets us work on them at lunch or after school sometimes. I wish my other teachers could teach classes in the I.T. room because it would really help to use the computers in class. He also doesn't let us work on other assignments in the I.T. lab.

From Technology Hater to Tech Girl

Definitely going to the Cyber Arts program in high school will change what I do next. I used to think that computers were so confusing, only for geniuses; now I'm the tech girl of my family, the one my family goes to when they need help on the Mac book. Of course, I don't actually know how to do many things on a Mac yet, but the initiative is what is important. I haven't just changed my opinion of technology; I've changed my opinion of myself and what I'm capable of.

— *Mairead Stewart*

We make meaning of what we read and think about it critically.

I remember years ago observing a colleague as she taught a novel, watching her hammer out with her class what seemed like hundreds of insignificant details that no reader would be able to notice or remember. I later asked her about her work with this particular book, and she told me that her students had to know the novel backwards and forwards. When I mentioned that schools and classrooms in her city were reading and teaching different novels, she stared at me, wondering aloud how those youngsters would learn about the book she had chosen.

The teacher came to realize that the students would all find different books in their lives and that how they made sense of them would depend on the strategies we helped them to develop. We don't share a book as a cultural symbol in our learning communities in order to remember irrelevant data — there must be better reasons for reading and reflecting upon shared texts in our classrooms.

We need to reconsider our roles as literacy teachers, to discover with our students the strategies that work, and to select interesting, worthwhile, and significant resources to read and write about. As teaching professionals, we often feel like Miss Narwin, in Avi's *Nothing but the Truth,* who no longer could cope with the pressures of teaching, and retires and moves to Florida.

Mr. Duval, as I see it, I have been working — working hard — as a teacher for twenty years. I've been a good teacher. Ask my principal if that's not so. Do you know, she was once my student?

Cause for Reflection

It is not surprising that we often have students perform on demand, instead of finding ways to help them learn about the processes of reading and writing — many of us began our careers feeling ill prepared as literacy teachers. We know that evaluation is not teaching but, if we are constantly using testing situations in lieu of methodology, how will our struggling readers grow?

A Changing Definition?

What does *illiterate* mean in the 21st century? I cannot read efficiently many different forms of texts — manuals, schedules, guitar magazines, sheet music, and almost anything with numbers in it. Does that make me illiterate?

I want the students we teach to know the possibilities that rich literacy processes can tap into. If they do, they can alter their futures, see the world from different viewpoints, construct their own ideals, transform their world pictures, own their lives, resist manipulation by corporations or governments, find pleasure and laughter and satisfaction in all types of texts, feel worthy as readers who make important choices, risk and fight for valued beliefs that will benefit all, and be awake to the imagined possibilities that surround them.

We aren't what we read; we read what we are, and what we can become.

On Negotiating Text Choice

Effective teachers enrich their programs with texts that are new to the students, or different from their standard reading materials, while building opportunities and respect for the resources that are owned by the students. I think it's a matter of negotiating the literacy territory, recognizing that every student has a right to read what he or she wants to read at some time during the day, but, as wise parents and teachers also know, we require the strength to ensure that the students experience texts that can change their lives, texts that make them laugh and cry, novels that portray lives so like or unlike their own, articles about science and geography and health that move them further into ideas and issues.

Constructing Meaning

Meaning making with print is developmental and can expand exponentially over time, if we have wise others to support us. We want our students to be in the company of others who are considering similar issues and ideas generated by the text — classmates, critics and reviewers, teachers who share and direct their learning, other authors whose writing connects to their work, and references that add to their background knowledge.

The landscape of our minds is constantly shifting as we read and reflect on what we have read. Our comprehension alters as our life goes on, as we consider the ideas and opinions of others. Our response to a single text is never frozen in time. Reading, of course, is more than pronouncing words; it is more than attempting to second-guess the intent of the author. It is a process of interpretation and negotiation from the locus of our lived and vicarious experiences at a moment in time. We need to constantly expand our abilities to process print, from a single word on a billboard to a dense novel translated from the Russian.

Texts will continue to present challenges to us for the rest of our reading lives — the words, the language patterns, the structure and organization, our purpose for reading a particular text and, especially, the connections we make. The reader is part writer; a text is like a printed circuit that the reader's life flows through. The text furnishes the hints, the clues, the framework, and the reader constructs the meaning. The reader writes the story by bringing self to the print, engaging with the text to create a thoughtful and mindful experience. Comprehension is now viewed as a complex process involving background knowledge, personal experience, thinking processes and responses. Reading shapes and even changes our thinking — reading *is* thinking.

Insightful versus fake-readers

How do we help those readers in the middle years who think that reading is pronouncing words rather than making meaning with the text? Are we, as teachers, following an unwritten and sequenced curriculum of literacy that seems to say, "Learn words in the primary years, find main ideas and details in the junior years, and examine author intent for the rest of your school lives"? How is it possible for students to have success in school without thinking deeply and struggling to construct meaning with what they read?

In her book *I Read It, but I Don't Get It*, Cris Tovani describes these students as *fake-readers*, people who make their way through school by pretending they can read, disguising their limitations, using their listening skills and powers of memory to make up for being unable to handle print. They have no intellectual involvement with the text; they rely on the teacher's summaries or on copying what others say; they quickly grow frustrated by a lengthy or complex selection, waiting for the teacher to tell them what to think.

However, non-readers, unmotivated readers, reluctant readers, and limited readers can all grow with the right set of conditions. We know stories from those who work with illiterate adults how their students eventually, and with support, come to be print powerful. We hear, from teachers who work with youngsters in remedial reading classes, of the great strides many students make with guidance and instruction. And we listen to the stories of those who struggled with reading — some of them teachers and writers — who, with the help of someone who understood the reading process, gained membership in what Frank Smith has called the "literacy club."

When people develop strategies for understanding different texts and for monitoring their reading, they are on their way to becoming fluent, independent readers who assume control and responsibility for their learning. Along the way, they need secure environments in which they can experience success in their reading ventures, where they feel safe to experiment and make and modify errors or miscues in their reading. They need to take charge of their own development as readers.

Discovering Reading Strategies

So, let's base our teaching on sharing the strategies that proficient readers use to build meaning and comprehend text, showing our students how to think deeply about what they read as they read, helping them move beyond the superficial. Explicit instruction through mini-lessons and demonstrations can clarify procedures for them and enhance their abilities to work with texts. They can discover their own ability to understand, to reflect on what they have met in print, and to move towards the insight that comes from connecting and considering their connections to the text. They can thus avoid pretending to read or giving up on a text. Like proficient readers, they can come to use strategies automatically and seamlessly as they work in real reading situations.

As students grow comfortable using a certain strategy, we can ask them to write about how the strategy works and how it helps their reading. The act of writing about it can make the strategy concrete for the students and allow them to move forward to include other strategies in their own reading.

Be sure to check out Cris Tovani's 2011 title, *So What Do They Really Know?*

Fixing Sense

Once, while reading the newspaper, I made a miscue that startled me: instead of "Basketball star *signing* with Raptors," I misread the word as *singing* and couldn't make sense of what was going on until I reread it.

Let's keep a list of the miscues we all make when we read and celebrate our abilities as readers to fix print that doesn't make sense.

Strategies and processes are, to a large extent, intangible. Because of this, we can never be certain how students employ them. Instead, we need to watch for evidence of specific strategy use and notice the degree of success students meet when using them.

Making connections

When we are engaged with a book, we bring the sum total of our life to the meaning-making experience: our previous experiences; our background knowledge of the content; our connections to other "texts of our lives" — the books, computer programs, or songs that are suddenly conjured up; our emotional frame; our knowledge of the nature of this particular text, how it works, the author's style; and the events of the world at large that are somehow triggered or referenced by our reading. Much is happening in our minds.

When we are engaged in reading, connections are occurring constantly and simultaneously as we recall personal experiences, summarize what has happened so far, synthesize information and add it to our constantly expanding mental storehouse, analyze and challenge the author's ideas, and change the organizational schema of our minds. Making connections with what we read is a complex process.

Our main goal as literacy teachers must be to help students build bridges between the ideas in the text and their own lives, helping them to access the prior knowledge relevant to making meaning with the text, the information that the brain has retained and remembered, sometimes accompanied by emotional responses or visual images. When we help students enhance their reading by activating their own connections, we offer them a reading strategy for life.

In my own work in the teaching of reading strategies, I am seldom satisfied unless the learning stretches outside the classroom lives of the students, connecting reading to bigger world issues so that perspectives and assumptions are challenged or altered. I am grateful to Paulo Freire for giving us the expression "*reading the word, reading the world*." Somehow, when we read powerful, significant texts, we travel outside ourselves, exploring what lies beyond our immediate neighborhood, extending our vision, and encouraging our personal meaning-making.

Questioning the text

We read because we are curious about what we will find; we keep reading because of the questions that fill our reading minds. Of course, readers ask questions before they read, as they read, and after they have read. As we become engaged with a text, questions keep popping up, questions that propel us to predict what will happen next, to challenge the author, to wonder about the context for what is happening, to fit the new information into our world picture. We try to rectify our confusion, filling in missing details, attempting to fit into a pattern all the bits and pieces that float around our sphere of meaning making. Constant self-questioning causes us to interact with the text, consciously and subconsciously. As we read on, our questions may change, and the answers we seek may lie outside the print.

The deeper and more complex the text, the more questions we will bring forward as we try to make sense of it. The greater our interest in what we are reading, the more substantive our questions will be. Monitoring our reading involves

Recognizing the Already Met

My son came home from Grade 9 excited about his history class: "Dad, did you know that Caesar is not just a salad?"

Now we laugh together at that memory, but the incident highlights how we can recognize only what we have somehow met before. Our knowledge is built from and based on all we have experienced, and those connections are being made all the time, consciously and subconsciously.

Two Millennia in a Word

British poet Ted Hughes reminds us that the word *crucifixion* contains 2000 years of history.

paying attention to questions that arise as we read, as well as those that remain when we are finished.

We begin to make our connections to what we already know, wrinkling our brows at incongruities or seeming inconsistencies, accepting that our minds work in this inquiry method while we read and that the questions that remain after the reading can form the basis for our text talk, for doing further research, or for pondering and wondering about the complex issues that the reading has conjured up.

Often our most limited readers ask themselves the fewest questions as they read — instead, they wait for us to interrogate them. They have not learned that confusion is allowed as we read: that authors count on it in order to build the dynamic that compels us to continue reading. As students grow in their ability to self-question, their understanding of how authors think and of how meaning makers work increases.

We have a much greater chance of having our students invest themselves in the reading experience if we help them to take ownership of their own questions. They may begin to participate in text-generated meaning making if they believe that their questions really matter and that others are interested in grappling with them. Those who are wondering why they are not making sense of text might begin using their own questions to move them forward as they seek answers, information, or at least clarification. They read as real readers do, moving back and forth between their own lives and the worlds created by the author, wondering, pondering, challenging, inquiring, rereading, searching, summarizing, and always questioning. That is the way humans learn, and the way readers read.

The questions I ask of students will grow from conversations with the text, from the honest revelations of the students' own concerns, as I try to guide them into deeper interpretations. Now I try to ask questions driven by our inquiring dialogue, as I would in a conversation with peers during a book-club session, based on my listening to their interactions rather than on my own scripted agenda. I want students to engage in thoughtful considerations about the text and its connections to their lives, not struggle to find the responses they think I want.

Inferring for deeper meaning

We spend our life making inferences, noting all the signs that help us to make sense of any experience — the face of the salesclerk displaying a product, weekend weather reports, the body language of the students we are teaching.

As readers or viewers, we make inferences when we go beyond the literal meaning of the text, whether it is a film, a speech, or a book, and begin to examine the implied meanings, reading between the lines to hypothesize what the author intended, what he or she was trying to say and why. When we read, our connections drive us to infer; we struggle to make sense of the text, looking into our minds to explain what isn't on the page, building theories that are more than just the words. We conjecture while we are reading, the information accrues, our ideas are modified, changed, or expanded as this new text enters the constructs in our brain.

Inferring allows us to activate our connections at deeper levels and to negotiate and wonder until further information confirms or expands our initial meaning-making ventures. Predictions are inferences that are usually confirmed or altered, but most inferences are open-ended, unresolved, adding to the matrix

In their book *Guiding Readers and Writers*, Gay Su Pinnell and Irene Fountas give this good description for using the questioning strategy: "The teacher's questions are a light scaffold that helps students examine text in new ways" (p. 294).

Prompts as Questions

Consider using prompts rather than recall questions in your interactions with students during group sessions and individual conferences, and in your responses to their reading and writing journals. These prompts can expand or deepen the offerings of the students, help them clarify or expand their thoughts, and nudge them into expressing their opinions and ideas. We have questions to ask and we need to ask them, but we want to teach our students to ask their own as well.

of our connections. Often we need to dialogue with others to further explore these expanding thoughts, and to become more adept at recognizing the need for digging deeply into the ideas of the text.

Visualizing what we are reading

Words are only symbols, a code for capturing ideas and feelings. When I was growing up, I listened to radio dramas and comedies, where the airwaves delivered the images to my mind, aided by sound effects, the narrator, and the actors. When we read, a similar process occurs, and we create pictures of what the print suggests, making movies in our heads. Each of us builds a visual world unlike any other. Our imaginations are at work.

We can demonstrate this strategy for youngsters and help make them aware of its strength in supporting our meaning making with print texts. We might read a folk tale to the students and then have them share the images that they created throughout the listening experience. They could draw the images suggested by the text. Reflecting upon the meanings suggested by an artist's illustration can be an effective means of demonstrating visualization and the need to reconsider our thoughts as we learn more. That is why graphic novels can be a stimulus for young readers to begin seeing in their minds what the print conjures for them.

Summarizing as we read

We summarize constantly as we read, sorting out significant ideas and events and other bits and pieces of information. If we are reading a longer selection or a complex and difficult piece, we need to pause and regroup every so often, coming to grips with a means of classifying the barrage of information we are receiving. We might make notes to help us connect and remember details so that we can focus on the big picture, check the table of contents to strengthen our awareness of where a section fits into the whole, and reread the introduction to clarify the framework of the information we are meeting. As effective readers, we use the strategy of summarizing as we read, getting the gist of the text.

At the beginning of a literature group or conference session, it's a good idea to ask the students to summarize the events they have read about so far. Doing so can establish a supportive context for the next section and help clear up any misconceptions about what has happened previously.

Determining important ideas

My own books are full of different-colored, self-adhering sticky notes; they hang out from the tops, bottoms, and sides of almost every book on my shelves. So why, I wonder, did it take me so long to make the teaching/learning connection and begin using these markers with students of all ages?

As readers, we have to read the text, think about it, and make conscious decisions about what we need to remember and learn. Sorting significant information from less important information means picking out the main ideas and noticing supporting details. Flagging text can help students begin the lifelong process of learning to notice what is important in a text, to prioritize the information, sort through it for significance and mark in some way the points they will want to use or remember. Computers also give us ways of highlighting and sorting texts.

We know now that finding the main idea is not a simple process. Traditionally, we taught that finding it was the first step in understanding a text. However, sometimes when we called for the main idea, we meant a plot summary; other times we wanted to find a theme.

Now we understand that there may be *many* ideas in a reading selection. Through mini-lessons, conferences, and demonstrations, we can assist young readers in learning how to determine what is important (especially in non-fiction material), what is necessary and relevant to the issues being discussed, and what can be set aside.

In my own teaching, I try not to ask a student to locate a detail unless that piece of information is necessary for a deeper understanding of what is being explored. I want the student to search out the facts necessary for understanding, for supporting an idea or clarifying a point, not to rely on a treasure hunt for details that I determine to be important.

Analyzing the text

Each of us has had in school the strangulating experience of analyzing a poem or a story to death, so by the end of the lesson we had lost whatever appreciation we had for the selection. Often, the teacher felt this to be a necessary building block for future independent learning, but seldom did many of the students internalize the learning so that they could use it later.

Our goal is not to dissect the selection but to notice how it works, how the author built the text, whether we are reading an emotion-filled story or a resource containing information. We can help students discover the underlying organization, the elements that identify the genre, the format of the selection (including graphic support), and the overall effect of the work. For me, these are opportunities for guiding readers into a deeper awareness of the text, the author's techniques, and their own developing responses.

Noticing text features

One Grade 8 class examined tables of contents I had gathered from six different history textbooks. I wanted them to make connections about how the books appeared to be structured, why the information had been arranged in such a way, and how the intent of each author team could be deduced from these opening pages. The activity became a literacy adventure, and throughout the year we used the discoveries we made with our own textbook. The students came to see how their text and the other texts were designed and formatted to help make sense of history.

Students need to be immersed in texts of all kinds in order to become proficient readers and writers. We will need to be aware of and constantly renewing our resources — building our classroom libraries, supplying our book rooms or school libraries with new titles, and locating our own significant texts for book talks and demonstrations. Students need to share in demonstrations of how different texts are constructed and used, since texts vary in purpose, audience, format, and organization, as well as in the publishing devices and designs they employ.

Critical Reading

Critical reading relies on the students employing all the strategies they know in order to come to thoughtful, carefully determined conclusions about the

---

Beyond Analysis: Synthesizing Ideas

Stephanie Harvey and Anne Goudvis, in *Strategies That Work*, say that "synthesizing involves putting together assorted parts to make a new whole." We synthesize the issues and ideas generated by our reading of the text in light of our own lives. When we synthesize, we change what we thought we knew — we expand our personal understanding. We move from recounting the new information into rethinking our own constructs of the world. We synthesize our new learning in order to consider the big ideas that affect our lives.

Often, classrooms forget the difficulties inherent in using a single textbook in mathematics or science, or the complexities involved in reading information books or information online, especially with students at different levels of proficiency as readers. How to handle specific types of texts often requires instruction.

value of a text. As citizens, they will need to think critically about the life issues they will encounter, and analyzing texts with a questioning mind is part of the developing process.

During guided reading sessions or during literature circles, we can help students move towards a critical interpretation of the text they are sharing. Analysis should be a component of every discussion, as students share their personal responses and connections, raise concerns and questions, make inferences from the information, and talk about different aspects of content and style. Readers can move towards a critical appreciation and understanding of the text, as the group members analyze and synthesize their ideas and responses. After the discussion each member should feel wiser about the text.

Engaging the class in analytical discussions about a shared text is often helpful. Keeping a record of what is said on a chart or having students keep notes can support reflective talk about the process. Using prompts such as these, we can guide students' comments and questions about the text and about the author's role in creating it:

- What type of selection is it?
- Does the text represent characteristics of the genre?
- What special language does the author use?
- Are the characters believable? Do they behave consistently?
- Is the author's background relevant to the selection?
- What new information do we find? Is it correct and complete?
- Are the themes connected to our lives?
- Is there bias or the use of unfounded opinions?
- Whose voices are silent?
- Did the author engage your interest and maintain it?
- How does this text compare with similar ones you have read?
- Are you somehow better off for having read the selection?

Contrasting and comparing can lead naturally to a more critical understanding of the content and the craft in a text. For example, students can read or listen to several versions of a story; they can then chart similarities and differences in structure, style, content, language use, length of sentences and paragraphs, and use of dialogue and narration. That gives them some background and support for the comments they make — they have informed their opinions.

We want readers to carefully weigh evidence from a text in order to make a thoughtful decision regarding their own opinions, to combine textual information with their own background knowledge. They need to draw conclusions and apply logical thought to substantiate their interpretations. We want readers to make and to recognize informed opinions, such as those of respected newspaper and magazine reviewers.

One of our goals must be to have our students work towards independence, to develop into lifelong readers who see a variety of texts and text forms as friendly objects, who recognize the art of reading — as Louise Rosenblatt, the authority on reader response, said — as the negotiation between the text and the reader.

Literacy is a developmental, lifelong process, dependent on many variables — personal background, language and thinking processes, life experiences, familiarity with the type of selection, the purpose and payoff for reading, the situation in which the reading is taking place, and especially the readers' attitudes towards a text, often determined by experiences in school. We can open up the options that printed and online resources offer, and explore with readers how different texts work, what to look for, and what to expect, so that they can be informed

Long ago I stopped thinking that there was a master list of what everyone should read; instead, I moved towards supporting individual readers' decisions about the print resources they selected — their newspapers, novels, magazines, work and organizational materials, and what they read for fun and satisfaction.

in the choices they will make and select the resources that give them the most satisfaction.

Self-Monitoring Meaning Making

Different readers have different challenges to contend with. Some simply lose track of meaning by "spacing out"; others see no purpose in what they are going to read; others have insufficient background knowledge to understand unfamiliar concepts or ideas, focus on details rather than on important ideas and information, or maintain misconceptions as they read. When handling a variety of texts, they don't have enough strategies to select from; they can't recognize the features of different genres or formats of texts in order to see the underlying framework that will help organize the concepts.

What is the best way to help students monitor their reading comprehension?

In the past, we would often introduce a text and be ready to follow up with activities, but leave the students to read the text independently. Traditionally, we assessed their reading *after* they finished reading, instead of helping them to notice what is happening when their meaning making is interrupted or when they lose track or become confused.

But *during* the reading is when we should be helping. The content may be daunting, class noises may interfere with their reading, or the time may be too long for students to sustain concentration. Even proficient readers can find themselves lost or their thoughts wandering while reading.

We *all* need strategies for repairing a breakdown in understanding while reading; otherwise, we just plough on to the end of the selection, totally confused. Worse still is reading the text and waiting to be told what you thought you had read. Readers have to monitor their understanding and try to repair any breakdown in meaning making: to do what experienced readers do. Students may need to improve fluency, adjust their reading rate, perhaps slowing down, reread, and, what's most important, increase their reading stamina through sustained engagement with text as they read intensively for a significant time.

Students need to be aware of these self-monitoring strategies as they read:

- checking predictions and forming new ones
- checking unanswered questions and forming new ones
- checking comprehension by rereading
- linking prior knowledge to what they are reading

Readers need to overview the text, to do a form of skimming and scanning, in order to determine important ideas and information while reading:

- noting characteristics of text, such as length and structure, important headings and subheadings
- determining what to read and in what order, especially in creating websites
- determining what to pay attention to or ignore
- making notes in the margin
- highlighting necessary words and phrases
- noticing special cue words
- finding interesting or important information or facts
- noticing opinions
- finding larger themes
- deciding to quit the text or read it again carefully

Saying the Words, Missing the Sense

Often, oral reading practice in a group results in little or no comprehension for limited or struggling readers, as they wait their turn and focus only on pronunciation. These students need to employ word-solving strategies as they read silently and then interpret the words aloud.

Readers need to construct and as necessary, repair meaning as they go. Doing this involves going back and salvaging what they can, clarifying their thinking, noticing when they lose focus, rereading to enhance understanding, reading ahead to clarify meaning, questioning the text, disagreeing with information or logic, identifying and articulating what is confusing or puzzling about the text, drawing inferences, determining what is important, and synthesizing their new learning.

Identifying Words

It would be impossible to learn, one at a time, all the words we will meet in print. Therefore, our brain classifies information about a word we meet in a text, working from the knowledge of word patterns built up from our experiences with print. We want to encourage students to use all the different strategies available for recognizing and solving unknown words in their reading, long before they begin to read the selection aloud. We need to help students learn how to solve words *while* reading, not only before meeting the text or after they have read the text.

We need to be careful of our requests to have students read orally if they don't have an opportunity to explore the text silently beforehand. In reading a text aloud, a student has to pronounce each word while demonstrating through the voice what the words mean. Unless it is a rehearsed reading, the student is unable to use a variety of strategies necessary for identifying unfamiliar or difficult words. To *decode* a word means to be able to pronounce it *and* understand its meaning in the context of the whole text.

Supporting Students with Special Needs

One published set of texts, or a series of remedial exercises, can't, on its own, support the different approaches we will need to use as teachers in designing programs for students with special needs. Inappropriate instruction may delay or regress a student's growth.

Students in difficulty need to experience what successful literacy events feel like, to know that there is hope for recovery and that they will be supported in their struggle to grow towards independence. Although all readers need our time and attention, readers having difficulty benefit from individual attention.

- We may need to help these students set short-term goals or to break the complete task into smaller steps. They will need brief but regular conferences and checkpoints, in order for us to offer support and to provide direction that will move them ahead towards success.
- During sharing times they, too, need to present to the class and can do so with extra preparation and support. They need to show the books they have published, to present book talks about books they have read and enjoyed, to read a poem they have practised, or to share excerpts from their journals.
- We need to help these students struggling with reading to learn the problem-solving strategies that proficient readers use to make sense of print experiences. Margaret Phinney says, "They remember the meaningful, the outstanding and the useful first, and those are all determined by personal interest and purpose."

R-A-T

They were teaching us rats to read. The symbols under the picture were the letters R-A-T. But the idea did not become clear to me, nor to any of us, for quite a long time. Because, of course, we didn't know what reading was. Oh, we learned to recognize the shapes easily enough, and when I saw the rat picture I knew straight away what symbols would appear beneath it. But as to what all this was for, none of us had any inkling.
— From *Mrs. Frisby and the Rats of NIMH* by Robert C. O'Brien

- We can prepare them for testing situations with demonstrations and mini-lessons. We can often orally direct them to respond to test-like questions, where the pressure to be correct is less than in a testing situation. These little practice sessions can help prepare them for the formal testing events. After a test, it is useful to stress what the student knew and understood, to build on positive aspects of the experience, and to then move into remedial work.
- Most of all, students in literacy difficulty need to be recognized for their successes in reading and writing, no matter how limited they may be, to have their accomplishments celebrated.

Reading Workshops

Planning a guided reading session, where a group reads the same text during the reading workshop, allows you to focus on students who have similar needs for improving their reading strategies. You might also have groups of students participate in a literature circle or book club, where they read a section of the text before meeting and then share their responses to the text in conversation with group members.

Guided reading instruction

Books used for guided reading can be grouped according to level of difficulty. The most important consideration in assigning a level to a book rests on whether students at the level can read at a rate of 90 to 95 percent accuracy.

Guided reading works as a teaching strategy because it lets us observe students as they read, while they are in the process of reading, rather than after they have completed attempts at making meaning with the text. Instead of struggling to stop them from racing through to complete the questions they know are waiting, we can help them notice the strategies they are already incorporating into their reading, introduce new ones that may be useful in supporting their challenges, and help them connect their lives to the text.

After they read along silently in a small group for a while, we can ask them to stop. We then help them notice the strategies they are using and suggest the ones they might try in order to make informed decisions while constructing meaning. We can model the questions effective readers ask while reading, helping students to become aware of how fluent, proficient readers "think with text."

A crucial component of any guided reading session is the time devoted to discussion of the text — identifying connections the students made, discussing interesting vocabulary they met in the reading, assessing the accuracy of their predictions, identifying ways in which the text relates to their life, and sharing reactions and insights. We can direct students' attention to points in the text that support their knowledge (e.g., sound–letter relationships) or we can ask them to apply particular strategies. Together, we can revisit parts of the text or do a second reading to help students increase fluency. Students can then discuss the strategies they used while reading and those they need to develop further.

Literature groups

Students need to work in groups with shared copies of books they have selected from a limited range we have provided — some classes are using e-readers and iPads. These groupings for literature are sometimes labeled book clubs or literature circles. Students may suggest books for group readings as the year progresses. Each group should meet two or three times a week in order to carry on a conversation about their books. They will need to decide on how much should be read before each session — what I call "checkpoints" — and if they read ahead, group members should reread the portion that will be discussed. The in-depth discussions can be supported by the notes, comments, and sketches students have prepared in their reading journals while reading the text.

During a literacy conversation, participants may include personal insights, emotional responses, and connections they are making to the text and to the comments of others. As they begin to hitchhike on each other's comments, they build background knowledge and incorporate new meanings and different perspectives into their own world picture. It is important that students speak up and all take turns, and refer to the text when making a point. They should support one another's comments, too, moving the discussion along and helping to keep the talk focused on the ideas generated by the text.

Students learn many things through these conversations: to support their ideas with references in the texts, to pose questions that have real significance, and to accept, or at least consider, the opinions of others when they disagree. They think and read about the text in a collaborative activity as they interact with others, learning about themselves as they deepen and expand their meaning making.

As teachers, we need to establish the routines that will make possible the management of literature groups in the classroom, making the expectations clear and repairing any disruptions in the flow of the work through demonstrations and direct instruction. We can contribute to the functioning of literature circles in a variety of ways, depending upon the needs of the group or individual students.

Independent reading program

During *independent reading*, students select books and read them silently. Often, because we need to build an atmosphere in the classroom, we introduce our program at the beginning of the school year with uninterrupted and sustained silent reading time. We then gradually implement an independent reading program.

A key part of the teacher's role is to guide text selection and to increase reading competence through book talks, conferences, and mini-lessons, as well as promoting reading journals. I like to promote independent reading during the community time with a book talk. Typically, I feature new additions to the classroom library, new books by favorite authors, books that I need to "sell" to the students because they are less familiar, books on relevant issues or with media connections, or books representing different genres. When doing this, I talk about the issues involved in the story, connect the text to other books and issues, briefly outline the text, note the plot or the people, show the cover or illustrations, and offer a personal response, being careful not to overinflate my influence as the teacher.

Students should be encouraged to read at their own pace, using books they have chosen to read. We can ensure that they make good choices by including a range of books in our class and in the school library/resource centre, and by giving advice and help if asked. We need to represent a wide range of genres, including non-fiction and novels, graphic texts among them. Over time the students' concentration can be extended, as can the level and range of reading material. By keeping up-to-date records of the books they have read, students can notice their reading patterns and widen the range if necessary.

Text Talk Recordings

Recording a group's book talk can offer a powerful demonstration of the kinds of text talk the students are engaged in. Sections of the dialogue — critical moments in the discussion — can also be transcribed by either the teacher or a group of students and used as a text for group members to observe their own thinking in progress. Accompanied by an analysis of the strategies being demonstrated, this report could be part of their self-assessment review two or three times a year, a record of their own reading progress.

In-Depth Writing Projects: Group Inquiry

Our classrooms have come a long way from demanding that projects submitted without our guidance be artistically beautiful creations, often relying on parental support. Now we see them as in-depth writing projects that demonstrate the students' high-level learning in both content and process, and that open up opportunities for them to teach others about what they have discovered.

If we want students to develop as writers, we need to help them set up a system that enables them to experience personally the learning that grows from an inquiry. In that way, they will acquire information-handling skills. We can help youngsters in the middle years come to grips with assigned projects and papers, so that they are not left to flounder, but gradually accumulate the strategies necessary for working with a variety of genres of information.

Steps for implementing a group inquiry approach to project work are as follows:

1. Selecting a topic
2. Forming an inquiry group
3. Building background knowledge
4. Classifying and categorizing the information
5. Interpreting and assessing the data
6. Presenting and sharing the inquiry

Student inquiries and investigations can grow from a topic or an issue drawn from the students' own interests and questions that stimulate their curiosity and cause them to want to find answers or solutions. Research can grow from science or social studies as well, or from the themes in novels and picture books. These inquiries can last for a few days or several weeks. Some aspects may be covered as homework, but the classroom is the best place for identifying a topic, formulating questions, and developing a plan of research. Intensive long-term research projects immerse the students in authentic reading and writing experiences; they also offer valuable opportunities for media-supported presentations.

Students often need help in planning how to structure the information they have found through their research inquiry. We can help them with ways to sort, select, and arrange their data by conducting mini-lessons. Examples of student writing we collect often give them frames for organizing their own investigations. Rather than demanding outlines for writing projects, we need to offer guidance and models for building effective structures. In the end, we want to be able to see what they have learned through their intensive research writing, and the results should document their growth.

Occasions in which students present their inquiries offer opportunities for both oral communication and written and visual demonstrations of the research. I am impressed by the power of overhead transparencies to cause students to carefully consider how they will represent their findings. In some schools, they can move into presentations using the computer. Displays and bulletin boards let other students benefit from the research, and young investigators may want to distribute a guide sheet for observers to note their learning and to ask further questions.

Evaluation rubrics are useful for letting the students reflect on their learning processes, and for recording the types of writing and research they explore. The class can set up standards that affect how others will view the work: using media effectively; representing the information neatly with careful handwriting or computer printing; arranging the graphic display artistically; and using captions and headings to stimulate interest and to give cohesion to the study.

Completion of an in-depth study of a topic that students found interesting means that the students will have explored the types of writing that will be valuable throughout their school years and in their future lives. They will come to recognize that the process of writing occurs in the content subjects and that when they are involved in subject disciplines, they need to see themselves as readers and writers. Literacy does not raise its head in language arts only; it is a lifelong interpreting and constructing process.

We talk and blog with each other, with our teacher, and with the world.

Students need opportunities to deepen and expand their understanding of different texts in involving ways. When their reading experiences are extended and supported by their own written and artistic responses and those of their classmates, they can move into interpretation and appreciation, understanding the negotiation that is required in order to truly read what others have written. They are learning to consider the complexities involved in the relationship of text and reader.

Giving Rich Responses

What we look for in responses to reading are instances where students
- challenge previous notions they had about a topic
- gain new learning through interacting with others
- discover a new way of viewing a character or an event
- see the text in a larger context, noting the big ideas
- check the accuracy of their predictions
- consider questions that were answered, and others that were unanswered
- review the main themes of the text
- think about what they have gained from reading and link it to their existing knowledge
- question, compare, evaluate, and draw conclusions from their reading of the text
- reflect on the experience of the text and incorporate it into their lives
- represent their interpretations in a different mode, such as poetry

Sometimes, however, students spend more time responding to a text than reading it. We need to encourage them in their reading, for the accumulation of positive, meaningful reading experiences is what will drive them forward to become lifelong readers. Through carefully designed response activities, we can nudge them into different and divergent levels of thinking, feeling, and learning.

Keeping a Reading Journal

In reading journals or note books, students can record their thoughts and feelings about the texts they are reading, as well as keep a list of what they have read. We often need to write about our thoughts before we can really come to grips with them. The act of revisiting and reconsidering our responses to a text is often possible by reviewing what we have written in our journals. In doing so, we are connecting the processes of reading and writing, formulating thoughtful and personal reactions to what we have read.

Keeping a journal or a note book during the reading of a text has several benefits for students in the middle years: they can engage in a conversation with the author, record critical interpretations, monitor their own progress, and note observations for later use in their writing projects or in a dialogue with the teacher. They may also include sketches or charts that support their responses. Ideally, they would write in their journals when ideas occur as they read, but it may be necessary to develop this as a technique. We can select a time in a group session or perhaps have students write an entry during every other reading occasion.

The teacher's response

Reading student journals allows you to have a conversation, often a private one, with each student several times throughout the year. Therefore it is extremely important that you read their journal entries as a truly interested and involved reader, and as an enabling teacher.

- As you reflect on their learning and the connections they seem to be making, your written responses can guide your students towards a deeper consideration of what their reading has meant to them. The art of teaching lies in your comments: celebrating their insights, deepening their awareness, and sharing your own connections to the texts of their lives.
- If you ask authentic questions and offer genuine comments and opinions, your message can connect with the student's in some way.
- By posing questions that involve rethinking or rereading on the part of the reader, you can help students consider what they have read in a different light or from another perspective. You can ask for more information or a clearer interpretation.
- You can recommend other authors, titles, genres, or websites featuring similar themes or events.
- You can model quality responses with your personal interactions.
- You can share your own experiences as a reader and writer, commenting on the authors and books you enjoy.
- You can come to know your students in more personal ways and learn more about them as readers and writers, and as people.
- You can gain important knowledge about their literacy abilities that can be used later as issues for mini-lessons and conferences.
- You can look for literacy growth, how the students are developing and refining their knowledge and opinions about reading, how they are discovering new authors and new genres, and how they are gaining greater awareness of themselves as readers and writers.

Some teachers write responses to five journals each day, while others have the students write them a weekly letter to summarize responses from their daily journal entries. In this type of letter, students can discuss what they have read or frame their reading experiences by synthesizing their thoughts. Occasionally, students will write back and forth to each other, having conversations about the different books they have read, as in a class blog or wiki.

Even if you haven't read the book the student is writing about, you can have an authentic conversation. Ask questions that will help you understand the text. Be sure to value the student's responses and acknowledge his or her thoughts and feelings.

A Teacher's Response

Here is part of how teacher Nancy Steele responded to a student's entry on Philip Pullman's *The Amber Spyglass*, annotations added:

Have you ever thought of the ethical component of these teen sci-fi/fantasy books? (*raising issues connected with the text*) You mention that the "dust" seems to have some relationship to good and evil but it is ambiguous. (*drawing attention to the unusual symbolism of a word in the text*) Do you think that Pullman is dealing with the theme of good and evil? So many sci-fi fantasy writers are. Madeleine L'Engle, whom I know you have read, has a very strong Judeo-Christian element in most of her books and most often the conflict involves destroying the agents of evil. (*directing the student into other texts with similar themes*)

Representing Responses Visually

Some students who experience difficulty writing their book responses or summarizing their reading may benefit from presenting their material through use of a graphic organizer. The organizer should be a rough draft of the reader's thinking, not a product to be mounted on the wall.

- *Semantic maps* can be used during pre-reading to record students' thoughts about what may be in the text, emerging from a brainstorming or discussion session. The activity focuses on activating prior knowledge and connecting to personal experiences. One way to build a semantic map is to write a word that represents the main idea of the text in the centre of a piece of paper, then write related categories in squares that are attached to the main word. Students then brainstorm details related to the categories.
- *Plot organizers* provide a visual means for organizing and analyzing events in a story. They help students summarize a plot and understand its organization, and they act as models for students writing their own stories.
- A *Venn diagram* can represent comparisons and contrasting information within one story or book (e.g., settings) or between two or more books. It consists of two or more overlapping circles: the parts of the circles that do not intersect represent unique or contrasting attributes, while the intersecting sections depict shared or common characteristics that can be compared.

Representing ideas through art is not just for those who can't write fluently, and creating pictures is not just part of rehearsal for real writing. For readers of any age, images are part of the serious business of making meaning — they partner with words for communicating our inner designs. For example, what relationship exists between the visual and verbal in picture books? on websites? Responding to a book through art frees students from worrying about their language abilities, a concern that many at-risk readers and ESL students share. Nonetheless, students of all ages can draw and paint as well as write responses to stories, and technology presents them with a variety of useful modes.

Ways to Respond Visually

Timeline
Story map
Mask making
Illustration of most powerful moment
Personal picture book
Graphic comic strip
Sketches in journal
Calligraphy for significant words
Prezi and iMovie

Reading Orally

In today's classrooms, students and teachers read aloud throughout the day: stories and poems composed; excerpts from other stories we love or wonder about; words that touch or puzzle us; tales from before; stories about today and tomorrow; episodes from people's lives; poems that cry out for sounds in the air; emails from friends; anecdotes about places where we have never gone; information about dogs and horses, mothers, granddads, and eccentrics, students and school, and city and countryside; poems of hope and death and wonder and fantasy. We read aloud short stories and long stories and chapters that build up the tension for days. We read brief biographies from CD covers and music sheets, blurbs about authors from the backs of book jackets, reviews, and recommendations.

As we read aloud, we fill the classroom with voices: the voices of our ancestors, our friends, our authors, our poets, our documents, our native peoples, our researchers, our journalists, our ad writers. We story aloud.

Can we give students the strategies required by oral reading so that they will approach the process with interest and excitement, accepting the challenge of bringing someone else's words to life? Oral interpretation is perhaps the most complicated and sophisticated of all response modes. We need to carefully re-examine our motives and strategies for including it in the language programs in our classrooms.

Whenever possible, we need to create situations that call for *repeated* readings of the same text. Familiarity with a text can support a struggling reader's attempts to make meaning, to acquire word knowledge, or to read aloud successfully with a group. Regie Routman tells of a student who said that her first reading of a book was like a rough draft of her writing.

Choral reading is one situation that *demands* repeated readings. I remember being in Larry Swartz's classroom years ago as they were preparing for a parents' night. The class was chorally reading six poems by T. S. Eliot from *Old Possum's Book of Practical Cats*, not the versions adapted for the musical *Cats*, which the students had listened to as well and enjoyed. Their rambunctious and joyful interpretations of the complicated rhymes and unusual language still ring in my ears.

Presenting to an audience

- Introducing Readers Theatre experiences will allow the students to dramatize narration or selections from novels, short stories, folklore, picture books, or poems, instead of reading aloud only scripted material. Little or no body movement is used in Readers Theatre; instead, emphasis is placed on polished and well-practised vocal performance. The students can have one person read the narration while others read the direct speech parts, or explore who could read the different lines. For example, a character who speaks dialogue may also read the information in the narration that refers to that character. Several students can read narration as a chorus.
- Middle students can join others as they read songs, verses, and poems aloud from books, individual copies, overhead transparencies, or SMART Boards, in a theatrical sharing, perhaps texts chosen to represent a theme.
- Play scripts are such useful texts for having students read aloud: each voice reads only the agreed-upon part or lines, and there is an expectation of rereading before the scene is to be shared.
- Middle students can work with buddies from a younger class and delve deeply into the context of the story as they find ways to bring it to life. I am impressed with buddy programs that require the older students to have some training in how to assist a younger reader and where they prepare for the session, debrief with the teacher, and even keep a notebook chronicling their progress.

Learning the Lyrics

Teachers are usually surprised when I mention that teenagers prefer interpreting text aloud to almost any other method of communication until I remind them of the music that they download or buy in the millions, learning the lyrics so that they feel part of music literacy.

3

On Page, Online, and in Workshop

When I began teaching, I scheduled creative writing for Tuesdays at two o'clock, ignoring the fact that students were writing throughout the day in various curriculum subjects. I chose each topic for all the students to address, and I waited for them to be finished. Revision and editing were demanded, but instruction was seldom offered. Sometimes I provided a prompt for a student staring at a blank page but, on the whole, I ran a performance-based program, where students completed a first draft and then wrote a good copy that I would mark. What was missing, I now know, was any understanding of the writer's work, of the writing process, and of the strategies that might be of help to developing student authors.

We write on page and online.

In our professional collections today, we have books by educators who have studied, taught, and reflected upon how writers write, and we can use those models to create classroom programs that nurture and teach youngsters to write like writers. I am grateful to the educators who began examining the writing process, researching and reflecting on how we might begin to support our students: Donald Graves, Lucy Calkins, Shelley Harwayne, Mary Ellen Giacobbi, Nancie Atwell, Ralph Fletcher, Shelley Stagg Peterson, and so many others. We now have a body of work that can inform our teaching and offer us methods and inspiration, strategies for assisting young writers in their development, and information about the writer's craft.

How to Approach the Teaching of Writing

Today my students are studying to be teachers, and I model how to approach writing. I write collaboratively with them. I talk out loud in front of them, using a SMART Board, revealing how I revise and rethink my work as it develops, make decisions, edit the conventions — how I write down my life. I share my writing: letters, stories, vignettes, memoirs, summaries, reviews, and reports. I want the students to see me as a developing writer who understands what and why he teaches.

Think about what we can do as writers: think in print, brainstorm ideas and observations, scribble down our thoughts, test ideas, ponder our problems, record and plan our lives. We record disjointed thoughts, ask questions, move around ideas, organize our bits and pieces and surprise ourselves with our discoveries. Occasionally, we communicate our writing in a permanent form with others, personally or professionally. Often we don't know what we really think until we try to write it down.

For some of us, writing brings back difficult memories of red-covered edits, failing grades, and mandatory topics of little interest. The only audience was the instructor, who seldom found our ideas interesting. And then we find ourselves teaching writing to a class of students . . .

How can we change our writing backgrounds and become professional, knowledgeable, and literate writing teachers? One way is to begin behaving as writers ourselves and helping students to act as real writers who write because they have something they want to say.

Quality writing occurs in a classroom where students write about things that matter to them, where a language-rich, supportive environment fosters their desire to see themselves as writers and increases their ability to capture their ideas and feelings proficiently. We want students to have real purposes for writing, to speak in their own voices with clarity and accuracy. Writing may not be easy or fun, but it can be satisfying and purposeful, an important aspect of living.

The Five Cs of Writing

We can help students to

- consider the *context* for the writing
- determine the *content* of the writing
- develop the *craft* of writing
- apply the *conventions* of writing
- value the *composing* of ideas, feelings, and information

Recognizing different functions of writing

We need to have our students writing frequently during the day in a variety of situations: note-taking during a mini-lesson, working on an idea web for an inquiry project in social studies, completing a final draft of an extended independent piece on the computer. But only the last example requires extensive editing — we publish our writing when we have something special to share and to keep.

We can consider the act of writing like other functions of communication, such as talk: sometimes we chat with neighbors, argue with our boss, present a formal proposal to colleagues, talk to ourselves in the car on the way home, whisper to our partner in bed.

Linking writing function to strategies

We have not always included all of the writing events that occur in the classroom as acts of written composition, but, of course, they are. At least we have replaced the inappropriate term *creative writing* with *writing*, but we still don't want to lose opportunities for exploring the different functions of writing.

Each writing function requires different strategies, and we need to help our students become aware of them. However, one thing true of all writing is that students write best about issues and topics that matter to them.

It may help to classify classroom writing events with your students as one of the following:

1. *Independent writing projects:* Regular opportunities for them to work independently on topics they (usually) select for themselves
2. *Research inquiries:* Topics drawn from the curriculum, although at times we may assign the topic from a theme or genre we are exploring as a community
3. *Guided writing instruction:* Lessons with a group of writers gathered together temporarily to work on target areas of writing techniques and strategies, such as conventions, genre study, or tools for technology (e.g., cutting and pasting text).

An open and accepting writing environment in our classrooms will offer a range of writing experiences and products, including social networking, diaries, journals, letters, surveys, how-to books, games, résumés, bibliographies, autobiographies, lyrics, poems, articles, editorials and opinions, essays, memos, advertisements, commercials, brochures, questionnaires, instructions, petitions, dialogues, screenplays, and legends.

Determining what to write about

"What will I write about?" Students have asked this question for generations. The first significant set of strategies we need to focus on should involve helping them to create an array of ideas that they care about, topics that call for their personal responses. For years, I thought it was my job to provide those topics, but now I know that my role is to work with my students in negotiating what is significant in their lives.

In their independent writing projects, students will need to choose a topic that matters to them. Since they will be working for an extended time composing and revising, and perhaps publishing, what they are writing about becomes paramount. Students need to explore their interests as they hone in on topics, probing issues, deciding on the genre and format, the style and audience, and referring to the models they have experienced in their reading and in their life connections. It is important to determine which ideas should be developed further before beginning the writing process.

Students can note the mentor or touchstone texts — memorable texts in a variety of genres and formats that can act as reference points for their own writing, providing suggestions for motivation, ideas, formats, and styles.

Keeping a Writer's Notebook

Ten Notebook Ideas

Special events at home
Unusual pet behaviors
Holiday or camp experiences
Book incidents and character memories
Family stories
Book and film lists
Moments in time
Story ideas
Problems and worries
Hopes and dreams

In *What a Writer Needs*, Ralph Fletcher, one of my favorite educators on writing, says we require a place to record "our thoughts, feelings, sensations, and opinions or they will pass through us like the air we breathe." Young writers need to explore, experiment, look inward, discover what matters, and as Nancie Atwell writes in *In the Middle*, "name and examine their thoughts and feelings." In writing notebooks, students can write about things that matter in interesting ways, clarify their personal concerns, and explore social issues — I wish I had kept a writing notebook while I was growing up.

Writing Down Their Lives

When personal stories are developed and shared, young authors become aware that writing can reflect their lives. By linking personal experiences with their writing program, students find that their lives hold the potential to provide starting points for significant writing.

We need to encourage our students to tell the stories of their own lives. They can borrow the shapes and cadences, the words and phrases, of the professional authors whose work they have read or that they have heard read aloud by generous parents and teachers. A student's identity, culture, and origins may be revealed in each story told, and the resulting experience will give the original tale a pattern and texture that will enrich both the teller and the told-to.

We can strengthen the students' story lives in so many ways:
• Make the classroom a safe place and a starting point for sharing life tales.
• Encourage spontaneous personal storytelling whenever it is appropriate.

High-Speed Fiction

Of course, writing fiction is a complex task, especially for young people. In *A Fresh Look at Writing* Donald Graves sums up the difficulties: "Most of the fiction that children write reflects their impression of what fiction is like. They want their stories to be exciting. Thus, their focus is on high-speed events reminiscent of Saturday morning cartoons. Older children choose bizarre and violent chases, space shootings, or war with modern weapons." (p. 287)

- Ask students to connect their own experiences to what they have read about or listened to.
- Use special events — a touring play, a professional storyteller, a visiting guest — as an occasion for sharing memories stimulated by the experience.
- Allow time for students to recount life stories formally during current events or informally on rainy day recesses or at cleanup times.
- Use polished life tales as building blocks for sources for role playing in a drama lesson.
- Help students to use real-life stories as the basis for their fiction creations, both strengthening the believability of their writing and offering them a means for handling sensitive issues.
- Design opportunities for deep listening to the stories of others with a visit to a home for senior citizens or to a hospice.
- Arrange for sharing stories with a buddy class of different-aged students in the school, or have a local high-school class come and tell polished life tales about their years in middle school.
- Tell your own life tales from both your teaching world and your personal life to strengthen or model a point that arises during a discussion or a shared reading. Swapping tales is still the best way of motivating your students to tell their stories.

The many biographies and autobiographies of authors who write for young people can be useful as both reading resources for your students and as opportunities for exploring viewpoints about the art of writing. Here is a selection:

A Girl from Yamhill by Beverly Cleary
Boy: Tales of Childhood by Roald Dahl
The Abracadabra Kid: A Writer's Life by Sid Fleischman
Childtimes by Eloise Greenfield and Lessie Jones Little
On Writing: A Memoir of the Craft by Stephen King
Little by Little by Jean Little
Looking Back by Lois Lowry
Bad Boy by Walter Dean Myers
Guts: The True Stories Behind Hatchet *and the Brian Books* by Gary Paulsen
Knots in My Yo-Yo String by Jerry Spinelli

Distilling the Poetry of Their Lives

At 1 a.m. on the day my son was to graduate from Grade 8, I found him awake in bed, reading the yearbook from his Grades 7 and 8 class. The yearbook was a collection of writings from the class's writing workshops that the teacher, Nancy Steele, had collated into a booklet. What Jay was reading and rereading represented the lives of the classmates he had been with for those two years.

The writings were mainly poems. Somehow Nancy had been able, in her carefully structured program, to offer this genre to her students as a means of capturing their very beings at this stage of adolescence. The emotional swings, the shocking observations of the adult world, the new awareness of strong feelings — all seem to fit inside the shapes of poetry that she modelled and shared with them.

The following samples are from that year's booklet. They still make me want to find a class and read and write nothing but poetry for the next two years . . .

Cottage Morning

Small familiar sounds create
the sounds of nothing
ripples over the smooth lake
the water — almost like ice
so perfect and black
undisturbed.
I descend the stairs
creaky and slippery
from the night's sleep
rocks and pebbles roll
under my bare feet
step onto the water
my foot makes rings
of indignation
the water freezes my skin
runs up my leg.

Walnut

brown and wrinkled
smooth in the palm of my hand
it protects itself
resisting my attempts
to pry it open —
until it shatters
and shards of sharp shell
fly everywhere.

Mystery Object

My great-grandfather's watch
Smells faintly of cigars and brandy
Staring into its golden surface I see my reflection
Along with that of my grandfather, and his father before him
Though cared for on its long journey
It shows signs of erosion on the delicate silver knobs
Thousands of hours contained in its weary metal hands
It has become a grandfather
Wiser than the modern-day contraption
It now
Is time itself.

We revise our words along with our ideas.

Like most writers, my own work is cyclical: I write, revise, read, write, edit, read, write, think, dream, and begin again. Students need to realize that writing, by definition, is recursive: we consider ideas, revise, find more information, edit what we have written, count how many words we have typed, share our draft writings, find a published model that interests us, reorganize what we have so far, and sometimes give up and start on another project.

Revising as Rethinking

We need to help students understand that revising and editing are important and essential processes to undertake when preparing a piece of writing for publication. If we share our own draft writing with the students in a demonstration, they can offer suggestions. Having the chance to see a teacher revising writing helps them understand the reasons we all have for drafting and redrafting. (Computers have eliminated much of the drudgery of recopying and increased our stamina for revising.)

Ralph Fletcher has helped us all look more carefully at the elements of writing. As a result of *Craft Lessons: Teaching Writing K–8* and *Nonfiction Craft Lessons: Teaching Information Writing K–8*, authored with JoAnn Portalupi, we now know a variety of strategies that we can open up to our students about the craft of writing.

Many students realize the need for revising and editing. Through rereading the writing, by reading the work out loud but privately, by conferring with peers and with the teacher, students can see changes they want and need to make in their writing as they refine their drafts. Students may, however, have difficulty revising their ideas and changing the structure of their writing.

When examining early drafts, then, we need to look beyond spelling and grammar errors. In our initial conversations with young writers, it's important to focus on ideas and coherence, considering issues such as these: Will a reader understand what is happening? Is the information organized for easy access? Are there details that, if included, would paint a clearer picture? Will the reader be connected emotionally to the writing? Is the writer showing rather than telling by describing action and events? Is the writer incorporating natural-sounding dialogue? Is there a powerful lead and a strong conclusion? Is the writer making good word choices — precise nouns, strong verbs, effective adjectives and adverbs — not always the first words that come to mind? Is the writer replacing overused words, such as *nice*, *said*, *a lot*, and words that are repeated?

As a young teacher, I didn't know the elements of the writer's craft, and I didn't know how to help my students develop their writing. As I read fine books written for young people, took education courses, and read professional books, I began to understand how writers work and what goes into making our writing stronger. But not until I began to write myself did I recognize the struggle writers go through to move ideas from the brain to the page so that others can have some hope of understanding what they want to say. Before, I thought I knew what it was I wanted to say; now my thoughts grow because I write.

There are many things to teach about writing through mini-lessons, demonstrations, or conferences. As well, students can brainstorm a list of craft items to master and add to it throughout the year. But acquiring the bits and pieces of the writer's craft requires as much time, I find, as it takes the cabinetmaker to learn how to handle different kinds of wood, to know and use the correct tool for the job. Mentoring, mistakes, and reflection will be part of the learning.

Editing for Improvement

Editing, as discussed here, is concerned with the conventions of print, the standardized norms of spelling, punctuation, and grammar. It represents polishing. Students may be motivated to polish their work when they are preparing it for

Support Cues for Writing

During a visit to our faculty British poet Gareth Owen was asked a question about improving students' writing. One simple suggestion he offered was to place prompts around the room that could act as support cues for young writers. He mentioned that, after demonstrating a list of clausal conjunctions with his class, their writing structures altered almost immediately.

an authentic audience. To assist them, we can have a variety of writing resources available in the classroom: dictionaries, thesauruses, and computers.

- For a demonstration, you can create a piece of writing that demonstrates the specific editing issues you want the students to examine. Transcribe the piece onto a SMART Board or make individual copies. Then, in small groups, the students can read the piece as editors and indicate where change is needed. To model the editing process, incorporate their suggestions by crossing out, adding, and deleting information.
- Computer technology has much to offer writers with spellchecks and syntactic warnings.
- Peers can edit each other's work for specific problems. Sometimes a checklist can be used as a guide for a peer editor to follow.
- One practice that may be helpful is for a writer to read aloud a piece to a partner and for both to listen for disparities and syntactical errors.

Preparing to Publish

The computer has forever changed our school publishing projects; however, there is still room for handwriting certain types of writing (e.g., thank-you notes), for personal illustrations, and for the art of calligraphy.

I enjoy seeing student work carried to the publishing stage, for it provides purpose for the students' writing and a valid reason for revising and editing. Each student can publish or display one piece of writing each month, and students can share their writing on networks of young writers on the Internet. Young writers can enhance their work through fonts, color, spreadsheets, graphs, and photos. They can make books in dozens of formats.

All students need to see themselves as writers. Sharing a published piece by each student in the classroom at various points in the year is a positive reinforcement for their work. It also recognizes that all students are members of the classroom community of writers.

The writing conference

The goal of any writing conference is to support the student's life as a writer. To meet that goal, we need to act as wise and compassionate instructors and editors. Our feedback as they engage in revisions, students tell us, is the greatest help they receive in becoming better writers.

As for me, I have worked with hundreds of graduate students, mainly teachers, and they have represented as complete a range of abilities as any grade in any school. Most need help in choosing and focusing on a topic; most need help in finding resources to support their projects; most need help in revising their ideas, rearranging sections, moving chapters, adding and clarifying details, finding references to support their opinions, and validating final drafts. A doctoral thesis will not be accepted until it is bound in leatherette with embossed title on the cover. (Today in my university, theses are submitted online to be accessible internationally.) Everything matters — just as it does in our middle-school classrooms.

A conference may last one or two minutes, or be a longer engaged conversation. You can hold a writing conference at any time during the writing process — at the beginning of an idea to be developed or during the revision of a draft. It is an opportunity to help students clarify what they want to write about, to offer feedback about what they have written, and to reinforce what they are learning as writers.

Gay Su Pinnell and Irene Fountas suggest that students co-direct the conference, "analyzing and evaluating their own writing projects and initiating questions about their own writing."

We solve linguistic mysteries!

I consider myself an adequate speller, but there are word demons that still stump me. I have, however, developed some skill at recognizing when a word does not look right, when I think that it may be misspelled. Of course, my computer spell-check program brings up all Canadian–U.S. spelling differences — matters of style — but misses homophones consistently. Most of my errors are typos created by my inadequate keyboarding skills.

What if we built our students' knowledge of how words work by helping them to see these language issues as problems they can solve as linguistic detectives? We can have students locate evidence of the intricacies, origins, patterns, and abnormalities of the English language through researching, comparing, analyzing, and constructing the words they need in their writing lives.

We can also show our students how to approach words the way proficient spellers do. Proficient spellers have a high degree of competency in frequently used words and know how to use multiple resources for dealing with the challenges that occur in writing. We can teach our students to use a variety of strategies when checking the questionable spelling of a word. We can help them to raise their *spelling consciousness*.

This approach reflects the fact that spelling is not just memorization. It involves processes of discovery, categorization, and generalization. It is a thinking process where students can learn the patterns, regularities, and unique features of spelling as they read, write, play with, and attend to words. With that in mind, we can draw students' attention to specific patterns or groups of words to help them see a rule or generalization; we can begin each day with a spelling conundrum for the class to solve; we can play word games on the computer.

Building Word Power

The more exposure students have to reading and writing, to the strategies of spelling, and to a variety of spelling resources, the more they will reinforce and strengthen their spelling patterns.

We can assist students in learning to spell with a variety of strategies. At a daily word study session, we might present just one point we want to bring to the attention of the whole class. Mini-lessons focusing on common patterns in groups of words or meaningful generalizations can also be held two or three times a week. Students can record their notes in a word study book or in their writing journals, along with their personal word lists. We want to promote information and discovery about language with this interactive structure.

Mini-lessons and demonstrations incorporating a SMART Board can call attention to spelling problems students are experiencing (e.g., doubling final consonants, adding *-ing* to a word ending in *-e*). Approaches to solving a problem can be verbalized and visualized, and students can learn how an effective speller

I was surprised when I asked 10 colleagues in my faculty to assess their own spelling competence, and to a person they labelled themselves as inadequate spellers. Is it because they are now using academic references that require constant confirmation or specific terminology? Or, do they, like most of us, simply need to check their spelling?

Words for Lunch

In one school I visited, the principal had just purchased a new collection of 12 boxes of different word games. The intent was for middle-school students to play the games at lunch.

Circling Around a Word

I am pleased to see a student circling a word in a rough draft; it's good when a young speller knows what he doesn't know.

Of *huipil*, *pelerine*, and *sorites*

Online you can find the spelling words used each year in the National Spelling Bee contest (e.g., *huipil*, *pelerine*, *sorites*, *qigong*). They can be fun to examine, helping us to realize that the students who win this contest have a special gift for understanding how spelling functions and that they work all year with references, learning and confirming unusual spellings of little-used words. The rest of us can improve and learn strategies for increasing our word knowledge and celebrate these word-smiths and their talent.

uses some words to learn other words. A brief conference can help a student come to grips with a troublesome word or pattern.

Let's keep the requirements of standard spelling in perspective. Each new piece of information gained about how words work alters the student's existing perception of the whole system of spelling in English. Sometimes, a student may appear to regress by misspelling words previously known, but the student may be integrating new information about words into his or her language background.

Spelling as word solving

Jack Booth's *Word Wise 1* and *2* (published by Tree House Press) are useful resources for building word muscles.

- Learning to spell is clearly related to students' general language development. Students go through developmental stages in learning to spell, but not necessarily sequentially or at the same rate.
- Students need to attend to the appearance of words and to check their encoding attempts. As they try to spell words, they often discover the underlying rules of the spelling system.
- Struggling spellers need to focus on a small amount of information at one time, especially in examining connections among words and word families. Our task is to help struggling spellers with particular strategies for learning and remembering word patterns: word families (*water, watered, watering, waterfalls*), mnemonic tricks (the principal is our *pal*), and personal lists of words we know or need to reference.
- Most of us fix our misspellings as we go along, correcting those words we already know — "one minute" words — rather than waiting until we have finished. We can teach our students to do these quick checks, heightening their ability to know when a word looks right.
- We can suggest that students circle any word in doubt. When they return to it, they can write it over until it looks correct. They should find a pattern or generalization that applies, or say the word slowly, stretching out the sounds. Teach them to picture the word in their mind.
- Before telling a student how to spell a word, we need to ask, "What do you know about this word?" We should build on the student's knowledge.
- Computers can help students develop a means for identifying and then correcting errors during revisions.
- Writing is the best way to learn about spelling.

The Role of References

When it comes to writing and checking spelling, the dictionary and spell-check are last resorts. We want to encourage students to practise their word-solving strategies *before* turning to a reference. Dictionaries are valuable resources for literacy, especially for expanding vocabulary, but only if they are used as aids in authentic language events (e.g., checking the spelling of a word in a report or the usage of a word in a poem). Many kinds of dictionaries can be found in a literacy-centred classroom (e.g., etymological, slang, proverbs — in print and online). Different dictionaries are useful for students looking up word information and noting differences in style, content, mode of recording, and so on. Games (such as Scrabble) and word-building activities (e.g., how many words a team can make from the letters in *onomatopoeia*) can help students see how references support their literacy learning.

Handwriting in Relief

Style grows over time with each student, but it is important to demonstrate the formation and flow of letters with mini-lessons when necessary. Practising handwriting should be kept to a minimum, but neat and legible handwriting should be a part of each student's efforts.

Computers have saved the writing lives of many students, including lots of boys, whose handwriting skills are minimal — my son is one of them. Using a computer, we can select fonts that amaze the eye, format our ideas, and strengthen the words; however, handwriting has some value, too, especially with younger children. It can help students notice words and letters — their shapes and sizes, their uniformity and design.

Teachers should not dwell excessively on the quality of handwriting. Instead, they should encourage students to focus on developing their writing into a style that is uniform, aesthetically pleasing, and legible. Handwriting used to be a time-consuming component of the elementary school curriculum, but in recent years, teachers have realized that students need to focus on what they are trying to say, rather than just on the shapes of their letters.

Most young people choose to print rather than use cursive writing.

Putting Grammar and Usage in Context

For many years, teaching specific grammar lessons to the whole class was thought to have an impact on the students' writing. Research today tells us that students learn about language by using it and then by noticing how it is used.

We usually speak the way our family or community speaks. To alter language patterns requires creating an environment and encouraging frequent interaction with significant models — speakers, coaches, peers — and, of course, listening to a variety of language patterns and incorporating them in our storytelling and writing. Reading scripts aloud and discussing the way characters speak can highlight usage patterns and build awareness. When to use standard and when to use non-standard English depends on the context — consider formal essays and text messages. What matters is *appropriate* usage rather than *correct* usage.

However, examining language allows students to detect differences in oral and written language forms, and note the language used by authors. Students may benefit from knowing common terms such as *verb* when discussing how language works.

Writing as Readers

Our students need to see themselves as writers who have something to say, either to clarify their own thinking, to share aloud with others, or to let others read.

We think with print, and we rethink because of our attempts at writing down our thoughts. We rewrite, we revise, and we start again.

So, we jot down our notes, we text or twitter, we collect our findings for an inquiry project, we express our thoughts in poetry or letters, we tell a story about our lives, we write down our information, our ideas and feelings. And we explore the modes of encoding all of this — the genres, the forms, the formats. We learn how written communication works, how each mode functions, how we can shape our initial responses into more meaningful articulations of what we want the people who read what we write to understand.

We want our students to know that writing is a way of being in the world, of remembering and recording, of interpreting and revaluing, of persuading, of organizing, and of wondering. A human attribute, to be valued.

PART B

Helping Students Find Their Voices

4

Engaging Students in Learning

Achieving Student Engagement by Seeking Social Justice

by Kevin Sebastian

Kevin Sebastian teaches Grade 8 Literacy at Mackenzie Glen Public School, Ontario. Integrating technology into the curriculum is an important focus in his teaching, along with his passion for making social justice the heart of his teaching.

Any teaching professional who has attended a workshop over the past few years has undoubtedly heard the title "21st Century Learners." Used to describe our current group of students, the title is usually followed with statistics citing the millions of emails that have been sent over the past two minutes, the fact that some of the jobs our intermediate students will eventually fill have yet to be invented, and the impact that technology will have on this world. Usually much is said to promote the power and innovation of computers, and the first super computers, their power contained within several rooms, is compared to those that can now be held in the palm of your hand.

While all of these facts are indisputable, there is, I think, one aspect they are forgetting: the Power of People. I believe it is an error when we apply the term *21st Century Learner* and use it to refer to technology alone — it is too narrow a viewpoint. Twenty-first-century learners are students who have a huge amount of influence in this world, but who are unaware of their own power. They are students who can make a change in their communities, provinces, or foreign countries about issues that they know nothing about. They are global citizens in waiting.

Wrestling with Opposing Models of Teaching

Social justice and the movement towards global citizenship came into my classroom out of necessity. As a math and science teacher for six years, I had thought everything made sense. We used a problem-solving approach that involved authentic situations, experiments, critical thinking, and student-based learning opportunities. Everything was fine until I was assigned my own language class. I found the curriculum overwhelming and was lost within minutes. In the science curriculum document "density" is listed and we study density. In math, "fractions" are listed, and we learn about fractions. In language, the curriculum talks about various forms of texts and writing for a variety of purposes, and all I could think to myself was, "So, where do I find these various texts and purposes for my writing?" After a few panicked emails to colleagues and grade partners, I was assured that all was fine, and we could plan together and create a balanced literacy program founded on the principle of the Gradual Release of Responsibility.

That's when I got really lost. In our approach to the mathematics program, we pose a question and then "let go," allowing the students to think, explore, debate, and then present their findings. I love it and the students seem to embrace this idea. Then I started learning about the Gradual Release of Responsibility, where I model my thinking before entering into a shared experience with the class, which is followed by small, guided groups, all before students are allowed to work on the task independently. I could not fathom how these two models could co-exist.

How could I ask students in math and science to be problem solvers and divergent thinkers and then, in the afternoon, ask them to sit and listen while I modelled my own thinking? Were these models not polar opposites? Could both exist in a class? Was there a problem asking students to think about a piece of text before I shared my own thoughts? If I'm modelling my own ideas and students share their thoughts, are those thoughts really their ideas or my own being bounced back to me?

I continued to struggle with this until one fateful afternoon. We were writing a hypothetical letter to a hypothetical person about an issue that didn't exist. One student asked the most brilliant question: "Why are we doing this?" Upon realizing that I had no response, we stopped the lesson, and I went home that weekend and re-planned my entire outlook on my language program. What I deemed lack of motivation and students not caring about anything was incorrect. My students wanted to do; they were just waiting for the opportunity and for me to point them in the right direction.

Social justice became the vehicle that drove my language program as it gave students a chance to explore real issues, in a real manner, arriving at real solutions. Over the past several years, social justice has spread to my mathematics, science, and social studies programs and recently to an intermediate leadership project, similar to the 40 hours of volunteer service that students do in secondary school (part of our requirements to graduate from elementary school; the one part of our program that students never complain about having to complete).

Writing for Real

Just as the scope of social justice has changed in my classroom, so have the topics. We have explored international issues, such as the conflict in Sudan, child labor, women's rights, and the accessibility to food in light of rising prices. Students have also examined childhood obesity, war and conflict, cancer, and poverty. While all of these topics provided valuable leadership opportunities and meaningful learning experiences, they have paled in comparison to our exploration of child soldiers in Northern Uganda.

An under-reported story

When we first began looking at this situation in 2004, it was, according to the United Nations, one of the 10 most under-reported stories in the world. At that time, we learned about the Night Commuters, children who would walk several kilometres every night to avoid being captured by a rebel group called Lord's Resistance Army (LRA). The LRA is notorious for committing murder, raising terror, and forcing children into their army or into slavery.

Over the past seven years, we have expanded our program into a cultural exchange between our school and a secondary school in one of the hardest hit areas in Northern Uganda. Our students have worked on raising awareness and finding sustainable solutions; meanwhile, Uganda is beginning to experience peace, and people are slowly returning to their homes. We have worked on shared projects, written letters to share ideas and experiences with one another, talked to one another about concepts such as peace, family, and life goals, and helped one another grow as individuals and as global citizens. Although we are separated by more than 11 000 km, we have become neighbors.

Throughout this process, the hardest part is saying yes. Yes, I'm willing to go where the learning takes me. Yes, I will put in the little bit of work to reap the rewards. And yes, my students and I can learn and make a difference in our lives and someone else's as well.

Unfortunately, too often the answer is no, not right now, or I can't. What follows is my open letter to my fellow professionals as to why social justice can change their program and their students.

An Open Letter on the Importance of Social Justice

Dear Colleague,

We all share a common thread in this world. We are trying to make a difference in the lives of our students as someone once did for us. What if that difference could be extended beyond the walls of our classroom and the "difference" we make is not just contained within that student, but shared among the masses? The key to this idea is teaching through social justice. The opportunities it offers will benefit your practice, your students, and the lives of everyone involved.

I know that we are bound by curriculum documents, report cards, and parental and administrative demands; however, social justice is not an add-on, but a means to an end. One of the biggest challenges we face daily is student engagement, while still meeting the curriculum expectations. I have found that the solution to this issue is to let students explore real-life issues in a real-life way.

In Geography, what better way to learn about factors that influence migration than to study the way of life of people that immigrate to our country? We have made Uganda our case study. We studied the peoples' way of life, the 25-year conflict, their cultures, and their customs much like any other class, but we supplemented that learning by connecting with students in the heart of the conflict. We wrote letters and communicated with former child soldiers, and we interviewed people who fled their home country to start a new life in ours.

Our class was moved and motivated by these experiences and wanted to do more. We took this opportunity to learn about economics and sustainable solutions. We compared our economy to theirs and used it to answer questions such as, why doesn't everyone go to school in Northern Uganda and how has Canada been involved in the problems and solutions in a country so far away? We discovered that buying goods here and shipping them to Uganda, even with the best intentions, could have dire consequences by affecting local businesses and economies. We found sustainable solutions to problems, while also supporting businesses and families in Uganda.

I used to think that my students didn't care about anything but themselves. The reality, however, was that they wanted to care about something else, but didn't know what that "something" was. By offering experiences or exposing our students to various situations, they will respond. They will learn content, but most important, they will learn about themselves.

The empowerment that students have felt through our studies in social justice has surpassed all other areas, as this is not limited to those with the highest grades or the strongest athletic abilities. In our language class, our students have written letters to our prime minister and minister of foreign affairs, trying to persuade them to adopt our slogan "Being part of the solution, not part of the problem." They have used the media as a medium to have their voices heard, contacting local outlets and writing editorials to raise awareness and exposure on a variety of issues. Our students have created blogs and realized that the supposed obstacles that stood in their way aren't really there. Ultimately, our students discovered their own voices and that they have a place in this world. People listened, responded, accepted, rejected, and debated with the newly empowered students. Regardless of the results they achieved, all the students left the class realizing that they had something to say and the power to say it — no one could take that away from them.

Isn't that the goal all of us strive for: to instill something within our students that will never leave?

In new curriculum documents, literature, and workshops, the term *critical thinking* has made its way onto everyone's tongue. But how can we think critically about issues that are not relevant to the lives of our students or worse yet, not even real? Social justice issues allow our students to think and truly become leaders among their peers.

Once we did some learning about Uganda, I said to the class: "So, now what? We can turn our backs or we can do something." I was amazed with the ideas the students came up with. They ran charity soccer tournaments with thousands of dollars in donations from local businesses and organizations. They organized awareness assemblies and kiosks for the rest of the school to share in their learning. They prepared a Movie and Letter Writing Day for the local schools, urging them to support their work, complete with support packages to take back to their schools. And perhaps most important, they started and joined social justice clubs at the high schools once they graduated — once we give our students skills to think critically and reason to be passionate, the resulting leadership is inevitable.

Removing the barriers

Before I began my journey down this path, I always came up with the same excuse as to why I couldn't take it — I didn't know anyone to get started to do the things I wanted to do. Aside from the encouragement I hope you feel from this letter, the other thing I hope to do is remove the excuse that plagued me. We all belong to the same family of teachers, and if we are asking our students to remove the barriers of their classroom, then we should as well. As a fellow colleague, you now know one other person to support your journey into social justice whether it is Uganda, connections with First Nations in Northern Ontario, or an issue affecting your community.

Through social justice, we have learned the true meaning of 21st century learning. Not the computers and technology, but the leaders that we develop and foster will truly make a difference to our world. There is not a computer powerful enough to match the gift that we can offer students to support their development and help them realize the influence that they have in this world, to cultivate the idea that they truly can make a difference not only in the lives of others, but the places where we live and how we choose to live. Once our students realize they have this power, it will not be easily removed. It will stay with them and grow. It will be passed on to others, and when we consider those possibilities and the impact it can have in the 21st century, our outlook suddenly appears much brighter.

Most important, imagine the change in our world when we don't define ourselves by borders, but identify ourselves by relationships, whether they be in our community, province, country, or world. The thought of our intermediate students going out into this world as compassionate, yet critical thinkers will surely be the defining feature of the 21st century.

P.S. I can be reached at Kevin.d.sebastian@yrdsb.edu.on.ca to share an idea, build capacity, or find ways to collaboratively push the learning of all of our students forward in a global classroom.

Relationship and Relevance: How Two Middle-School Teachers Approach Their Students

by Monica McGlynn-Stewart

Monica McGlynn-Stewart has been a classroom teacher, consultant, and administrator. Currently teaching in the School of Early Childhood Education at George Brown College, she is completing her doctorate in teacher education.

As a teacher educator and former classroom teacher, I know how important it is to engage students in their learning. As part of my longitudinal research with beginning teachers, I have had the privilege of observing in many classrooms over the years, and I would like to share the great work that two beginning middle-school teachers are doing.

When I walked into Kelly's and Kendra's classrooms for the first time, I was immediately struck by the relaxed, yet purposeful way their students worked. They smiled at one another, appeared to get along well, and worked cooperatively. Classroom discussions were lively, with most students offering an answer or opinion. The teachers were warm and supportive, and everyone seemed "at home" in the classroom. I spoke to the teachers several times over the first years of their teaching to try to understand how they had achieved these positive learning environments.

I learned that Kendra and Kelly understand that the foundations for effective learning and teaching at the middle-school level are positive student–teacher and student–student relationships, and curriculum that is relevant to the lives of their students. Both teachers are now teaching in large, diverse urban schools in Central Canada — neither teacher expected to be a literacy teacher. Kendra specialized in teaching Mathematics and Kelly in Physical Education and Health during their pre-service education. While they have taught these subjects over the first four years of their teaching, they also have been the home-room literacy teacher.

Like all new literacy teachers, Kendra and Kelly worry that they don't know enough about literacy or how to teach it effectively. This concern has motivated them to continually seek out new learning opportunities in the form of teacher resources, workshops, courses, and mentoring from more experienced teachers. Although Kendra and Kelly feel that they did not begin with a deep knowledge of literacy teaching and learning, their ongoing learning and their commitment to a fair and respectful learning environment have brought them far.

Forming Positive Relationships

Both teachers believe that forming and maintaining positive relationships at school is a key part of their teaching, no matter what the subject area.

In order to build relationships with her students, Kendra takes the time to talk to them about their interests and activities outside of school. Doing this builds trust that allows the students to take learning risks in the classroom.

As Kendra says, "If they don't trust me, it's not going to work out very well for either of us."

While the students are working, Kendra schedules mini-conferences to check in with the students to see how they are doing. The content of the conference may be an academic issue, but it doesn't have to be. It is the regular, predictable, personal contact that is important.

"So, for every day, I have a couple of kids who are expecting to have a little chat with me. If they've got nothing to talk about, then we just talk about the weather or something."

In addition to this in-class check-in time, Kendra has organized an after-school homework club for all the Grades 7 and 8 students. For some of the students who come, this is a time for needed academic help; for others, it is a time for extra encouragement and emotional support.

Kelly, too, uses mini-conferences to get to know her students and to build trusting relationships with them. She knows that if the students are not feeling safe socially and emotionally, then effective learning is unlikely to occur. She establishes the goals for her program by trying to put herself in her students' shoes: "If I was in Grade 8, and feeling really insecure with myself and socially awkward and going through puberty, I wouldn't want to be singled out in class and made to feel stupid."

As a Physical Education teacher, Kelly feels that she has an edge in the area of building relationships. She uses the more relaxed and playful atmosphere of the gym or playing field to draw out students who may be harder to reach in the classroom.

Both teachers work on building bonds with their students through humor, but never put-down or belittling humor. As Kelly says, the students need to know that she will always treat them with respect: "A really important aspect of your teacher–student relationship is mutual respect. They need to know that you are not going to belittle them or yell at them."

Part of that respect involves showing their students that they are learners, too. Kendra shares with her students that she struggled with reading comprehension as a student, and Kelly confides to her Grade 8s that she felt "Oh, I can't do this!" in Grade 9 math. Both reveal their past struggles with learning, but also focus on how working hard and seeking help pulled them through.

Not only do these teachers reveal their past learning struggles, they also position themselves as ongoing learners. Kendra reminds her students that if they don't "get" something she is teaching, then she needs to figure out how to teach it better. She says to her students, "We learn together. So, if you mess up, then I realize that I've messed up too. I need to readjust."

The Importance of Classroom Community

In addition to building positive relationships with individual students, Kelly and Kendra work hard to establish supportive classroom communities. According to Kelly, achieving this begins with the students' belief that the teacher likes the class and wants to be with them. "I like helping them and I like being here," she says, "and I think the kids can pick up on that energy." Kendra makes sure that there is always time for the class to enjoy one another's company through celebrating accomplishments, playing group games, or doing Tribes activities (a professional development program). Both teachers use classroom jobs, such as tending to class pets or dealing with recycling, to give their students a sense of ownership in the classroom.

Consistent routines and clear expectations also help to foster a positive and safe classroom atmosphere. Kendra and Kelly find that the more organized and clear they are, the more organized and less anxious their students are. Fostering this includes putting a weekly and daily agenda on the board so the students know what to expect and ensuring that materials are accessible so the students can get what they need.

Kendra knows that the students' energy should be going into learning, not trying to figure out what's going on. "If they are constantly worrying 'What's coming up next?' or 'Where am I going to get that?'" she said, "there's no way they can devote any energy to working on math skills or writing a paper."

Finally, Kendra and Kelly believe that if they want their classrooms to function as positive communities, then they need to be models of appropriate, respectful behavior, and gently but firmly call the students on their behavior when they are less than respectful to one another. Neither has any tolerance for name-calling or put-downs.

Relevant Curriculum Content

Kendra and Kelly "hook" their students, many of whom have had struggles with school attendance in the past, with curriculum that is connected to what is going on in their lives and in the wider world.

Kendra uses newspapers to link current events to concepts in the curriculum. She brings in articles, but also encourages the students to bring in articles and to form opinions about what they are reading. "It's not just show and tell anymore," she says. In addition, at the end of each math unit, the students need to complete a project that demonstrates their understanding of the usefulness of the concepts "just to show them that things have a real-life application — it's not all about tests."

Kelly works to connect what she is teaching to what is going on in the world and to her students' immediate lives. She says, "I try hard to make it applicable to their lives and their interests." If the students are reading *Twilight* and enjoy creating comics on the computer, she works that into her literacy program. She is always on the lookout for opportunities to teach "life lessons," to point out how what they are studying matters in their everyday life.

Relevant Curriculum Processes

Group work is used frequently by these teachers because they know that peers are particularly important at this age. Kelly finds that group work is particularly useful for discussions of social issues and problem solving. Both teachers encourage their students to voice their opinions, and to question and challenge each others' ideas in a respectful way. Kendra cites this as a major goal of her literacy program. "I really want the kids to be able to find their own voice," she says, "and to be able to write and speak intelligently about things that they're interested in, in a way that convinces other people of their understanding."

A wide range of knowledge and skills among their students motivates Kendra and Kelly to offer choices in how the students learn and demonstrate their learning. Kendra makes general teaching plans over the summer, but then tries to "let the students direct the flow, to tell me how they want to learn and show their knowledge." Kelly assigns projects with many different deliverables from which the students can choose, perhaps a report, short story, comic, or play, on paper or on computer or presented orally.

Early in their teaching careers, Kelly and Kendra have discovered the benefits that result from focusing on positive relationships and classroom communities, and relevant content and teaching practices. This respectful approach, coupled with their ongoing professional development, will ensure that they continue to grow as teachers and to deepen their understanding of literacy teaching and learning.

Photovoice: Our Photographic Truth

by Lynda Marshall

Lynda Marshall is an English teacher working with Grade 10 boys and with students in Grade 12 University English. She is the Lead Literacy teacher at Widdifield Secondary School, North Bay, and coordinator of the New Teacher Induction Mentoring program.

Engagement is the key! Keeping students engaged as active participants in their own learning is critical. Teaching boys, many of whom are having difficulty with literacy, is challenging and rewarding.

This Photovoice project involved 14 boys with 14 digital cameras. The students were given the cameras and asked to photograph their lives outside of school. Handing them these cameras further developed the trust and mutual respect needed in a classroom. It also made the students active researchers, as well as participants. They were given a voice through photography.

These photographs were to include
- physical environment — their homes, bedrooms, yards
- hobbies — Xbox, reading, television habits, skateboarding
- friends and get-togethers
- transportation — how they get to and from school, the mall, and movies
- extracurricular involvement
- out-of-school activities — sports, classes, and clubs
- people who are important in their lives
- what they are reading, wearing, and watching

- what they eat for breakfast, lunch, and dinner
- where they eat their meals
- family interactions

The boys were asked to document their photos through captions in either a writing journal or a video journal or both.

What the Research Hopes to Find

Why is it that a boy will claim he cannot read well and will refuse to complete assignments, but will spend 40 hours online researching and reading gaming manuals to improve his gaming skills? How can we bring his interests into the classroom and validate them?

Consistency

What interests are shared?
What similarities are found in the family units?
What literacy is available in their lives — at home and at play?
What literate behaviors do they share?
What are their favorite classes?
Why are they engaged in these classes?

Gaps

What are the differences in these photographs?
How much variety in interests exists?
What literacy behaviors are missing?
What differences can be found in the family units?
What are their least favorite classes?
Why are they their least favorite?
What are the gaps that exist between the world of school and the "other" world?

Anticipated outcomes for the students

- Active involvement in their own education
- Being heard and acknowledged
- Presentation skills
- Planning skills
- Journal writing/documentation
- Photography lesson (Media Arts teacher)
- Confidence building
- Writing, editing, polishing
- Computer skills (Mac Lab)
- Creation of a graphic novel using *Comic Life*
- Making recommendations (being heard) concerning plans for future classes for boys that will engage them in such a way that their literacy and success rates will increase as their confidence and desire to be active participants grow

What happened?

1. There was 100 percent participation!

2. Through the sharing of their lives, interests, and fears, the boys formed the strongest bond I have ever witnessed. They were supportive, attentive, and encouraging to one another and continue to be in the regular school setting.

3. Students who previously had no interaction with each other in the room became friends as their interests surprised and even shocked their peers. Questions were asked; plans to "hang out" were made; new seating evolved daily.

4. A strong, cohesive group of young men, respectful of each other's differences and abilities, emerged.

5. Once literate behaviors were discovered and identified, student confidence soared, and their abilities began to shine. Rather than saying, "I can't" or "I don't," they began saying, "Oh, yeah, I know how to do this!"

6. Recommendations from the students include having smaller classes; being offered more choice through differentiation and a variety of resources and reading materials; having more access to technology; and having the opportunity to know one another early in the semester, thus creating a safe and respectful environment (This last-listed recommendation ranked first.)

Participants Are the Researchers; Researchers Are the Participants

If engagement is the key to closing the gaps and getting boys involved and performing at their best, they must have the central voice. We can speculate, and we can ask, but we cannot truly know until the students open their world to us.

Through picture and the written word, boys were given a voice. They were given permission to tell educators what they need in the classroom to be successful.

A few scenarios

- Terrence discovered a talent for photography and visual art that set him on a path to college programs in film and photography. His talent shone through to the class, and we watched his confidence grow and his future plans emerge. Terrence had struggled with school, authority, and alcohol and had turned a corner in his life. When handed a camera, he documented his journey and his new choices and interests. His talent was obvious from the very first photo shared with the class. Students immediately praised his work and enjoyed his narration of his adventures. What talent!

  As a final product, Terrence chose to create a DVD of his life, which included photos, oral narrative, music, and the use of technology. His DVD has been shown in our school to motivate struggling students. It has been shown to faculty of education students and to teachers at staff meetings as an exemplary example of one student's success, talent, and growth.

- Tyler announced he had nowhere to live. Of course, he could not take pictures like the other students. The other boys in the class were dumbfounded. They may all be from different backgrounds, beliefs, likes and dislikes, but they all had a home. Immediately, the class supported Tyler and echoed my own sentiment that I was so proud of him for being in his seat, in this class, period five when he had no bed last night. Would he mind documenting his journey?

  Tyler quickly agreed; he would call it his "couch-surfing adventure." True to his word, he shared daily, as he mowed lawns in exchange for a bed, bought broccoli for supper, and hung out with friends. Regardless of his lack of sleep, strange eating habits, and family problems, Tyler attended class every day, sharing and being supported by his peers, who were now his friends. At the end of the course, the boys were asked to respond to the most amazing, surprising, exciting, or unexpected outcome from this project: *Every* boy wrote about Tyler: Tyler with the droopy jeans, Tyler with the supposed attitude and the ear holes, Tyler with no home for three weeks. They wrote about how proud they were that he came to school and how much they respected him for his perseverance and resilience. They also wrote about appreciating their own homes and families even more after experiencing Tyler's journey.

(Unfortunately, Tyler is representative of a group of students who often fall through the cracks. Being able to share in a safe environment was healthy for Tyler and a life lesson for the rest of the class.)

- Shane waited a few days before speaking out. He watched the photographs of his classmates' bedrooms, Playstations, families, collections, and so on before raising his hand to say, "Ms. Marshall, I don't actually have a bedroom, so I do not know what to take pictures of for my project." The class went quiet as I asked, "Where do you sleep?" Shane explained that he slept in the living room at his house. He was told that that is his space then and he should begin there. Two or three weeks before this sharing began, the students might have made jokes or comments or ignored him. Due to the sharing and the trust that had been building so quickly through Photovoice, the boys supported Shane immediately. They made comments like, "Cool! Do you get to kick everyone out of your room when you want to sleep?" and "I guess you get the TV all to yourself whenever you want? Must be great to watch the basketball games!" For Shane, a teenage boy, to share this information with a group like this is very telling. The instant support he received catapulted him into photographing every corner of his home, his yard, his family, and many other intimate parts of his world. He stood proud knowing he had nothing to hide.

Photography by Terrence Phillips

Exploring Web 2.0 Tools to Deepen Knowledge

by Kate Shields

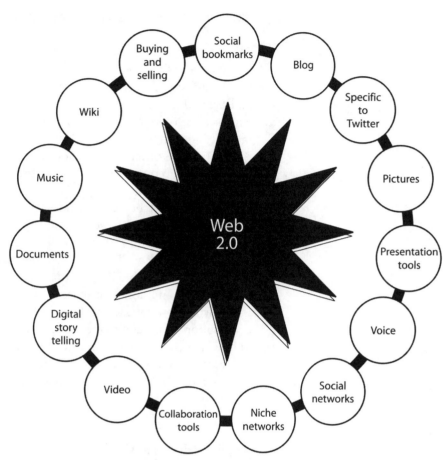

Kate Shields is the teacher-librarian for all the secondary schools in the Near North District School Board. She is also well known for her technology skills and enthusiasm for using technology in the classroom.

This graphic provides a structure for organizing and classifying the different tools that are exploding all over the world and are becoming part of the greater term *Web 2.0*. What makes tools such as YouTube (Video), Facebook (Social networks), Glogster (Presentation), and Flickr (Pictures) different from the first generation of websites is their ability to be interactive with the user. Generally, these tools will require a signup process and give you the opportunity to collaborate and share with other users. The other thing that makes these tools different from first-generation tools is that they are Web based. That means there is no downloading software to the machine being used, nor are these tools stored on a particular machine's hard drive; instead, they can be accessed through the Internet anytime anywhere.

There is no doubt that these tools are already becoming part of the daily routines for our 21st century learners. They are quickly moving from being digital natives to being digital residents. They understand how these tools can help them succeed academically, professionally, and personally.

Questions for you as an educator in the 21st century: Do you consider yourself a resident on the Internet? Do you know what it means to be a resident on the Internet? Can you identify some labels from the graphic? Are you willing to learn about Web 2.0? Are you willing to incorporate new tools into your practice to help differentiate your instruction? Are you willing to let students experiment with these tools to demonstrate their knowledge and understanding of a subject?

When will I find the time to learn all of this? How can my students learn from me?

Ideas for Becoming a Resident on the Internet

The most successful residents on the Internet create a personalized digital dashboard to help them organize their favorite tools. There are hundreds of on-the-dashboard tools, but some of the most popular are iGoogle, Netvibes, My Yahoo, and Symbaloo. These personalized digital dashboards allow you to customize your access to your favorite tools. From this one location you can access your favorite blogs to follow, your Twitter feeds, Facebook, email, and so much more. Again, like the other Web 2.0 tools, these dashboards are Web based with no software required to be downloaded; they can be accessed from anywhere with Internet connections.

Once you start becoming more familiar with these tools, you will start to notice symbols on other websites to help you connect to the tools. For example, one is the "like" button from Facebook: once you press it, a link appears as a post on your Facebook wall. There are other sharing buttons, twitting buttons, RSS feed buttons, and more buttons to come. The idea is to be aware of the power of these buttons and not to be an expert on every single one.

You will know you have really made it when you start to understand the embed code options on many of these sites. The most common example is under You-Tube videos, where you will find the word *embed*. By pressing this button you get to copy the html code, or website language, for that section so that you can incorporate it onto your own Web tool and continue to share it across the social networks.

Why Use Web 2.0 Tools?

These tools are designed to emphasize collaboration — an essential skill for our 21st century learners. They have the ability to cross any geographical boundary; being completely Web based, they can be accessed anywhere over the Internet. Learners will find themselves often networking and collaborating in these types of tools through their professional and personal lives. As educators we should prepare them for their future learning. These tools can be used to expand their knowledge prior to, during, and after reading. They provide a unique way for students to ask questions while reading, bringing a certain level of excitement and encouragement to help struggling readers stay motivated.

Examples of Web 2.0 tools used to deepen knowledge after reading a novel

Tool	Example
Glogster http://edu.glogster.com	Create a digital poster. *Example:* Ask the students to create a digital poster that advertises the movie version of the book that includes video, images, and hyperlinks.

Prezi http://www.prezi.com	Create a slide show, incorporating video and hyperlinks. *Example:* Ask the students to create a timeline of events from their novel. It should include video, images, and hyperlinks to more information.
Kerpoof http://www.kerpoof.com	This tool gives some basic themes and characters to help generate story ideas. *Example:* After students read their novel, have them create a short story with the same plot and themes as the novel.
Voicethreads http://www.voicethreads.com	This tool allows you to post an image or video in the centre and then have multiple people comment around the image either by typing a comment or by recording their voice. *Example:* Ask students to create a digital story with their own images and read it out loud with expression. Ask the viewers to leave a comment.
Blabberize http://www.blabberize.com	Record voice over an image. *Example:* Students choose a character from their novel and record how their character answers interview questions.
Tagxedo http://www.tagxedo.com	This tool is similar to the popular Wordle tool, but it lets users determine the shapes in which their words appear. *Example:* Ask the students to make a list of words from the novel they are reading and incorporate them into an appropriate shape.
Wallwisher http://www.wallwisher.com	Use virtual sticky notes. *Example:* While reading a novel students can post digital "I wonder" questions on the wall.
StoryJumper http://www.storyjumper.com	Create a digital storybook. *Example:* Have the students design and create a novel of their own. Consider getting the books printed professionally and adding them to your own library collection.

Taking the Next Step

The best way is to jump in and try something. Just one thing. Don't set out to be an expert on all the tools all at once because the tools are always changing, new ones are being developed, and some areas have not even been thought of. Try to focus on the bigger picture of offering your students more options to present their work and allowing choice in demonstrating their knowledge. Embrace the idea that the teacher does not have to be the expert — the teacher is the facilitator.

Level 1	Take one of the ideas suggested and just try it.
Level 2	Check out these websites for more ideas and adapt to make your own: http://elemliteracy.wikispaces.com/Web+2.0+Tools http://www.web2teachingtools.com/index.html http://50ways.wikispaces.com/Tools+A+to+Z
Level 3	Find ideas from websites recommended by using a social networking tool such as Twitter or Delicious.
Level 4	Create, contribute, and share new ideas across social networks to other educators. Encourage your students to find a tool they haven't used before and to expand their own learning.

Engaging Students in a Media-Saturated Environment

by Jon Lewis

Jon Lewis is a Grade 8 Literacy teacher and Intermediate Lead teacher at Mackenzie Glen Public School. He fills his classroom with media tools and events, and negotiates literacy choices with his students, building a collaborative environment that supports deep and intensive learning.

As educators, we are required to provide experiences that engage, challenge, and meet the needs of our students, and still get through the curriculum expectations. There is a growing sense that students are more difficult to capture, as the standard for entertainment is forever being raised due to the often numbing effects of overstimulation, accessibility, and consumption. How, then, do we engage students in a media-saturated environment?

One thing is certain: the entertainment value of an awkward, 30-something teacher, who gets fired up about embedding Web tools into blog posts (no matter how amazing the blog post) cannot compete with Black Ops, Katy Perry, or, for that matter, Jersey Shore. Nonetheless, the voice of the teacher in the middle-school classroom is still vitally important; it is, however, better suited as the "implied" voice that is heard through the overt voices of the students. As one considers the above realities, it appears that in order to effectively reach our audience, a new triangle for deconstruction needs to be constructed . . .

The foundation for engaging the intermediate audience is *choice*. Students who choose their outcomes will inevitably be more engaged than those who are told what to do. However, the foundation of the triangle both supports and is supported by student voice and teacher knowledge of students. Without the understanding of who the students are and what they care about, it will be difficult to hear their voices in the classroom or provide an appropriate environment for self-selected outcomes.

The Middle Years Triangle

(triangle labels: student voice / teacher knowledge of student / choice)

Encouraging Student Voice Online: Voicethread

Voicethread is an online collaborative tool built to encourage student voice. The simplicity of the design and its ability to receive and display almost any file format makes learning the tool effortless to our media savvy audience.

The most important feature of Voicethread is the way in which students can interact with their work and the work of their peers. It has really helped to bridge the gap between trying to guess a student's thought process on a particular task and really knowing what thoughts shaped the outcome. Students can underline directly on the work posted as they type or record their thoughts about the specifics. They can interact with documents, photos, artwork, and video directly through Voicethread.

Voicethread has proven especially useful as we challenge students to be mindful of strategies they use as they read or interpret texts. Students can underline specific references within Voicethread and record their thoughts relating to those references. Comments can be moderated — public access prohibited — or made available to be shared so that others can hear and see strategies their peers are using. It has become common practice in my classroom to begin our learning with the voices of my students modelling metacognition.

Voicethread is especially adept at handling highly visual content. Picture books, videos, and advertisements have been shared and thoroughly analyzed through the tool's interactive nature. Likewise, student-generated artwork, public service announcements, clay animations, advertisements, audio recordings, and graphic novels have all made it onto our Voicethread network for feedback in order to deepen effectiveness.

By using Voicethread, my students have become incredible resource "gatherers" for the class. When deconstructing effective advertisements, students were challenged to find powerful examples and post them to Voicethread to be shared and discussed by others. The richness of content chosen by the class was inspiring. It is fascinating how much ownership students take in engaging with the content when they become its source. It also serves as a looking-glass into the interests and values of the specific students in the class.

Providing a Framework for Choice

There is no perfect tool or method for deepening engagement; however, with tools such as Prezi, Aviary, Glogster, Comic Life, or the Google suite of apps, the menu of choices is often limitless. As students work their way towards the intention of the task, the challenge becomes about providing a framework of reference as they chart their course through a sea of tools. Students need to remain focused on their destination in order to arrive at the end with an outcome based on the assigned criteria, not just a product that is a really well-designed advertisement for the chosen tool.

Whether designing their culminating task for Visual Arts, working on group advertisements in Media, choosing the method of recording their thoughts as they read, or brainstorming their research topic for a social justice unit, students must be able to provide a rationale for their choice. As they begin to grapple with making choices, it is critical for us to build structures in our classrooms for dialogue and feedback to help facilitate choice.

In my classroom, the framework that often helps to facilitate choice is similar to the creative process, as outlined in *The Arts*, a 2009 curriculum document from the Ontario Ministry of Education:

Inspiration $\longrightarrow$ Planning $\longrightarrow$ Exploration $\longrightarrow$ Producing and Revising

Begin with inspiration

The intermediate students I have had the privilege of teaching are often inspired by content that is relevant to them as learners and that introduces them to larger communities of learning so they can see the importance of being part of the learning.

I have found that middle students are captured by material that raises awareness of how the world around them functions and how they can be instrumental in influencing its function. It also seems they are more drawn to content that has high visual appeal or somehow incorporates aspects of their own pop culture.

Considering this, we decided to use Ishmael Beah's *A Long Way Gone* as a source of awareness into issues of injustice. We wanted students to be able to relate the large disparities between Global South and Global North to their world, and consider what it looks like for some to grow up in areas where the realities of this disparity are much more evident. Through this investigation, we have been able to confront issues of violence, specifically in the media, with a much less narrow perspective. Before launching into the book, students were challenged to consider their own values relating to violence: they examined the effects of violence within the media they consume. We were able to expose the harsh realities of violence, and how it is often glorified in our experiences in North America.

Our goal through this investigation was to somehow help students to be confronted with the realities of a world often removed from their experience. In order for this to happen, we realized that stories alone would not be sufficient — we had to bring faces, names, and people to the experience.

Through a contact my grade partner had in Uganda, we began writing letters to students whose realities were more similar to those of Ishmael Beah in Sierra Leone. We received letters back and thought it only appropriate to create a more meaningful connection between these two worlds. We wanted our faces to be seen, and our voices heard, so that our friends in Uganda could understand who we were and what our experiences were. Due to the lack of resources in Uganda, we were unable to connect via the Web, so we decided to have each of our students sit in front of a camera and record what freedom meant to them. Their short videos were compiled and sent on a disc to be hand-delivered to our contact school in Uganda.

At time of writing, we had not heard back from our friends in Uganda. As a result of the clear disparity, specifically in access to technology, our students began writing letters to companies, challenging them to support our efforts and provide technology that could be delivered to Uganda. The students jumped at the opportunity to write to these companies. Most important, they began to feel as if their voices could be heard.

Plan for success

As students are inspired and challenged, the next step of the process is for them to plan their outcome. Planning needs to include what content will be used, how it will be communicated, and what tool will help in the process.

Planning, this year, has come in many forms. In some cases, it was as simple as a written proposal or completion of a graphic organizer. Other times it developed into using group blogs to dialogue and brainstorm ideas related to themes or post rationales on blog homepages for cross-class discussions.

Regardless of the form, the main goal of planning is to build accountability into the process. Students need to be able to articulate why they are making the choices they are at the beginning of the task, so that at the task's end, they can identify the specific elements that worked or needed to be changed. Without time to dialogue, share, or rework ideas, I have found the depth of learning limited.

Explore guilt-free

The process of exploration becomes more important, especially in light of the vast array of tools to be used. It is a refreshing activity to participate in learning that has no other purpose than to explore. Often, the most difficult challenge in exploration is convincing the students that it is not about getting a mark, something that can prove to be difficult since many middle students judge the worthiness of a task by its impact on the report card. However, to have time for students to explore what tools are available with feedback that has a collaborative, rather than an evaluative, focus builds an environment for pushing learning to new depths.

We make it common practice to introduce at least one new tool for every unit of investigation. Below is a brief list of some of the tools and the tasks we explored this year. "Purpose of Exploration" was the introduction to the tool. As the year progressed, students could use any of the tools specific to their planned outcomes.

Term	Tool	Focus	Purpose of Exploration
Term 1	Voicethread	Reading, creating online portfolios, beginning an online identity	To share our use of reading strategies for common texts while exploring what it means to find the deeper meaning To share current books we were reading and create online profiles about ourselves as learners
	Prezi	Communicating meaning from text	To share deeper meanings from our independent texts in a range of ways
	Bitstrips, Comic Life	Narrative writing, graphic novels	To use the graphic novel format as a means of communicating narrative writing
	iMovie, Garageband	Visual art and media production	To create claymation and live-action, stop-motion animation, including use of photos, while exploring how to create soundtracks for movies

Term	Tool	Focus	Purpose of Exploration
Term 2	Aviary	Communicating "voice"	To create "audio walks" to communicate the voices of the citizens of Africville through narrative storytelling
	TodaysMeet	Reading and media deconstruction	To share thoughts relating to the elements of literature used by authors and media creators as we viewed videos or did class read-alouds
	Google Apps	Researching, discussing, and sharing issues of social justice	To learn what social justice is and share links to research specific to group themes; to investigate the use of Google Apps for collaboration between two Grade 8 classes

Produce and revise to share

The culture of sharing is alive and well in the intermediate classroom. Students are much more networked as a result of technology, and most come into middle-school classrooms with some experience in sharing information about themselves. While true that some students are more critical about what they share than others, the process of making information "public" is still a learning process for many students. Since most scour hundreds of images in order to find the perfect online identity, they understand the concept of critical sharing; however, some still lack critical thought when it comes to "sharing" work. They may be used to completing their work, only to hand it in to the teacher for feedback, to be sent back to them with a "grade" — this linear process does not encourage critical thought. Once students begin sharing their work with peers, and sometimes, multiple peers, they learn to view their work more critically before presenting it.

Our journey into sharing began early in the year with Voicethread. Many students were familiar with the tool before. However, we really wanted to push students towards collaboration. We began "sharing" our reading experiences by creating a common thread in which students could edit by adding images of book covers they had read. They were challenged to provide a brief synopsis and then explain why (or why not) someone should read their book. This simple activity of sharing what we were reading exposed many of the students to books they had never read and encouraged many to pick up the recommended reading.

The real power of sharing emerged much more strongly in the writing process. We feel that sharing should be about harnessing students' knowledge to promote peer learning. As students worked through their drafts, sharing became a vital step in turning exploration into production. We dove back into Web tools for assistance once again.

After generating the criteria for the writing task, students can easily edit each others' work using collaborative online tools. The two we found most effective were Google Docs and, of course, Voicethread. There are many positives to both tools; however, the downside to Google Docs, and why it is not on the chart above, is that an email account is required, which brings a host of considerations before use. Voicethread users can register a non-active email; however, they cannot directly type on the document online. Instead, they can download the file or use the pen tool to circle and record their voice as they edit. The enormous benefit for both tools is the online record of how students are editing each others' work, which can be used to inform assessment and practice.

Finally, when students "re-share" their work for teacher feedback, work is much more refined due to the critical process that has been involved. In my class, this critical process has had an impact not only on students' writing, but on many facets of my program, including media production. This process requires deep student engagement so cannot be completed the night before assigned due dates. When students are proud of their work, they are inspired to share it. No matter the mechanism of sharing, their final display often encourages future learning. Web tools have made the process of sharing easier and more critical; however, the old school bulletin-board display of a job well done still brings joy . . . even to intermediate students.

5

Creating the Conditions for Learning

Laying the Framework for the Ideal Classroom
by Lainie Holmes

As an Intermediate teacher at Reesor Park Public School, Lainie Holmes worked with her students to develop their program timetable collaboratively. At time of publication, Lainie is serving as a resource consultant supporting literacy through mathematics education.

It was the end of August, only a few weeks before a new school year would begin. I was starting to plan the activities I would do with my new class during their first week back at school. In past years and for this particular year, I planned on stating the rules in my classroom. Every teacher is different, and I wanted the students to know the expectations in my room. I still had the four laminated posters that I put up on the wall each year; the posters outlined four Tribes rules: mutual respect, no put-downs, the right to pass, and active listening. But this year, posting these rules didn't make sense to me; it didn't seem right.

A few weeks earlier, I had attended a math conference in Barrie, Ontario, for three days, and had begun to change my practice as a result. But it was not the well-known, motivational speaker who inspired me to think differently, but the modelling of three classroom teachers, who facilitated our small-group sessions each day, that prompted me to question my practice.

The first morning together, the facilitators guided us through the process of creating group norms. Anonymously, we were asked to make a list of things that were important to us when working in a group. It was completely quiet in the room as 30 adults jotted down what was important to them. I wrote down: "no side conversations while others are talking" and "no texting." We were asked to hand in our sheets to the facilitators.

The facilitators came back that afternoon with our comments summarized and on chart paper. I can remember looking for my comments up on the sheet, pleased to see that they were included. We were told to read the sheet and were asked, "Is there anything on the list that you can't live with?" Some people said that they didn't mind side conversations because sometimes when someone is speaking, it sparks a thought and they want to discuss it with someone next to them. The group was asked if they were okay with keeping side conversations to a minimum, and if they did happen, to keep the discussions math related. We all agreed. We continued with the other items and after further discussion, we had fine-tuned our list and agreed to the norms.

The time that it took was well worth it. Side conversations were minimal, and as a result, we could listen to and focus on the ideas shared by others. Cell phones stayed out of sight and as a result, more people were sharing their ideas. There were days when I wanted to stay outside in the sun for just a few more minutes during our break, but I found myself really watching the time because I knew that my colleagues wanted to stay on schedule (a group norm). I wasn't following the rules of the facilitator — I was showing respect to my colleagues by considering their feelings and needs.

I thought to myself, I need to do this with my students. I want them to be more concerned about how they affect others and considerate than following my list of rules and hearing threats of consequences. I knew how it was done with adults, but what would it look like for students?

I began to think, How would I picture and describe my ideal classroom? Kids sitting together. Working together throughout the room at their desks, on the rug, stretched out on the floor. Kids excited about learning. Kids helping one another, sharing ideas and thoughts, listening to one another. A place where judgment, fear, and insecurity were left outside the classroom door.

I wondered, how will I be able to create such an environment all by myself?

Of course, I cannot. In order for this environment to be created, the students need to be a part of it. They need to help shape it. They need to have a voice. That's how I would do it: to create our group norms, we would discuss our ideal classroom.

Asking the Big Question

On the second day of school, I asked my class: "If you were to picture the best possible learning environment, how would you describe it? What would it sound like? look like? feel like? What would make our classroom ideal for you?"

With excitement, I waited for the flood of responses.

Instead, I had a room full of kids staring at me with puzzled looks on their faces. "What do you mean?" they asked.

I rephrased the question for them: "Well, if we wanted to make our classroom the best possible place to learn, what would it be like?"

After I had rephrased the question and there was more discussion, the kids quickly began to write down their thoughts. The room was silent — only the sounds of moving pencils could be heard. In nine years of teaching, I had never asked my students to share what they envisioned as an ideal place to learn. I wish it wouldn't have taken me so long to do so.

Acknowledging the Students' Ideas

After they had lots of time to think and write, I collected their sheets. I told the class I was going to summarize their responses that evening and bring them in the next day to share with everyone, so we could see what we all had in common. That night, I retyped all of their comments into Wordle, a website where text can be typed into a box and an image will be created that shows the words most often mentioned in the text. The words that are mentioned the most become larger in size, compared to those that are repeated a few times. I thought it would be a great way to show the kids what we valued as a group.

The next day I shared the Wordle by projecting it on our SMART Board. I asked the kids, "What is something that is ideal for the majority of our class? What other things are important to us?" The kids pointed out words that surprised them and began to notice themes. After our discussion, I posted a colored copy of our Wordle on our classroom door as a reminder of what was important to us.

The next day, I took the kids' initial statements and combined those that were similar so I could create a master list on chart paper. Beside each statement, I wrote a number in brackets to show how many times it was written by students in the class. Even if only one student mentioned a particular need, it was written down. I remembered looking for my own comments when we created norms at the math conference and the feeling of acknowledgment when I did see them — I wanted the kids to feel the same sense of acknowledgment: that what they had to say was valued.

The first statement written at the top of the page reflected what was the most important to students in the class: "Respect everyone (teachers, peers, self, classroom space)." The second item that was important to the group was to "be quiet when working, when others are talking, and during independent work time."

I posted our list in the classroom and explained to the kids what the numbers in the brackets represented. I read each statement aloud and asked them if they had any questions about what their peers had written and if they could live with everything on the list. The kids then asked for clarification and for additional comments to be added. In the end, the kids all signed the list to show that they understood what everyone wanted and needed from one another, and that they would do their best to follow it. I signed it as well.

"It's Their Voice They're Hearing"

Now that we had created our ideal classroom, I needed to let my students know that their list served a purpose. It wasn't just a fun activity to do the first week back to school; it was something that would be used throughout the school year. I told my students that, as their classroom teacher, I was responsible for ensuring that they had an ideal learning environment and that the list was to remind us all of what we could do to make the classroom an ideal place to learn. In my role, I would remind them of items on the list, if need be. For example, when the volume in our room began to increase, I would simply say: "Just a reminder that 14 of your classmates, almost half of the class, mentioned that they need a quiet work environment to learn. Let's respect their needs and bring the volume down, please." I didn't use the list to say, "You're breaking this rule or you said . . ." In the end, it's their voice they're hearing — not mine.

It's now the beginning of May as I write this story, and I still refer back to their list when needed. I don't see this as a bad thing. I think it would be strange if every day for 10 months, everyone listened, worked hard, and stayed completely focused. We would be teaching robots, not humans. We need to understand that kids are kids. And if we truly value an ideal learning environment, it is something that we will continue to work on, continue to discuss, and continue to uphold.

The process of creating group norms took about a week from start to finish — maybe 30 minutes each day. Not only did the process bring us closer together as we learned more about each others' needs, but we saw that we had things in common, we were able to work together, and the tone for the year was set — we needed to consider each others' feelings, work together, and value one another.

Not a bad way to start off the year . . .

Working in Groups in the Literacy Classroom

by John Myers

John Myers is a curriculum instructor in Elementary and Secondary Education at the Ontario Institute for Studies in Education, University of Toronto. John has a special interest in collaborative and cooperative team building, both with his college students and with students in the middle years.

Group work has come some distance since we had reading groups based on perceived ability and given such names as Robins, Crows, and Buzzards. But are we clear on what works when we put students in groups for any purpose?

Co-operative and Collaborative Learning Compared

The two common terms are *co-operative* and *collaborative learning*. While these terms are often used interchangeably, they are not synonymous. Nor are they mutually exclusive. While both value the work of students in small groups, advocates of these two traditions seldom talked to each other or read each other's work until recently. This is not surprising, given the volume of research in small-group learning and the need for researchers to ground their work in a particular theory. Unfortunately, in the past, advocates have misunderstood the value of considering co-operation and collaboration as complementary and taking the best from each.

The following chart offers a comparison:

Collaboration	Co-operation
Dictionary definitions of *collaboration*, judging from the Latin root, focus on the process of working together.	The Latin root word of *co-operation* stresses the product of such work.
The classroom roots are British: largely language arts aimed at more active student response to literature.	The educational roots, largely American, pertain to examining the social nature of learning and the nature of group dynamics.
The collaborative tradition takes a more qualitative approach, analyzing student talk in response to a piece of literature or a primary source in history. Here, process is important.	The co-operative learning tradition tends to use quantitative methods that examine achievement, that is, the product of learning.
Advocates stress relatively unstructured group processes promoting purposeful talk and doing engaging work. If the task is rich and authentic, the positive interdependence among group members will evolve.	Advocates of the various forms of this teaching model stress the explicit structuring of the learning environment to induce co-operation among group members through positive interdependence and individual accountability.
Critics worry about the possibility of unequal contribution to the group product: the "sucker" and "free rider" effects.	Critics worry that the talk in groups is wasted on tasks that are more busywork than authentic or engaging.

Interaction is a key element of successful student groups. It may be the mechanism of purposeful quality talk that promotes the learning in small groups. Talk turns the passive reception of information into an active struggle to explore, clarify, refine, shape, and reshape complex ideas. Those who talk more, learn more: their thinking and their writing improve. The silent classroom is often not a learning classroom. On this point my colleagues in both the co-operative and the collaborative learning traditions agree.

But how do we encourage better learning groups among students?

Bridging the gap

Here, I take a detailed look at a popular procedure within the overall group work arena: Think-Pair-Share. It may bridge the gap between co-operative and collaborative approaches. Here is the original procedure.

1. Teacher poses a question.
2. Student thinks about an answer for 5 to 10+ seconds depending on the question or prompt.
3. Student pairs with a partner to share and compare answers and come to an agreement if possible.
4. Pairs share their responses as part of a whole-class discussion.

The structure is relatively simple and low risk: after all, it is hard to hide in a pair. Furthermore, it is flexible with more than a thousand combinations when you consider the many ways to think, to pair, and to share. Here are three of the more popular options.

- Think-Write-Pair-Share: Individual students write a response before pairing.
- Timed Pair-Share: Each member in the pair has a specific time limit to present a response while their partner listens; then, they switch roles.
- Think-Pair-Square: The pairs share with another pair before the whole-class discussion.

When Should Students Work in Their Groups?

For the promotion of learning through purposeful talk, the following kinds of tasks are suitable for designing group activities for pairs or larger groups. These include tasks that stress engagement for the collaborative advocates and tasks that structure the interaction for the co-operative advocates. Some opportunities and variations for Think-Pair-Share serve as examples.

Tasks involving exploratory talk: Sometimes, you may want students to struggle with new information by talking through ideas. Small-group brainstorming to generate ideas and reactions to a provocative question posed by a teacher (or another student) are two examples.

Point-of-View–Pair-Share: An initial prompt directs students to imagine themselves in the situation. For example: "As you read the story about the flood, imagine having a farm in the path of the flood water. How might you feel?"

Tasks involving checking for understanding: You might have a student turn to a partner and review the key points of a film or a presentation. Students may be more willing to express uncertainty in a small group or with a trusted partner than in front of a whole class. That's why the often-used "Any questions? Any comments?" directed to an entire class may not work.

Think-Pair Paraphrase-Share: One partner responds to the teacher's prompt about the main point of the passage; the second partner paraphrases the response: "Are you saying that . . .?"

Tasks involving problem solving and/or decision making: Members of a small group can combine different perspectives, either based on their own experiences or on the task you have created. They must talk it through in order to achieve a consensus and in so doing achieve a deeper understanding.
Think-Pair Consensus-Share: "What is the message in the poem?"

Tasks in which a variety of abilities are required: Different students may bring different talents and experiences to a task. Using roles can help here. For example, if students create a propaganda poster for the First World War, some students can draw while others work on the caption. While working from strength is important, your ultimate goal is to help students develop strengths in many areas of learning.
Think-Pairs in Role-Show: One member of the pair draws and the partner writes a caption explaining the drawing. The showing is done as the pair holds up the drawing and caption, representing their view of the event they have just read about for all to see. Follow-up class discussion assesses similarities and differences in the responses, if the passages read are similar.

Tasks involving review of previously encountered ideas or material: If you ensure individual accountability, students can review material in small groups prior to a quiz or major test. If you used direct instruction or another whole-class approach for the initial learning, change the approach for review. After all, students who mastered the work the first time do not need review, while those who struggled with a teacher-centred approach the first time are not likely to learn through more of the same. This advice is reversed if the initial teaching used a group learning format. Depending on what is to be reviewed, there are many think-pair-share options including the above. One variation could be this:
Think-Interview-Share: Each partner asks questions of the other about the content of the reading. This interview could be done in role. "Please explain to our viewers how a combination of diet and exercise promotes good health."

As a substitute for individual practice in a direct instruction lesson: Some co-operative approaches consist of peer-tutoring in the practice phase of direct instruction. In my own experience, and the research seems to bear this out, we often overuse seatwork or implement such individual practice sessions without much effect. We usually concentrate on misbehavior, thus making it difficult to help those who are struggling, especially the "closet confused" who do not want others to know of their academic difficulties, for fear of being labelled.
Think-Rally Table-Share: Partners take turns writing or performing a task, going back and forth several times as in a rally in tennis; for example, contributing ideas with evidence to support an argument in a position paper on an issue such as "Who won the War of 1812?"

As a vehicle for reflection on the learning: This works in the same way that people talk after a movie, play, concert, or other event. It promotes synthesis of information.

Think-Unpack-Suggest: During their debriefing, partners explain their reasons for their thinking and responses; then, each student, pair, or larger team of four (pairs of pairs) suggests an alternative procedure for use next time they face a similar learning task. "Next time I will try to get into the role of the character in the short story from the beginning so I can more easily figure out the motivation behind the character's action."

The one strategy can be extended in many ways, often determined by the students.

The School Library as a Learning and Leading Hub

by Tania Sterling

Tania Sterling is a teacher-librarian and literacy coach in the York Region District School Board. She has a passion for implementing all aspects of technology into every classroom, and for supporting collaborative teams of teachers. Tania is completing her Ph.D. in education.

Learning spaces are no longer defined by four walls, brick and mortar. Learning and collaboration between individuals from all around the world happens within organic soft-walled, virtual communities, and new information is being written and rewritten every day. Many of our students spend countless hours in these spaces, interacting with a wide range of digital tools and texts at home.

As educators and leaders who are charged with preparing students for the future, part of our job is to help students become critical and responsible consumers *and* producers of information in a fast-paced, technologically rich world. While some educators have embraced technological change and regularly use these same digital tools personally and professionally, other teachers feel anxious and do not know where to start.

The Library as Learning Commons

By leveraging the school library as a *learning commons*, new relationships can be formed between teachers and learners, exciting opportunities to collaborate can be developed, and emerging technologies and information can be accessed and harnessed. In the process of reshaping a school library into a *learning commons* to address the challenge of harnessing "the unfamiliar yet incredibly fascinating opportunities presented by this [technological] transformation" (Ontario Library Association, 2010, p. 2), we need to ensure we build teacher capacity and foster opportunities for collaboration to truly prepare teachers and students for the future.

Long before the notion of libraries as *learning commons* became mainstream, my school principal was convinced that our library could and *should* be the hub of student critical thinking and inquiry, teacher professional learning, and collaboration in the school. As the newly appointed teacher-librarian, I was to make changes to the library's physical layout and schedule to realize this vision. What's more, dividing the library into separate sections where people could learn and work simultaneously would require the creation of a new culture among staff and students. To transform our library into the school's learning hub, I needed to help staff understand the value in doing away with the *silent library* archetype and embrace the library as a dynamic shared space where learners access new technologies and information, and teachers and learners collaborate. Clearly, transforming our library into the learning and leading hub of the school required the shared commitment of all school community stakeholders: students, school staff, and parents.

The Library Experience

Having just completed the Librarianship, Part One Additional Qualifications course, I knew that the physical appearance and layout of the library have a lot to do with its success. Taking lessons learned from *The Starbucks Experience: 5 Principles for Turning Ordinary into Extraordinary* by Joseph Michelli, I wanted to make coming to the library a pleasant, modern-day inquiry and reading experience.

Physical change

With the co-operation of my school principal and custodian, we purchased bright-colored paint and moved furniture to make the library more welcoming. Next, we redefined spaces according to their function: the computer lab, the instructional space, and the collection.

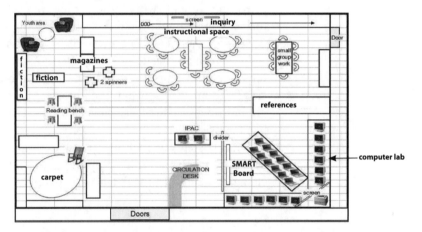

Our outstanding primary picture book collection was moved to one corner of the library. Picture book posters were re-hung in the same area as the rocking chair. Durable play furniture was purchased for students to practise choosing *just right* books on their own, or to show and share their independent reading books with one another.

In the opposite corner, I created a section for older students to sit and read on two red comfy chairs such as you would find in a Chapters bookstore. There, students could access popular, brand-new graphic novels and magazines. All of the junior–intermediate novel sets were moved out of the collection to the book room to free up space for more independent reading books.

The circulation desk and book drop were moved right beside doors to welcome users when they entered and exited the library.

Scheduling

By dividing the library floor plan into three distinct spaces, we tripled the number of students who could access the library at one time. This change forced us to rethink how teachers reserved library time slots.

Within the new *learning commons* model, it quickly became obvious that the paper signup system whereby the teacher-librarian daily posted the library time-table on a clipboard outside the library doors would no longer work. In consultation with staff, the library signup system was moved online for teachers to access anywhere anytime. Staff embraced this change because it allowed them to schedule regular book exchange slots, as well as plan opportunities for students to conduct research using the library technology months in advance.

Resource collection

Once we had ensured more equitable access to the resources in the library for our school community, I focused on reshaping our library's technology and collection to reflect the needs and interests of our school community *and* the world at large. The information technology technician, technology lead teacher, and I determined that the majority of the school's computer hardware required updating. As a school, we also realized that newer technologies had become available to support student learning.

Together we developed a three-year *Literacy through Technology* budget and implementation plan. This plan included procuring document cameras to aid instruction and assessment, ebooks for auditory learners, MP3 recorders for providing students with audio feedback, iPods for students to listen to and view instructional content, netbooks for creating digital media works, and SMART Boards for shared reading and writing lessons.

I then did an inventory of our fiction and non-fiction print resources, weeding the collection of outdated material and books in poor condition. This process freed up shelf space in the library and revealed gaps in our non-fiction and graphic novel sections. I surveyed each grade to find out which books they would like to have added to the collection.

The last step was making a presentation to school council to inform parents of and garner community support for our library renewal project. Aware of the changing needs of today's learners, parents wholeheartedly endorsed the vision and changes.

Ripple Effect

While procuring the new titles and technologies took time, everyone was patient and committed to the new learning commons model.

Initial feedback from staff, students, and parents about the *new* library was resoundingly positive.

- Students remarked the library was a fun place to work and learn with students from different grades in the school.
- Teachers had immediate access to a range of new tools to support their practice, and they began to use the library for division meetings and grade-level team lesson writing and unit planning.
- It was wonderful for students to see caretakers come into the library and sit in the red chairs during their break to read the newspaper or a favorite book, or listen to a podcast.
- Thanks to an amazing teacher who supports English Language Learners, the library is now used before school for a project where a parent volunteer conducts read-aloud sessions in the different first languages found in our school community. As a result, the dual language section of the library has become one of the most popular areas in the collection.

- We're planning to work with children's authors to gain copyright permission to audio-record parents reading the stories aloud for students to listen to as they read along with the print text in their first language and/or in English.

The new space and culture that we created in our learning commons fostered collaboration in an organic way. Teachers learned and explored new technologies in pairs and teams. This team planning and collaboration resulted in the development of new ways to teach fundamental skills and concepts. Teachers were learning along with students and had renewed energy for their practice. The "library as learning hub" idea was taking hold.

Supporting Teacher Learning

Oftentimes, technology is brought into a school under the assumption that teachers will intuitively know how to use it in their practice. Having surveyed staff at the beginning of the year, our library team knew this was not the case. Many teachers indicated they were *lagging behind* when it came to using technology and made learning how to integrate more instructional technology into their practice a priority on their personal professional annual learning plan. Therefore, as the literacy lead teacher and teacher-librarian, I was to find ways to embed the use of technology in our school effectiveness framework.

In my role as a teacher-librarian, I toured the instructional software on our school network with classes to help students select the right tool for the right task when researching, revising, editing, or publishing in the computer lab. I also modelled to students and teachers how to critically search for information online.

As the literacy teacher, I modelled the use of instructional technology to teachers by using a different technology or Web 2.0 tools when I presented at our staff meetings or co-taught literacy lessons in the classrooms.

Literacy through Technology PD model

Research tells us that when teachers experience technology as a *learning* tool, chances increase that they will use technology as a *teaching* tool. With the support of administration, to further support teachers in finding innovative ways to engage students with the new technology tools we brought into the school, we offered job-embedded hands-on learning sessions with the help of our school's computer resources teacher.

Together, we designed a three-part teacher professional learning model for a whole range of topics, including how to create and use MP3 audio files, use the document camera, and access lessons using the SMART Board.

Part 1: Give a Prep With their grade-level partners, teachers signed up to meet with our computer resources teacher during their planning time to select a focus for their professional development.

Part 2: Get Two Preps The following week, supply teachers were brought in to release teachers for two periods during the school day to learn with colleagues and the computer resources teacher to design a technology-embedded activity to implement in the classroom.

Part 3: Hold a Staff Sharing Session Six weeks later, teachers shared their learning at a staff technology-sharing carousel. As teachers presented their student work at the six stations set up around the library, I had light music playing in the background so the atmosphere was casual and fun. The presenters did a masterful job of making the teachers who had felt anxious about trying the technology feel safe, and before long, the teachers were advancing the slides to the next screen or manoeuvring the tool. In this case, teachers became open to change because it was modelled in a social, risk-free setting.

Exciting Grade 8 Cross-School Collaboration

Following the three-part Literacy through Technology professional learning model, we invited teachers to collaborate on several class projects involving Web 2.0 tools.

Our two Grade 8 classes were in the midst of teaching persuasive writing and wanted to do a debate. They were particularly interested in using videoconferencing with students. Coincidentally, the Grade 8 teacher at a neighboring school was also teaching persuasive writing to his students at the time. Through email, it was decided that the three Grade 8 teachers would leverage online collaboration tools to allow their students to form cross-school debating teams. The topic: *Should below level 3 students attend mandatory summer school before entering Grade 9?* The students had one week to structure their *for* and *against* arguments.

The culminating event for the activity would be a live cross-school debate using a piece of free Ontario-licensed, video-conferencing software tool, Adobe Connect. We arranged to have technical support on site at both schools, and fortunately, the chat function that was moderated by a student at each site, and all of the audio and video equipment, worked well. The cross-school video-conference debate was a success.

In this case, the technology was not just used for technology's sake. Video conferencing was used to bring two parties together that would otherwise not be able to work together; therefore, its purpose was relevant and authentic. The Grade 8 teachers were impressed by the focus and commitment of students as they presented their position to an authentic audience, and the students thoroughly enjoyed working and learning in a way that they imagined happening in the "real world" of work.

Reflective Practice and Student Involvement

As the technology evolves, so, too, do teacher professional learning models and our library as learning hub. Valuable student and teacher feedback told us that our library collection needs constant revisiting to include a range of etexts and print texts for independent reading that meet students' changing interests. We have also made more technology tools available for teacher sign out, and they can be reserved online. Most important, our Literacy through Technology professional development model has evolved to include *students* in the planning and delivery of the hands-on technology learning sessions with teachers. By adding student voice into the professional learning model, we help ensure that the needs of the students in the classroom will be met.

Students as teachers

Moreover, teachers feel better supported and the learning activities are set up for success because of the availability of *built-in tech support* by students. As one student commented, "I love to use technology to help me when I learn, but I like it even more when I get to teach with it!"

In this revised model, teachers model what it means to be a lifelong learner, and students are empowered by having an active role in the teaching, leading, and learning process.

Evidence that the collaborative learning commons model has been operationalized can be seen in the way that teachers now use the *Teacher Share* drive on our school's computer network: they post and collaborate on long-range planning, resources, and lessons. When we develop our learning intentions and success criteria for an upcoming unit of study, we plan in teams instead of one-on-one to build on one another's ideas.

Sometimes we even connect with grade-level partners beyond our schools. Doing this helps foster creativity and allows us to more effectively schedule and share the technology tools on site. From an environmental standpoint, we are proud to have reduced the amount of photocopying at the school by allowing students to submit work online instead of on paper for teacher and peer feedback. Throughout the implementation process, we have learned much about how technology can positively change practice and have an impact on student learning.

Learning beyond school walls

The library as a *learning commons* model has provided key learning that has extended beyond the walls of our school. More specifically, the Grade 8 video-conference debate was highlighted in an educational newsletter, and the three-part job-embedded Literacy through Technology model to raise teacher capacity has helped inform the design of teacher professional learning within our network of schools and in our district. Finally, our school team presented a session, "Innovative Approaches to Involving Students in K–8 School Leadership," at an international educational conference to inform participants of how students and teachers work, learn, and lead in collaboration with and beyond our school community.

Becoming Literate in Mathematics

by Kevin Sebastian

Kevin Sebastian teaches Grade 8 literacy and math at Mackenzie Glen Public School, Ontario. He recognizes the power of both math literacy and the connections that math events offer to print literacy development in youngsters.

Any fan of *Curb Your Enthusiasm* will be quick to recall the neurotic Larry David "protesting math" after the clubhouse added a mandatory 18 percent tip to his breakfast order. For those of you who have not seen the episode, David could not figure out how to add in an extra 2 percent because, in his own words, "I don't have a system."

After watching this episode, I wondered two things: How many students feel like Larry David, sitting in math class without the *right system*? And how many people would feel comfortable announcing to the world they couldn't read or write with the same comfort level that David expressed towards math?

I believe that the answers to these two questions are inextricably bound to one another. Many students, teachers, and parents seem to be searching for this mythical system. Mathematics is *not* a system; it is a language and can be taught using the same approaches we take to teach reading, writing, and virtually any other form of communication.

I wonder how many of us would feel comfortable with the following situation. A student walks into a foreign language class, and the teacher asks the student to repeat a variety of phrases that could be used in everyday conversations. The student feels confident and is ready to try them out. The next day is the evaluation, which is comprised of an essay written in the foreign language. In this case, the *system* has failed because the teacher did not provide the necessary skills and language for the student to be successful; the phrases the student learned on day one were empty; they did not build the necessary understanding.

Now consider a similar situation in math. A student walks into a class and is asked to repeat a variety of equations, similar to the one the teacher modelled on the board. The student feels confident and is ready to try out the new skill. The next day the student is presented with a variety of tasks, including reasoning, estimating, problem solving, and communicating.

Has the system provided given the student the necessary skills and language to be successful? Probably not. This situation is more recognizable than the former, or at least it should be, as some of us grew up in that kind of math class.

So, what is the solution? I believe that the answer lies in the language of math. There are several ways in which we can build this into our everyday programs.

Let Them See Mathematics

Most of our students can successfully perform simple multiplication statements such as 3×2, yet when students are asked to show what that looks like, the success rate drops. For those students who struggle in math, numbers, variables, operations, and constants might as well be hieroglyphics.

How can we expect our students to be successful communicators, thinkers, and problem solvers if they first do not understand the basic vocabulary of mathematics? To address this, take the mystery out of math — make use of manipulatives to represent these numbers and operations.

The beginning of our school year is heavily rooted in number sense as this becomes the language we will use throughout the year to address the other strands. For example, in fractions, most of the students entering our classrooms can tell us that the numerator represents the *part* and the denominator represents the *whole*. They know this as they have been repeating the same sentences for the past four years. But ask that same group to shade in where all regular fractions occur on a number line, and I routinely get answers that are negative, whole numbers and well beyond the 0 to 1 range.

To address this, we spend a considerable time representing fractions using pattern blocks, Cuisenaire Rods, geoboards, fraction tiles, paper, water in graduated cylinders, base-10 blocks, and drawings. Within a differentiated classroom, there are many levels and questions that can be posed to challenge all of our students, but at the end, I am confident that my students have the basic vocabulary to address some of the deeper concepts related to fractions and all the other strands in which they appear.

Seeing mathematics goes well beyond the use of manipulatives. If, like me, you have ever uttered the phrase "Math is everywhere," then allow students to experience it. That could mean that math for the day is held in the hallway, in the gym, in front of a computer, or during a walk through the community. Anything we can do to help our students decode these numbers and symbols, and have them become part of their vernacular will make them more successful.

Let Them Engage in Mathematics

One of the most difficult battles to fight in a mathematics classroom is to engage the student who hates math. Several resources out there claim to engage students in math by giving them real-life questions. After reading some of these books, we would believe that most of our students are carpenters, painters, fence-builders, truck drivers, and pilots. Although these are real-life applications of math, they don't do anything for the uninterested student. Knowing your students goes a long way in a mathematics classroom — their interests are the easiest selling point — but it rarely seals the deal.

Allowing students to engage in fewer, yet better, more thought-provoking questions is more effective than posing a larger volume of repetitive questions. For data management, students could explore and prove which gaming system is superior. Or they could consider which teen movie series, Harry Potter or Twilight, is the best. This kind of topic was more effective for my students than creating bar graphs on their favorite foods or TV shows.

I struggled for years on how to make integers accessible and relevant for students as most of the examples have either been overused or the students lacked the necessary background knowledge to connect to them. For example, golf provides an excellent opportunity to explore the concepts of integers and zeroes, yet I would spend more time trying to explain the rules of golf than I would integers. It was a *eureka* moment when I asked myself, "Why am I trying to explain this, if they can simply play the game themselves?" So, after setting up our 12-hole mini-golf course, where they kept track of their scores as integers, every student had an additional foundational piece to build conceptual understanding. Perhaps the most important aspect is that even the students who supposedly hate math smile and laugh during this class.

The other engagement tool at our disposal is the use of technology. I find that part of my job description as an intermediate teacher is wrapping mathematics up in the right package to eliminate all excuses of why we shouldn't, couldn't, or won't. Allowing students to experiment on programs such as Geometer's Sketchpad or a variety of data software allows them to use a medium they enjoy. It also takes away some of the tediousness from mathematics (as in drawing triangles and squares to explore the Pythagorean theorem). We can explore other aspects of the concept at a much deeper level due to the time that technology affords: perhaps using Web 2.0 tools such as Voicethread and Today's Meet to have a backchannel discussion and share ideas among the class or conducting a real or virtual experiment using Gizmos to gather their own unique data. The list could continue with blogging, SMART Boards, and cameras — all provide opportunities to make math accessible and engaging.

Once a student is engaged in a mathematics classroom, you have removed barriers that often prevent learning from occurring. If we can open students' minds, they will, in turn, be open to acquiring the language of math . . . even if they are not aware that it is happening.

Let Them Talk About Mathematics

If you grew up in mathematics classrooms similar to those I grew up in, you likely did little talking outside of yelling out the final answer to the question on the front board or from homework the previous night. Allowing our students to talk about mathematics is an important part of acquiring and consolidating their new language.

Once we have posed a question to investigate for the day, the dialogue between the students becomes an integral part in acquiring a new concept. As a teacher, I become a listener and a questioner to help guide the learning and allow students to draw their own conclusions. We all want to see our students succeed, and at times, we want to point out the obvious answer that seems to be sitting there. I often remind myself that they will get there, and if I'm patient, then so will the students be.

The students know the procedure for these investigations, as it is usually the same. They get 3 to 5 minutes of individual think time before they share in partners or small groups. Within the groups, all students are accountable for understanding the problem and group solution, as any of them may be presenting to the class to facilitate the learning of the entire class. I then select the 2 or 3 groups that will present their findings, based on the concepts I want the class to see.

Setting this up from the first few days of the year is essential for the long-term success of the math program. The students who are presenting should be talking to their classmates, not the teacher. It is the class that decides what is reasonable and what is not. At the beginning of the year, I often have to facilitate this discussion between the presenters and the class. But after a few months, the students are posing the questions, asking the presenters to restate, debating, and justifying the reasonableness of the solution.

I can't stress the importance of this consolidation phase enough: it "pulls out" the meaningful mathematical vocabulary and concepts. But the other benefit of these opportunities for the students to talk is that the students can practise using their new terminologies and understanding. My mother, a French teacher, often said the hardest part of her job was getting her students to speak to one another in French. All we are doing is getting our students to speak to one another in math.

Let Them Think About Mathematics

As a young teacher I remember my frustration when my students weren't successful problem-solvers. I decided that there was a simple solution: Problem-Solving Fridays. Every Friday we would leave our regular program behind and focus exclusively on a variety of problem-solving techniques. We got quite good during these sessions, yet on a test, their problem solving remained weak. When I confronted my class with this and asked why they weren't using any of the techniques we had talked about, one student responded with the perfect answer. He stated, "Because it's not Friday! We problem-solve on Fridays." It was then I realized that problem solving was not a skill that needed to be practised, but rather, the foundation of mathematics.

From then on, problem solving became the vehicle to drive math. It has evolved since then, as I've learned that problem solving is not simply the open-ended question we pose for the daily lesson. It goes beyond that to the smaller, differentiated questions that I pose to students. It includes the questions that students ask and answer among their group and class. It extends through the questions and investigations that arise from our previous lesson and ideas that students want to learn more about.

The reason this critical thought is so important is summed up in this question: What good is any language unless we can do something with it? Thinking and communicating about mathematics allows us to use our acquired language to accomplish tasks, ask questions, justify answers, estimate solutions, compare concepts; in other words, continue our development towards becoming mathematically literate.

Let Them Break the Barriers of Mathematics

I remember talking to a Grade 9 math teacher who informed me that one of my former students claimed we never covered equations in Grade 8. There were two possibilities: the student was exaggerating or he genuinely had no recollection of solving equations. I decided to give the student the benefit of the doubt and reflect on what we had done. We taught the unit early in the year and had some formative assessments, a test, and a summative task. Everything seemed okay, until I realized that we never revisited the unit and barely used it. No wonder the student didn't recall it! What was its worth? It was useful exclusively within one unit, in one subject area.

I began to wonder, Why did math have to be so compartmentalized? Why can we not just *do* math? With this approach, equations are embedded within our learning in all of the other strands of mathematics. While I, as a mathematics teacher, appreciate this idea, I can see that to a student, it still appears that math is useful only in math class.

Perhaps the way of making math relevant and purposeful is to break the barriers of math belonging only in the math classroom. Instead, we could establish that math belongs in our learning in all of our subject areas. That could mean a mini-lesson before a science class and using equations instead of the less efficient guess-and-check methods when exploring density and buoyancy. It could include reading, interpreting, organizing, and analyzing graphs and data to create a persuasive letter to a company, asking it to give support to a class project. It could be the use of proportional reasoning to create a scaled replica of a historical building for a history project. Perhaps if we remove the barriers around mathematics, our students will see its importance and relevance in their academic lives. If we can accomplish this, little will stand in their way to using the language of mathematics to its fullest capabilities and becoming fully literate in math.

Taking a new approach

The second question posed at the beginning of this section persists, though: Why are people so comfortable about admitting they cannot do math? Anyone who has taught in an intermediate classroom has heard this statement uttered by students, teachers, and parents alike.

The solution is not to embarrass people but to provide them with the skills and language that will enable them to think and do math confidently. As the professionals in the classroom, we have a tremendous impact on society and the reculturalization of all the stakeholders. That means the solution starts with us, but we are not alone. Many great books, workshops, and courses promote these same messages. Most of my learning has come through brainstorming sessions with colleagues and series of successes and failures in designing lessons and the subsequent reflective practice.

In becoming fully mathematically literate, we are often on the same journey as our students, something that can be used to our benefit. I continue to be amazed what I learn every year from my classes and how it can be used to support the learning for years to come.

What I Would Do Now: Supporting Diverse Learners in Reading and Writing

by Shelley Murphy

Shelley Murphy is an instructor in the Department of Curriculum, Teaching, and Learning at the Ontario Institute for Studies in Education, University of Toronto, and is completing her Ph.D. She has worked as an inner-city teacher, literacy specialist, teacher educator, and educational researcher and consultant. She is a frequent lecturer on the topic of inclusive strategies for students with characteristics of ADHD.

Middle-school teachers are confronted with complex demands and challenges in school. They are expected to know content and pedagogy, to meet the needs of many diverse learners each day, to develop positive personal relationships with each of their students, and to manage classroom climate and behavior. They are asked to keep pace with growing diversity in the classroom and to address the myriad learning needs that diversity generates.

Middle-school students are also confronted by unique challenges. To begin with, they are in the midst of a multitude of developmental changes: intellectual, social, emotional, and physical. As they move from elementary school to middle school, students must adjust to new expectations from teachers, courses, and activities. They have to transition several times a day, all while organizing and keeping track of their belongings and juggling the requirements of numerous classes. These students typically experience less structure and supervision, while bearing more homework and assignments and stricter grading practices.

Would it surprise you to know that, for many students, the shift to middle school brings a general decline in academic performance, motivation, confidence in ability, and attitude towards school?

A Tough Transition to Make

"As a teacher, as well as the parent, I have found that the key to the 99 is the one — particularly the one who is testing the patience and good humor of the many. It is the love and the discipline of the one student, the one child, that communicates love for the others. It's how you treat the one that reveals how you regard the 99, because everyone is ultimately the one."
— Stephen Covey, *Seven Habits of Highly Effective People*

The transition from elementary school to middle school brings challenges for many students, and the transition is even tougher for students with characteristics of ADHD (attention deficit hyperactivity disorder). Many students with ADHD manage in grade school but in middle school suddenly find it difficult to keep up. At this time students must navigate a much greater degree of independence, organization, planning, and self-management — the very things many students with characteristics of ADHD struggle with. As a result, grades often suffer and self-esteem plummets.

My image of a student with ADHD is 13-year-old Marcus, a student I taught during my early years as a teacher. Marcus was a bundle of energy and humor. He talked quickly and incessantly, and he had a sparkling kind of mind. He was original, creative, and intelligent. His behavior, however, was another matter; he would often act, it seemed, without regard for the consequences of his actions. Academically, he struggled, especially in reading and writing.

At the time I had little, if any, awareness about the academic implications of ADHD and the kind of instruction that could support his success. I assumed that if students had ADHD, it simply meant they would have a harder time managing their behavior, which would end up making *my* job more difficult. More difficult it was, but much more so for Marcus. He had a challenging time regulating his attention, remembering instructions, completing assignments, and keeping his behavior in check.

With more experience and training, I have come to realize a number of things. Many of Marcus's struggles (including his disorganization and inattention) were not matters of deliberate choice. They were, instead, a result of cognitive challenges related to his ADHD. I also realize now that there were many ways in which I could have supported him better.

Here's What I Wish I Had Known Then . . .

Many of the challenges our students with ADHD face are due to neurological events. Many students have weaknesses in executive functioning, sometimes referred to as the CEO of our brain.

Let's first consider the role of a CEO who oversees the operation of an entire corporation. The CEO generally orchestrates the planning, organizing, and guidance of the various departments that make up the company. He/she sets and manages the particular goals of those departments and acts as the final decision-maker. In essence, the CEO sets the tone and mood for the entire corporation.

Similarly, a student's executive functions are the overseers of the brain: they ultimately set the tone for academic performance and behavior. More specifically, executive functioning helps regulate attention, determines appropriate behavior, regulates emotions and actions, and helps develop, prioritize, organize, and execute a plan of action.

There's no surprise that a strong link exists between academic success and executive functions. Furthermore, weaknesses in these executive functions present serious academic challenges for many students with ADHD, irrespective of their level of intelligence — especially in middle school, where the demand for the executive functions increases dramatically.

Many teachers respond to students with ADHD primarily with behavioral management approaches, and many students do require support to help minimize their disruptive and impulsive behavior.

For students' academic success, however, it is even more important for teachers to help students regulate their learning processes — that is, initiating, planning, goal setting, staying on task, self-monitoring, and managing time. Think of this support as taking on a "surrogate" executive functioning role. By doing this, you would support your students according to their needs and set them up for successful learning experiences.

Executive Functioning in the Context of Reading and Writing

When it comes to helping many students with ADHD read and write, the executive functioning does its job much less efficiently. For example, weaknesses in executive functions cause many students with ADHD to have a hard time recalling information from stories, to be less sensitive to story structure, to have difficulties retelling stories cohesively, and to struggle with making inferences. These students often have messy or illegible handwriting and poor written sentence construction and story composition.

When I recall Marcus now, I can see that he had all of these difficulties. How could I have supported him better? Knowing about his and other students' CEO challenges, how can we better support such students towards success?

It is common for many students with ADHD to encounter difficulties in writing and reading, often a result of executive functioning weaknesses. With 25 students in one classroom, you will have 25 diverse learners. Yet every student has unique gifts, strengths, and challenges.

Here are a few ways in which difficulties in writing and reading can manifest themselves, an explanation of why this may be, and some supportive strategies to consider.

Writing

Difficulties: When asked to do anything that involved writing, Marcus found it hard to generate more than a short paragraph or two. He wrote excruciatingly slowly, and his paragraphs were often disorganized and, at times, incoherent. His writing was messy and difficult to read; it often contained spelling errors. Lack of knowledge and experience led me to believe, at the time, that Marcus simply lacked interest in his work.

Why this may be: Writing requires students to come up with ideas and then plan and organize the structure of their writing. Executive functioning weaknesses make coming up with *what* to write and *how* to express ideas two of the most common and impairing writing problems for students with ADHD. This was certainly the case for Marcus.

Many students with ADHD also have fine motor skill challenges, which make the act of writing fatiguing and ultimately, daunting. This is why Marcus's writing was so often messy and, in all probability, why he resisted writing.

Reflection: I realize now that these challenges interfered with his ability to communicate what he knew on paper. In discussions, Marcus often had wonderfully unique ideas and understandings, but was never able to demonstrate them in his writing because of these challenges. Unfortunately, his writing was often used as a measure to evaluate his understanding and knowledge.

Strategies: If I had Marcus in my class now, I would differentiate my instruction by increasing support throughout the writing process and provide alternative ways for him to demonstrate his knowledge. More specifically, I would do the following:

- *Increase support in the pre-writing stage and spend a few minutes helping brainstorm ideas.* Students with ADHD often get stuck at this critical pre-planning stage because executive functioning weaknesses result in poor planning and organization. I would help Marcus plan by having a conference of 3 to 4 minutes or by pairing him with another student, offering writing prompts (e.g., a picture, a song, a poem, or a news story), and teaching use of graphic organizers. I would provide examples of filled-out organizers as a reference.
- *Teach explicitly (and continue to revisit) the steps of the writing process: pre-writing, composing first draft, revising, editing, proofreading, and publishing.*

1. Teach and then guide practice in applying each step separately. Students with executive functioning weaknesses often experience cognitive overload when faced with several steps at one time; they might shut down completely. You can significantly increase and improve a student's writing output if you teach each step explicitly, and give frequent and immediate feedback, especially after each step. ("Here are the steps in the pre-writing stage, here's how to do it, here's what it looks like, you try it, show me what you've done, here's feedback, next step," and so on.) This level of support can be reduced once students show an increased level of independence.
2. Create a checklist that outlines the specific steps students need to take in each phase.
3. Have students write for 10 to 15 minutes and then stop to exchange work with another student to receive feedback.

- *Give the option of composing stories on the computer.* Let students use desktop, laptop, or AlphaSmart computers to compensate for weaknesses in fine motor skills.
- *Suggest the use of assistive technologies.* These include Dragon NaturallySpeaking, which helps students get their stories and ideas on paper by using a voice recognition system, and without having to type or write; Co:Writer 4000 Solo, which is a word prediction software that also provides grammar and vocabulary support for struggling writers; Write:OutLoud Solo, which is a talking word processor and writing software program that provides auditory feedback and purposeful revising and editing tools.
- *Substitute written reports with alternative reports that draw on student strengths.* Allow students to present their work through oral reports, audio recordings, dramatic presentations, singing, PowerPoint presentations, drawing, dancing, Readers theatre, or another way.
- *Give "time off the clock."* When written assignments (or tests) are timed, it is not always helpful to give students with ADHD the standard "extra time" accommodation. Problems with attention and concentration may increase. Instead, give students 2 to 3 minute breaks to stand up, walk around, or doodle, and do not include these minutes when you are timing the test or assignment. Breaking tests or assignments into smaller chunks and having frequent breaks helps to increase attention and concentration. Students will gain more time to write the test, but are not expected to sit through more active work time.

Reading

Difficulties: Marcus had a difficult time with reading comprehension. Although he read somewhat fluently, he wasn't always able to summarize, retell, or respond to questions related to the text well.

Why this may be: Reading is a complex process in which the construction of meaning is the ultimate goal. Students with ADHD quite commonly have difficulties with reading comprehension to some degree, due to inattention while reading. They often miss words and important details because their attention gets pulled away from their text. Once again, this problem can be due to executive functioning weaknesses.

Poor working memory also makes it difficult for students to remember what they have read. This is likely why Marcus had such a difficult time deriving meaning from his reading.

Strategies: If I had Marcus in my class now, I would teach techniques to help him process what he is reading. Doing this would ultimately help him with his comprehension. Specifically, I would do the following:

- *Teach and model* prior, during, *and* after *reading strategies.*
- *Teach how to be strategic.* Suggest metacognitive strategies, such as taking brief notes, highlighting, underlining, circling, using sticky notes, summarizing, visualizing, thinking aloud (making text-to-self, text-to-world, and text-to-text connections), diagramming, and keeping literature logs. All of these techniques require active involvement in thinking about or responding to what is being read.
- *Teach how to create a graphic representation of what the student is reading.* Doing this helps students organize and remember details and ideas from the text as they read. Examples are charts, storyboards, story maps, Venn diagrams, and character webs.
- *Suggest reading aloud quietly.* Many students with ADHD have a hard time reading silently. Hearing their voices helps them to keep their attention on what they are reading. They often need the auditory input to stay connected to their text.
- *Suggest the use of assistive technologies.* These include Kurzweil, a text-to-speech software that aids in comprehension through the use of highlighter tools, a built-in dictionary, and other supports. It also supports writing through brainstorming, outlining tools, and writing templates.
- *Suggest after-reading strategies intended to involve students in a deeper exploration of the text.* Examples are retellings, Readers theatre, an interview with a character, writing in role, a story map or art piece, and diary entries from a main character.

These are just a few of the ways in which middle-school teachers can support their students with ADHD. You may have students who have been identified as having ADHD, who have characteristics of ADHD, who seem to be struggling, and who may not be struggling at all. Indeed, these strategies offer ways to support *all* students in their reading and writing.

Middle-school students, particularly those who are struggling, need support in *how* to learn, *how* to study, and *how* to start and finish homework, essays, and assignments. Although middle-school students are expected to demonstrate responsibility and independence, the middle years is a time when many students need more guidance, care, and support. For students like Marcus, we must ensure that their unique ways of learning, being, and showing their knowledge are respected, valued, and reflected in our teaching.

6

Assessing for Learning and Teaching

Improving Student Learning Through Purposeful Assessment

by Amy Robinson

Amy Robinson is an itinerant literacy and numeracy teacher who works with teachers in Kindergarten through Grade 8. She also is an instructor for Literacy Additional Qualifications courses.

In my first year of teaching a parent told me that her daughter, then in Grade 7, was a terrible speller and asked what I was going to do about it. I fumbled through an uneducated explanation about spelling being developmental and that I wasn't too worried about it; that her daughter's spelling would improve through the year.

I look back now and wonder why the parent didn't call me out on such a poor answer — if I only knew then what I know now. Now I would administer a diagnostic assessment, such as *Words Their Way Inventory* (Prentice Hall, 2007) in order to understand what her daughter knew about words, vocabulary, phonics, and spelling and what she didn't know. From there I would be able to purposefully plan my instruction to meet the specific needs of her daughter.

Assessment is at the heart of everything we do as teachers. Without assessment our instruction as teachers is like searching for a needle in a haystack; we are aimlessly searching without ever finding what we're looking for. Furthermore, without assessment we are blindly trying to hit the target with each of our students, never knowing where that target is.

"The primary purpose of assessment and evaluation is to improve student learning."
— *Growing Success Assessment, Evaluation, and Reporting in Ontario Schools*, 2010

Getting to Know Your Students: Achievement and Attitudinal Data

Two sets of data I collect at the beginning of the school year. The first is achievement data which will tell me what students know or are able to do in relation to academic skills. The second is attitudinal data which tells me about the students' interests, learning styles, and preferences. These two data sets determine what I need to teach, how I'm going to teach it, and how I will address the individual needs of the students in my class.

Reading achievement data

At the start of the year I administer reading assessments to determine a student's fluency, comprehension, reading behaviors, and fix-up strategies. To assess fluency and reading behaviors I use a running record and miscue analysis. While conducting a running record I am also able to notice the student's reading fluency (with attention to expression, phrasing, intonation, punctuation, and rate) and use of fix-up strategies when the student comes across a word that is difficult. I also examine the running record to determine whether the student is using cueing systems to make meaning of the text: meaning (does it make sense?), structure (does it sound right?), and visual (does it look right?). After completing the running record, I use this information to plan for reading instruction. If the text used is a levelled piece, then I can also determine specifically the reading level of each of my students. To assess comprehension a teacher could ask a few quick comprehension questions after the running record to determine if the student understood what was read; another way that I have assessed comprehension is through an assessment tool such as Pearson's *Ontario Comprehension Assessment* (2008), which has students independently read a text and answer comprehension questions. Using a rubric with clear criteria I can then score the assessment and identify areas of strength and areas for further instruction. Using this achievement data allows me to plan for instruction and enables me to group my students for guided reading purposes.

Writing achievement data

In writing I use a writing assessment tool such as Nelson's *Ontario Writing Assessment* (2008) which has students write for a specific purpose and audience in a specified form of writing. Using a rubric with clear criteria I can then score the assessment and identify areas of strength and next steps. Whether using a formal assessment tool like *Ontario Writing Assessment* or a sample of student writing, I examine the writing to get a sense of students' knowledge and understanding of the forms of writing; their thinking in terms of the development and organization of ideas; their use of interesting details to support their ideas; and their communication using traits of writing such as voice, sentence fluency, word choice, and conventions. This achievement data enables me to plan for whole-class and small-group instruction.

Reading and writing attitudinal data

At the start of the year I also gather attitudinal data through surveys and questionnaires. I use a reading interest survey and a writing interest survey to determine what my students like to read/write, which authors and genres they prefer, what their interests are, how they perceive themselves as readers and as writers, how they think others perceive them as readers and as writers, and how students value reading or writing in their lives. I also use a multiple intelligences survey and a learning style inventory to find out what type of learner they are. I use this information throughout the year to assist me in my planning to ensure optimal engagement from my students.

Assessment in Reading

Three approaches to assessment of reading are offered by reading journals, book talks, and Guided Reading.

Reading journals

At the beginning of the school year I introduce reading journals to my class. Reading journals are a place where students track what they are reading and what they are thinking while they read. They are a place to record what texts are being read as well as practise the skills and strategies I am teaching. When we want students to refer to the mini-lessons taught to support them in their thinking they can simply refer to the back part of the journal. A book log could also be included in the reading journal for students to track reading and to ensure that over time students are reading a variety of text types.

In the reading journal, I would also have students include a space to cultivate metacognitive thinking. I want students to reflect on and understand the strategies they are using to make sense of the text. Students could also reflect on how they use different text features to gain meaning from the text. Some possible prompts to use to get students to think about their thinking are as follows:

- What strategies do you use effectively?
- What strategy works best for you when you come to a word or concept that is unfamiliar?
- What questions do you ask yourself to help you monitor your reading?
- What genre or type of text do you prefer reading? What do you do differently when you read a genre that is more challenging for you?
- What goals do you have for yourself as a reader? What will you do to meet those goals?

Book talks

In my class I regularly use book talks as a way to meet with students, 4 to 6 in a group, and support their learning. Through book talks I am able to observe what comprehension strategies students are using to make sense of the text, what areas they are struggling with, and how well they are able to communicate their meaning. I create a schedule for book talks that allows me to meet with a different group of students each day. I meet with the book talk group for about 20 minutes. Students bring their completed reading journal as a springboard for discussion. Initially I, as the teacher, facilitate the conversations, but as students become familiar with how a book talk works, they take turns facilitating. I also act as a group participant which enables me to model that I value reading but also to demonstrate what an effective book talk contributor looks like. My experience has always been that students place high value on the time they have with the teacher in small group.

As students become familiar with meeting in book talk groups, we co-construct success criteria that will be used for assessment purposes. Success criteria are put in student-friendly language and are posted in the classroom as an ongoing reminder of what is required for success in book talks. Success criteria are based on students' ability to demonstrate understanding of the text as well as use of critical literacy skills and oral communication skills such as listening and contributing to conversation.

Guided Reading

Guided Reading is just as important in the intermediate grades as it is in the primary and junior grades. Many students still require scaffolded support as they read in order to improve as readers. The biggest difference between Guided Reading and book talks is that in book talks students are facilitating their own discussions around the ideas in the texts they are reading; in Guided Reading the teacher is facilitating and supporting student learning about how to read and think in relation to text. Both Guided Reading and book talks have an important role to play in the literacy lives of our intermediate students. In my classroom I

structure my 60-minute literacy block or Readers/Writers Workshop in the following way:
- time to teach (mini-lessons): 15 minutes
- time to practise (collaborative and independent practice): 40 minutes
- time to share (reflections): 5 minutes

This structure enables me to meet with two groups each day. Usually this works out to be one book talk group and one guided reading group. Students may be different in those two groupings. The book talk group is based on the text and student interests, and the guided reading group is based on student need.

Assessment in Writing

Two ways I approach assessment in writing are represented by writer's notebooks and student presentations.

Writer's notebook

In my class, the notebook is a place for students to explore different ways of writing, to grow ideas, and to practise strategies being taught. When students want to take their ideas and use them to draft longer pieces of writing, then they pull the ideas from the notebook and begin writing on sheets of paper that can then be stored in the writing folder as they work through the process of writing. Despite not having any real format to follow I do have high expectations for my students' use of the notebook. I expect the following:
- that students write daily
- that students are willing to explore different strategies for writing
- that students start to reflect on their writing by rereading the notebook
- that students record and use the lessons on writing

I communicate these expectations and either post them on an anchor chart or create a checklist that is glued into the front of the notebook.

As I read through the writer's notebooks I am also becoming aware of areas for further instruction; I use the information I gather from their notebooks to guide me in the next steps for precision teaching. The writer's notebook is used for assessment as learning as well. On a regular basis students are encouraged to reread their notebooks and identify trends and patterns they notice. Students also examine their writing to see how they have improved and to identify next steps for themselves; students set goals for themselves as writers and develop action plans to achieve those goals.

In my practice I use the writer's notebook to generate and develop ideas and then, when students write longer pieces of text, they use the writing folder to guide them through the process. I use the writing folder to support the instruction and use of the writing process (drafting, rethinking and revising, editing and proofreading, publishing or sharing). It is important to note that not all pieces of writing go through the full writing process; some may stay in draft and others may get fully published.

Written work that is in progress stays in the writing folder, even if it is a piece that never gets to the published stage. The reason for this is because towards the end of a period of instruction or the end of a term, I encourage students to revisit their writing and choose one to two pieces that they will work through the process and publish. These pieces will become evidence of student learning and will be used for evaluative purposes.

When I want to see what is in a student's writing folder I conference with the student. We examine the work in the folder together, highlighting what the student has done effectively and identifying next steps. While conferencing I track my anecdotal notes and use those to guide my instruction. The student and I co-create descriptive feedback for the student work. At the end of the conference I should have a good understanding of where the student is at in writing, what the next steps are, and how I can support the student in realizing them.

Presentation

Presentations are another way to gather assessment of learning data. Presentations could be interconnected within the strands of language (oral communication, reading, writing, and media literacy). In my classroom students have been engaged in student-led inquiry which requires them to read, research, write, and produce a presentation of some kind to demonstrate and share their learning. Despite each inquiry being unique to the individual students, there is a common set of criteria that I use for assessment of learning. Prior to the presentation I ensure that I have taught students about presentation skills so that when they present based on what they have read, they are able to effectively communicate with the audience (the class). Again, I want to be certain that whatever I am evaluating has been explicitly taught and supported through instruction. I develop a rubric with clear criteria based on whatever has been the focus of instruction. For example, if students are presenting on a topic they have researched and I have taught certain comprehension strategies needed for research as well as presentation strategies, then I reflect that on the rubric. I share the rubric with students prior to their developing a presentation so that they have a good understanding of what is required.

On Point: Rubrics with a Twist

by Barb Smith

Barb Smith brings a background of expertise in the area of international curriculum, assessment, critical thinking, boys' education, teacher development, school leadership, and innovative school design. Barb has taught and been an administrator in Grades 1 to 12 schools. With work published in numerous books, in 2010, she co-authored *Mining for Gems: A Casebook of Exceptional Practices in Teaching and Learning*.

My students at the International School of Brussels have taught me plenty about being "on point."

When I first asked Grades 7 and 8 English students about rubrics, they yawned, sighed, and basically withdrew from the discussion in a surprising unison. The more I tried to convince them that rubrics were a tool that would direct their learning, the more they resisted, the gap between teacher and students widening steadily in polar opposition. On the one hand, teachers have accepted the language-rich prose aligned neatly in horizontal boxes with seemingly obvious compliance. I, for one, loved the idea that rubrics were transparent: students would not have to operate in vacuums; instead, the expectations, made explicit, would guide their actions and achievements. Rubrics could be that "missing link." On the other hand, students were clearly not embracing them. So, I asked them why and how we could make these assessment tools better.

Evolution of the Layered Checklist

The student responses helped us develop a leaner, more "on point" rendition of the classic rubric. Calling this tool the "layered checklist," we identified expectations, not in prose form, but in a phrase format. This learning tool made it easy for students to self-assess how well their work was completed. It also served as a guide to revise and renovate drafts in any subject area.

Grade 7 students used a layered checklist to guide the class's Reader's Forum. Students were asked to lead and participate as audience members in a literature circle conversation about Lois Lowry's *The Giver*.

Reader's Forum Assessment Tool		
Self *I*	Score *2* for meeting mastery expectations; *1* for partially meeting expectations; and *?* mark where there appears to be no evidence.	Teacher *You*
ACTIVE AUDIENCE SKILLS:		
	posed relevant questions	
	followed instructions well	
	added relevant contributions	
	presented ideas with clarity	
	used prior knowledge	
	made predictions	
	listened attentively and with civility to others	
CRITIQUING SKILLS:		
	gave instructions effectively	
	acknowledged and built on ideas and contributions of others	
	disagreed in a courteous manner	
	contributed accurate information	
	presented ideas with clarity	
	made connections to real life	
	paraphrased and summarized responses	
	monitored message for clarity and understanding	
	provided verbal and nonverbal feedback	
	took notes to organize essential information	

	identified imagery	
	identified and explained similes	
	identified multiple points of view	
	described how the character developed	
	identified the function of major and minor characters	
	described motives of the characters	
	interpreted causes for action	
	identified moral dilemmas that characters encounter	

This tool focused on teaching both audience and critiquing skills, using the novel and the understanding of the story as the backdrop or context for learning more universal skills of analysis and communication.

When students were asked what they thought of the layered checklist form of rubric they expressed opinions such as these:

- "I like how the teacher gets to the point so we don't have to read the same thing over and over in each box."
- "I have to think about all these things so it gives me a second chance to go back and fix stuff."
- "My scores usually match my teacher's scores. I get it. When I use the old rubrics, I'm never sure if I'm a 3 or a 4. This is clear that I met the goal. The old rubrics are only clear to the teacher."
- "I like having a say in marking my work."

As teachers, we ask our students to make improvements every day, so we need to step up, too. When I asked students for ways to improve conventional rubrics, they helped me find a way to make them more meaningful, fair, and "on point."

7

Weaving Threads of Purpose and Community: One School's Journey

All the features in this chapter are contributed by members of the same public school, Donald Cousens.

Sharon Moss is the principal at Donald Cousens Public School in the York Region District School Board. Her mandate is to enable and support a total school community.

Creating a Culture of Learning

by Sharon Moss, in consultation with Jeewan Chanicka, Community and Culture lead teacher

The work around creating a culture of learning within schools and school systems must be both intentional and purposeful. It begins with the structures that are created because these drive what happens in an organization and send a clear message about the beliefs and attitudes that are valued. This culture is a balance between both the administration and the types of leaders on staff.

At Donald Cousens Public School, we began with a clear focus on the types of leaders being hired at the school. While some may have been concerned about hiring too many leaders, the focus around hiring sought to balance the type of leadership offered by staff members with a clear sense of both character and common purpose.

Once hiring was accomplished, a leadership team was identified — it is here that an administrator's lens and role become quite important in moving away from traditional constructs of leadership. We determined that the lead team at our school would be comprised of a Literacy lead, a Technology lead, a Special Education lead, and a Community and Culture lead.

Opening Up Philosophies of Teaching

Jeewan Chanicka was hired in the latter role and in collaboration with me as principal and the lead team, he decided that, in order to set the context for the type of work to be done, he would begin with a philosophy exercise. Teachers were asked to think about why they do what they do in the classroom and to represent it in any way they wanted. They were presented with this opportunity in June and given the summer to complete it. In September, it was expected that the philosophies would be posted outside of classrooms.

In September, the philosophies provided an excellent opportunity to begin finding common threads that would bind the staff together on our learning journey. Staff members were asked to bring their philosophy statements to our first staff meeting and talk to one another about commonalities and interesting points.

Jeewan did a philosophy unit with his Grade 8 homeroom students that involved them in reading teachers' posted philosophies and making comments on sticky notes. The comments were then posted in the staff room for teachers to read. This qualitative data was used to further conversations about our core "business" and what we needed to do to ensure student engagement, well-being, and success.

A couple of student comments point to the value of posting the philosphies:

- *"It helped me notice that several teachers have many dreams, hopes, goals to move the students to a higher standard level and that they really care for us."*
- *"It made me feel that the teachers care about the students and their education. They want the students to learn and that made me feel comfortable in this new school."*

The data also served as a powerful communication piece to engage community members throughout the year.

Intentional Initiatives for Forwarding the Journey

Over the course of the year, other intentional work was done through the Community and Culture lead in collaboration with the lead team and the principal:

- a series of workshops to engage staff around the "critical friends" model of engagement in the building
- an exploration of the question What is the purpose of education?—Shift happens
- a *True Colours* team-building workshop, where teachers shared their "colors" with each other
- participation in development of the School Improvement Plan with lead team members
- activities that involved explicit expressions of appreciation
- use of TRIBES (a professional development approach) and common language to describe student behavior or achievement
- TRIBES refreshers: engaging TRIBES and the ministry of education's Social Emotional Academic Learning document
- anonymous staff surveys done in September and January to get feedback about teachers' thinking and how they felt about their ability to contribute and lead at school

The learning pieces were often short and targeted, and during the year there was a focus on *layering* the work so that staff would not feel overburdened by working with disconnected initiatives. What was most important during this process was the understanding that this was a journey. While we had a clear vision and purpose, the *what* and *how* were not always so clear. This process enabled us to dialogue with one another about what was best for our students. When it was not clear, it allowed us to disagree but continue working collaboratively. Overall, it has brought about many successes, *ahas*, and many more questions.

Our philosophy initiative helped us to establish a positive culture of teaching and learning, something that we have been able to sustain over the past three years. The philosophies and mini-me activities were foundational pieces that supported our work with Character Education and Tribes as approaches to build community at our school. Over the years, new staff members have included their philosophies on doors, on windows, and in classrooms throughout the school. (See "Mr. Demacio: Together on a Learning Journey — A Personal Philosophy.")

Our challenge will be to keep up with the booming growth of the community around us, our student population, and the addition of new staff members. We know that the time for reculturing the school is opportune, and to support student success, we will be going deeper with our quest for engagement and inclusion.

The journey continues.

**Mr. Demacio: Together on a Learning Journey —
A Personal Philosophy**

by Jeff Demacio

Becoming a teacher has been one of the most rewarding experiences of my professional life. The thought that my abilities as a teacher can shape the lives of my students is both overwhelming and exciting. I hold this responsibility close to my heart, and I engage all facets of my intelligence to provide the greatest learning experience possible for the students I teach.

My classroom is a place where my skills, background, education, and enthusiasm for learning combine with each of my students. Together we embark on a learning journey every day, and with the support of fellow staff, administration, parents, and families within the community, my students will have the greatest learning experience possible.

I believe it is my responsibility to provide a safe and supportive environment. Students will feel comfortable engaging and exploring their learning, and are positively reinforced whenever possible. My classroom is a place where exploration and experimentation are commonplace. It is a place where my students can use their prior knowledge to make predictions, and use available resources to investigate how things work. We sing, act and move each and every day, exploring the world, as children should, with enthusiasm and wonderment! We are partners in learning, so my involvement as a facilitator is paramount. As a teacher, I consistently guide my students through their learning process.

No two children are exactly alike. All of my students have different learning styles, and the pace at which learning occurs varies. Knowing and understanding all available research into how children learn give me insight into how to structure the environment and deliver the curriculum. Addressing the cognitive, social, emotional, and physical needs of my students is not only important, but is essential in the design of the daily activities.

As I have two children of my own, I appreciate when teachers create effective and open communication with parents. I want my own children to be successful, and I always take the time to support them in any way possible. As a teacher, I create the same opportunity for families of my students. I always keep them informed of their child's progress, as well as classroom, grade-level, and school-wide events. I am available before and after school to meet with students and parents, and I am easily reached by phone or email.

*Our future lies in the success of our children.
Let's learn together!*

Jeffrey Demacio, along with Natasa Vujanovic and Sultan Rana, whose contributions follow, are Grade 7/8 homeroom teachers at Donald Cousens Public School. They work as an amazing team, planning inventive, extensive, and co-operative literacy events with their students. With the support of their principal, Sharon Moss, they represent the school's staff, whose members function as a true school community.

How Engagement Leads to Inspiration and Passion for Learning

by Jeff Demacio

I have found it is absolutely essential to build a solid classroom community *early* and maintain it *often* through constant and consistent communication and classroom management. I like to use as many co-operative games that I can fit into the first few weeks of school. If you are fortunate enough to have participated in TRIBES training, you will know that an amazing number of community-building activities are available in the resources. During these activities, I like to challenge my students with time or external motivations when I have a chance. I like to keep things slightly competitive, but am careful to keep the competitor as the clock, a goal, or a group far enough away that there can be no hard feelings. You can set the goals, or find a colleague at another school that your students can challenge.

Always remember that failure at a challenge or game is a great learning experience for a group and moves the community-building process ahead. I will often play a challenging TRIBES game such as Fork & Spoon knowing that it may fail and that the facilitated discussion following that moment will be challenging and yet extremely valuable.

Building a Classroom Community

Learn who your students are! Find a few different multiple intelligence surveys and have the students complete them and work with the data. I like to have my students complete four different surveys and then gather the trends in a personal poster that will be displayed on our classroom wall.

The time is well spent because you can use this information throughout the year as you adapt your program to suit your students' needs. This knowledge will enlighten individual students as to their learning style and will foster a sense of group understanding that everyone in our community learns in a different way. This sharing has led to great discussion and activities around the ideas of equity and empathy in learning.

Establishing routines and best practices is also important early in the year, and I like to establish the following three right away.

First, all daily routines involving literacy responses establish a norm that our class will be involved in reading and writing activities from the get-go. In the past, I had my students complete this task on paper, but with the advent of Google Docs, I have moved this process online (see below for technology integration). Students are required to read daily and fill in a reading response form on our classroom website. It makes life easier for me, as I have one place to go to for a quick glimpse into what my students are reading. I can guide the responses on a daily or weekly basis, and can integrate them into my guided reading sessions to have certain groups respond in various ways, depending on student needs. These sessions provide a good forum for peer discussion.

A second area of focus is in the establishment of a Writer's Notebook. A number of good books can help you establish this routine, but I just stick with the idea that the notebook is used daily to write *anything* that interests the student. We work regularly to compile lists of notebook ideas, and I rarely dictate the topic. The students are responsible for the quality of the ideas and the writing.

Another amazing thing to get started early is a reflection writing process. I like to set aside an entire section of my classroom website for thought-provoking and potentially controversial reflection writing under the heading "How Do I Feel About . . ." There are so many curriculum connections that you can make here, from analysis to perspective and point of view, and there are many cross-strand or cross-curricular tasks that you can undertake from current events presentations to full debates. What I have found is that my students don't really know how to approach these reflections at first; in the fall they often have a difficult time piecing together a meaningful response. As we move through the year, we meet as a whole class and in small groups to read and share our thoughts on the topics and our writing. I use this time to give formative feedback related to areas of our reading or writing program. By mid-year, these entries are much longer; they are filled with depth, insight, and reflective meaning. As with everything that exists in the virtual world of our website, I print large-format copies for our classroom walls. When we have visitors to our classroom later in the year, it is amazing how passionate the students are about their writing, and how desperate they are to have a guest read their posts on the wall and respond to them in person.

One last area in which we need to build a solid foundation is communication. How you communicate with your students and parents can really make a difference in the success of your year. In my class, I use a website, email, and Twitter to drive two-way communication. I have found that effective communication can be an excellent way to stay on top of issues that may arise and to promote a team approach between teacher, parent, and student.

Engagement Through the Curriculum

We need to focus on big ideas and challenging questions. World issues, environmental and scientific challenges, social justice, and character-based big ideas are great topics to start with, and the new Science and Social Studies curriculum guides are filled with excellent examples. Over this past year, our division had three phases within our program and many big ideas to investigate:

- *What Does the World Look Like to Me?*
- *Where Do I Fit into the World?*
- *How Can I Use My Voice to Influence the World?*

Within these areas we investigated many interesting and thought-provoking issues, including human reliance on fossil fuels, consumption, consumerism, and how the economy works, what it means to be a hero, what makes us who we are and how we want to live, and even the notion of competition versus co-operation.

We didn't abandon the curriculum in favor of interesting ideas to ponder; instead, our program was driven by ideas, challenged by real-world experiences, and motivated by our interests. Students weren't working on a completion checklist for their assignments but were a part of a learning experience that yielded a real sense of accomplishment. Students became knowledgeable in research skills, comprehension and analysis, point of view, identifying bias, and many other important curriculum areas. They were becoming critical thinkers — and critical thinkers cannot get the answer from Google, but must use all of the resources and tools available to them to take a position, make an argument, and participate in the learning. The best part was that our journey didn't stop at the language curriculum document, but had an impact on many of the cross-curricular subjects.

When working with big ideas that push the boundaries of the traditional sources of information, it is important to engage as many real-world connections as possible. The obvious first choices are various forms of media. Any media texts you can utilize, including newspapers, magazines, videos, website content, and even YouTube, can be excellent, as long as students remain critical consumers of the information. A few other areas to consider are in the form of guest speakers, both live and via video conference. You don't have to be an expert on all topics, and having a speaker or guest via live video can often make the learning experience incredibly rich! I would even recommend connecting classes to each other via video conference for the sharing of ideas and perspective, as the learning experience can be advanced a great amount, even without an expert. Students will make incredible learning advances when given a chance to work collaboratively.

Assessment and Differentiated Instruction

Over the past few years, I have become increasingly supportive of the idea that solid evidence of learning is gained from the triangulation of data through conversation, observation, and products produced by students.

If I had to share one strategy with respect to my teaching practice that has made an enormous impact on my students' level of engagement, I would choose my ability to step back and share control of my classroom with my students. I have never been a lecture-from-the-front teacher, but over the past couple of years I have become much more skilled at defining what my end goals are in terms of learning, and mapping backward how I might teach, so that all of my students can be successful. *Differentiated Instruction* by Anne Davies is an entirely separate book you may want to pick up, but I will highlight one area that has worked for me, and perhaps you will give it a try.

As my students and I work together to gain familiarity with their skills and identify areas of interest that engage and excite them, we reach a point where the direction of their learning can diverge from the group. Throughout the process, I know what I require from them, and they are becoming familiar with how they will be assessed. Together, we can map slightly alternate paths to a similar destination and in doing so, create an amazing experience for each student.

An example from my classroom came as we worked through persuasive essay writing. Having followed a shared path towards the adoption of some fundamental skills that would be required to write an essay, we moved forward into uncharted territory, where students had to find a means of expressing their persuasive essay in a more personal way. The curriculum, success criteria, and rubric were constructed together and modified during teacher–student conferences to suit the needs of the individual student, with the core learning remaining the same. Student work included a song with a music video, a series of posters, a mural, rants, a recorded talk show, and even a 40-minute guided tour of a museum constructed in an unused classroom. I also had speeches, simple presentations, and paper essays, which suited some of the students very well.

The key success was in the engagement. As soon as I opened up the boundaries of the assignment, things burst to life! I couldn't get my Grade 8 students to stop working on their inquiry, research, and analysis, let alone control their passion for finding techniques that would persuade their target audience. Suddenly, I had teams collaborating with each other and extending the task well beyond my expectations. There were times when things appeared overwhelming, but we had our end goal, our success criteria, and our rubric, and so I continued to adapt, observe, and meet with students. In the end, I had covered and assessed much more than I had planned for, and my students had travelled to that special place where they forgot about "doing work" and basked in the satisfaction of learning because they wanted to.

Technology

Here are a few simple ideas for embracing technology in your classroom.

1. Get your hands on an LCD projector and a decent pair of speakers. If your school doesn't have enough, then beg, borrow, or buy these items and get started projecting media in your classroom. I am not suggesting watching movies all day, but I am suggesting that you bring youtube.com, ted.com, skypeforeducators.com, and docs.google.com into the classroom. I use a wireless keyboard and trackpad regularly to move around my classroom and create an interactive environment. Students can post comments that instantly appear on the screen, vote on a topic, or even get out a pencil and gather their thoughts on a sticky note to post.

2. Allow students to bring their technology to school in the form of hand-helds and phones. Be prepared for them to use them for "fun" purposes, but they will also use them to look up information to add to a discussion, find a video that makes your lesson more engaging, and pull in that crucial piece of knowledge that they need to make their point, I can assure you. Obviously, infrastructure work at the system and school level must be done to prepare the school environment for this kind of technological immersion — this is where you need to take on the role of advocate and push for technological change.

3. Take a media course and experience the value of blogging, podcasting, digital storytelling, and advertising. There are so many ways that students can express themselves through technology that a simple book report, poster, and speech are only just enough to engage our students.

4. Give students the opportunity to explore and create with technology, and when a student asks you about doing something that appears out of the box, say YES!

This idea leads back to planning and assessment. Take the time to plan your units with the clarity and detail you require to address the curriculum requirements and the needs of your students, plan for the use of media and technology, *and* leave flexibility to adapt to the differentiation needs of your students.

"Pack Your Bag, We're Going on a Road Trip": Building Engagement Through Schema and Purposeful Planning

by Natasa Vujanovic

What's in your backpack? For the past three years, I have asked my students this question at the beginning of each year. I hand out pads of tiny sticky notes, and on blank sheets of paper, everyone, including me, sketches an outline of their own backpack. We then start filling up the outlines with everything that we bring with us daily.

The exercise goes something like this: "If you speak another language, write it down and put it in your backpack — you bring that skill with you everywhere. Who do you live with? Are you an only child or do you have brothers and sisters? Are you the oldest, youngest, or something in between? Write that down; you bring that experience with you when you deal with others. Have you travelled anywhere? What's your favorite book, movie, video game, type of music . . . ? What are some things you really love to do? What are you really good at? What is one thing that makes you extremely happy, extraordinarily sad, tremendously nervous, unbelievably angry? What are you afraid of?"

The list is almost limitless, and we keep going until we run out of meaningful questions. The sticky notes are all but gone, and words (English and home language), pictures, and symbols are scrawled all over the backpack outlines. Anything goes.

The Value of Personal Experience

It's a simple exercise, and it's a metaphor, of course, but it's what I use to teach students about schema and the value of personal experience. The "backpacks" stay tucked into the front of their language books, and we come back to them from time to time throughout the year. Sometimes students share their thinking through classroom discussions; sometimes their "items" become an inspiration for writing; sometimes the items are used as a reference for character comparisons; and sometimes they're a great jumping-off point for personal reflection and goal setting. As a teacher, I can get a snapshot of some of the interests and experiences of my students with little more than a visual sweep of the contents of their backpacks. Nobody *really* knows what the seemingly random set of words mean or remembers the order in which the questions were asked, so it's safe, and it's a good reminder (or realization) that people bring many different skills and experiences with them.

The backpack is also a great analogy for life learning and something that every child can relate to. Every "backpack" — be it yours, mine, or that of any students we work with — represents all of the "stuff" we carry with us and all of the things we use to process our lives and surrounding environments — not baggage, but rather the *life experience* that helps us negotiate and understand our world and surrounding environment.

Do you use everything in your backpack (whether it's literal or metaphoric) all of the time? No. Absolutely not, but if you're going to engage students in classroom learning, they need to understand that their perspective and experience are unlike anyone else's, and that their schema has value. They need to understand that everyone comes prepared with different "stuff" and that sometimes we need to be able to "borrow" from someone else's schema to build our own.

Taking personal inventories such as interest surveys and multiple intelligence inventories has much the same effect. Inventories are a simple and easy way to understand who our students are, as opposed to what they know (in terms of curriculum content alone). They provide a great platform for teaching about self-awareness within the context of a larger learning community.

Purposeful activities, like the backpack-filling one, are easy to build on and revisit. They're easy in general — it's part of what makes them effective. Every student can participate because every student has some kind of life experience, and when it's time to "go deeper," they also have a tangible, personal resource to connect back to. Writer's notebooks and sketchbooks can serve the same function. They are an effective way to develop writing and communication skills, but they can also be daunting for students who don't always (or ever) feel like writers or artists.

Graphic materials such as "backpacks," inventories, and lists provide simple and meaningful starting points that convert to engagement in its simplest form

— accessing every student and then building on their interests, strengths, and needs in different ways.

Building and Sharing Knowledge

Rich learning tasks, regardless of how simple they may seem, are great building blocks for learning. However, for them to be relevant in the larger scheme of things, you need to develop a strong knowledge base in your students.

Rich literacy environments support literacy-rich learning tasks. It's that simple. Students need access to a large breadth of *connected* texts and resources. These include *good* literature that's easy to relate to, such as novels, storybooks, and poetry; graphic texts, such as advertisements, movie trailers, and graphic novels; informational texts, such as essays, articles, atlases, website content, and documentaries; and "expert" resources, like guest speakers. The larger the variety of text, the easier it is to access and engage the "audience." If there is something for everyone, then everyone has something to contribute.

The single most valuable (and accessible) resource I have had for building engagement in my classroom has not been the Internet, the library, or the bookroom but the input of my colleagues. I am fortunate to work alongside a strong and supportive team of teachers. We plan together and choose meaningful learning targets, texts, resources, tasks, and activities that will work for different purposes and learning styles across a variety of grade levels and interest areas. There is a diverse knowledge base and skill set among us, so the shared resources and tasks we come up with are far more varied and differentiated than individual unit plans. Our "units" span whole terms and include every subject area. Even though we work across grade levels (Grades 6 to 8), we plan with specific expectations and big ideas in mind, and then supplement our individual programs with content appropriate for the grade, interests, and developmental levels of our learners.

The "hook" elements of our program come from both student and teacher interest. One recent team plan developed out of a case study that was presented in the Grades 7 and 8 science classroom; a school commitment to pilot a new graphic novel and global issues–based resource; and a *eureka* moment that our Grade 8 teacher had when he stumbled across the trailer for Tom Shadyac's documentary film *I Am*. Our Grade 7/8 teacher found a guest speaker to help develop the background knowledge of our students and organized the "umbrella plan" for our unit; our Special Education teacher compiled a bank of quotations, articles, and rubrics; I found some online resources, as well as literary and supplementary texts, to support programming; our Science teacher worked with the intermediate classes on researching subject-related content; and our Grade 6/7 teacher pulled all of the related resources she could find in our school library. Our Music teacher started planning for an environmentally themed year-end Tree Concert. Since all of our students had taken part in an essay writing competition earlier in the year, they were familiar with expository writing formats and had been taught how to support thinking using direct examples. The initial debate and case study, as well as the rich variety of shared resources we came up with, provided lots of background knowledge to start teaching our students how to be critical consumers of text, develop opinions, and explore themes related to adversity and global issues.

Our backpacks were full.

REMIX Your Program

by Sultan Rana

Curricular instruction at the intermediate level is fulfilling both to the learner and teacher when passions from all sides are included in the planning.

In June 2010, we planned for the following year, as a grade team, the big ideas that the literacy program was to embody: *What does the world look like to me? How does my voice fit in with the world? How can I influence the world with my voice?* All curricular expectations and focuses in each school term would be in line with those big ideas.

Our Passions

The Grade Team's Passion: Colleague and grade partner Jeffrey Demacio was impressed with an unreleased documentary trailer he had seen for *I Am* (http://www.iamthedoc.com/). This documentary spoke about the inherent nature of human beings to be good, caring, global citizens who are innately programmed to be empathetic and democratic beings. Mr. Demacio personally reached out to the director and his team, and was able to get us a pre-released copy of the documentary to view in class. The opportunity presented piqued the interest of our entire grade team.

The Students' Passion: At the beginning of the second school term, students from Grades 6 to 8 were introduced to environmental and human rights controversies brought on by the Alberta oil and tar sands, and related manufacturing practices, from their science teacher, Kevin Mueller. Emotions of confusion, anger, disappointment, and empathy arose from the students. Clearly this issue was a topic of interest among the students.

My Own Passions: My own passions lie in current events, social justice, and the use of technology in education.

Our Literacy Experience, January to June 2011

January: *Birth of the Arab Spring: Tunisia and Egypt*
Students analyzed the point of view of all stakeholders in the movement through debate, writing reflections, blog postings, and graphic organizers with discussion. All of these items and artifacts were assessed as formative pieces, strengthening the students' concept of point of view. The students came to recognize the importance that Facebook, Twitter, and social media had on this movement. Through use of online streaming of 24-hour news sources, handhelds providing instant updates, Twitter feeds, articles, and blogs of participants in the movement, students received primary and secondary information instantaneously in the classroom environment.

February: *Guest speakers Lou Schiza (happycapitalism.com) and Tashi Harrow (30-elephants.com)*
First, Lou Schiza shocked the students by presenting the point of view of proponents for the Alberta oil sands, the alternate to what they had adopted; then, with Skype and Twitter, Tashi Harrow participated in a very engaging discussion as to what true global citizenship could be.

Summative Project: With online document sharing, students were able to use a 500 MB multimedia source file filled with documents, advertisements, media releases, videos, and podcasts to conclusively state the points of view of all stakeholders in the debate.

March: *Introduction of the pilot project from Pearson, CIDA, and* TEACH *magazine*

In March, our team was approached with the opportunity to pilot a social justice literacy unit presented by Pearson Education, Canadian International Development Agency (CIDA), and *TEACH* magazine. The unit focused on the concepts of democracy, global citizenship, human rights, and basic education. Here was an opportunity for our classes and colleagues to contribute to the effectiveness of a curricular resource.

Students were guided as to how one *analyzes* through the actual analysis of one of the four components in the unit: global citizenship. Since the entire unit was in line with an online graphic text, the use of computers and online access were imperative. In addition to the computers, chat applets such as TodaysMeet (www.todaysmeet.com) and the document sharing and collaboration of Google Docs (docs.google.com) facilitated full-group interactions.

April/May: *The Death of Osama bin Laden — News sources were filled with this news topic, yet not every source was disclosing the same information.*

Again, my passion for current events, and the understanding of how pivotal this event was in North American history, fuelled this slight deviation from our work on the pilot project. Nevertheless, it strengthened student understanding as to how one should analyze the validity and authenticity of various news sources. When students shared their analytical statements, they used handheld devices and laptops to fact-check and skim through the sources each student referred to in his or her analysis. Debate and enlightened arguments marked the sharing session.

May/June: *Analysis of the effectiveness of the literacy unit, by the students*

In presentation form, written summary, or information depicted in a website, students shared directly with the stakeholders of this project their analysis of the entire project. The task was differentiated to suit the students' strength in demonstrating their analysis.

In conclusion, the literacy experience from January to June 2011 did the following:
- It gave the students a voice.
- It engaged the teachers in the learning!
- The use of technology in the classroom engaged, enhanced, and increased opportunities for deeper and authentic learning.
- The experience met my goal to facilitate a dynamic and relevant literacy program with my students.

8

Promoting Reading as Literacy Events

Literacy: Real Winner of the Kids' Lit Quiz

by Rachael Swartz

Rachael Swartz is a teacher and librarian at Dublin Heights School in Toronto, Ontario. She encourages the wide reading of novels with her middle-years students by involving them in national literacy projects that require extensive reading.

The atmosphere was so tense you could hear a page turn. The players, coaches, and spectators were all on the edge of their seats, eyes glued to the scoreboard, as they waited for the final scores to be posted. After three hours of gruelling competition, it all came down to the final round.

What was at stake? Only the title of "top team" in all of Canada and a trip to New Zealand for the finals! And the final totals are in: Dublin Heights 79, Summit Heights 79.5. First place was determined by only half a point!

Kids' Lit Quiz

These weren't school basketball, baseball, or volleyball teams vying for a title. The event wasn't even about sports! At Canada's first Kids' Lit Quiz competition, it was all about books and reading.

The Kids' Lit Quiz is an annual literature competition where students ages 10 to 13 compete in teams of four to answer 100 book-related questions in 10 different categories. The categories change every year, and the students don't find out the questions until minutes before the event occurs. Wayne Mills, quizmaster and founder of Kids' Lit Quiz, creates the questions, affirming that he never asks a question from a book he hasn't read. National quizzes are held in New Zealand, the United Kingdom, South Africa, China, and other countries; the winners in each heat go on to compete in the World Finals in New Zealand.

As the teacher-librarian in a K to 8 school, I have found over the past few years it is easy to hook the primary and junior students into reading great books, but our middle-school students are a tougher market. This year I was able to increase book circulation and literacy interest with our tweens and teens through the following initiatives: creating a "Teen Corner" in the library (complete with comfy chairs and a coffee table), leading the Red Maple Book Club (part of the Forest of Reading initiative), extending library hours to include after-school and open periods for book browsing, bringing in magazines of interest to this target audience, creating technology connections (through Web tools such as wikis and blogs), and holding contests in which all divisions could participate. When the opportunity for the Kids' Lit Quiz Challenge came up, I jumped right onto the idea of turning reading into a competition and a celebration for our avid readers.

Reading as Team Sport

Right from the get-go we treated reading like a sport. We held "tryouts," assigned coaches and trainers, and held weekly practices. The first few months consisted of tryouts and practices. Different team combinations (based on grades, genders, interests, and expertise) were created, and the teams completed questions from practice tests that were provided on the Kids' Lit Quiz website (www.kidslitquiz.com).

We had a surge of interest in the event from Grades 7 and 8 students from different pockets of the school, especially from those who don't always have a chance to take part in the school team experience. As the Canadian coordinator, Nancy Davidson, says, "Giving students who read a place to be with like-minded peers is important at this age of 'fitting in.'" As students need to work together as a team, they share their expertise in a particular genre and acquire knowledge about areas of literature they might never have explored.

As facilitator, Davidson has noticed that "a long-lasting benefit of the program is experience gained through teamwork. It was great to see students working together as a team, respecting the knowledge of their peers in other genres. The power of the synergy of a team is a tremendous experience for these impressionable youth." Although the final team that represented our school at the competition was comprised of only four students, the other students played an equally valuable role as trainers.

In order to determine the makeup of the final team, we held a mock competition where students answered 50 sample questions individually. Once the final four students were selected, the other students remained an integral part of the team. They created sample questions, imparted their own personal knowledge and expertise, and brought in recommended books for their teammates to read.

"Each trainer was also assigned a training category in which said trainer was most proficient (mine being fantasy and fables/myths) and then trained a future contestant. In such a way, our team was well prepared and well versed in all genres of fictional literature by the time of the competition," said trainer Daniel Marin.

Another trainer, Madeline Leggett, commented, "It was so much fun to be able to talk about books we'd read and find out about books that we had never even heard of, and make some new friends too." Even though she wasn't one of the competing students, the Grade 8 student said she was "so happy that I chose to be one of the trainers because it made me feel like I helped our school try something new and do so well."

The excitement built up to a fever pitch as our team (participants, trainers, coaches, and parents) entered the school gymnasium at Maurice Cody Elementary School. The gym was filled with enthusiastic students and spectators waiting for the competition to begin. Some teams arrived wearing team uniforms while others dressed up in a theme (e.g., *The Wizard of Oz*). Each team had its own table, and each group huddled, checking out the topics (this was the first time they saw the 10 topics) and receiving last-minute support from their entourage. There was quite a variety of different categories: Bears, General Book Knowledge, Harry Potter, Aliases, and Mythology, as well as a visual category on symbols and an audio category, where students had to identify the book according to a song segment. Students could choose to "double down" on one topic, which meant they would double the points awarded for any correct response in this round.

In order to keep the excitement going between the 10 rounds, Wayne Mills would ask book trivia questions to the audience and to the participants for

One of the trainers, Grade 8 student Daniel Marin, said, "The spice of competition, along with the possibility of winning glory for the school, encouraged me to join the Kids' Lit Club."

on-the-spot cash and Indigo gift certificate prizes. The top school for each round of questions also received a book prize for each team member. These additional prizes helped to keep the momentum going and rewarded students for reading.

Gil Posluns (Grade 8) was one of the students representing our school. "The actual competition was amazing," she said. "Dublin took off quickly when my team successfully won the first category and, as a result, I was taking away a prize from the very start of the contest! The book I won was called *Leviathan*, and it was a very good read in a genre that I hadn't tried before."

While our team came in second place by only half a point, it was a win-win for everyone; second place netted our students $100 to share between the four of them; each participant took away a book prize; new friendships and bonds were made; students branched out their literature repertoire; and most important, students were recognized and rewarded for being readers.

Literacy was the real winner of the Kids' Lit Quiz experience.

When Students Read Texts for Authentic Purposes

by Lisa Donohue

Lisa Donohue is an elementary school teacher who incorporates innovative teaching techniques that nurture and support student growth. She has written several excellent books for Pembroke Publishers on different aspects of literacy education.

Not long ago, I was challenged to take on a group of struggling readers and create an after-school tutoring group that would target their reading skills. These students had trouble determining main ideas, providing supporting details, and formulating complete written responses that would clearly explain their thinking. However, the most serious problem these youngsters faced was a complete disengagement from reading. As struggling readers, the last thing this group of middle students would want to spend more time doing was, of course, reading.

As I shared this challenge with David, I asked: "How am I supposed to teach this disengaged group of kids to be better readers?" He responded: "You need to *stop* teaching reading."

Initially, I was perplexed. How could I help students become better readers without teaching them reading?

But the more I thought about it, the more the advice made sense. We had been *teaching reading* rather than teaching the students how to use reading. We needed to shift our focus from teaching reading to *using* reading as a means to get to the information they wanted.

We started by making sure that the name of the club was something that would "hook" the kids. Like most schools, our school has a team. Ours is The Storm. We wanted the after-school tutoring group to appeal to our students, we wanted it to represent the strength of our school and our community, and we wanted it to be something that the students would feel proud to be a part of. Instead of calling it a "tutoring group," we named our group "The StormChasers." Our group gained an identity that was strong, powerful, and positive.

Then, our challenge began. How can we teach kids the skills that they are lacking — without directly *teaching* them? We needed the students to see the value in reading, the power of researching, and the importance of thinking critically about the information they were finding.

As StormChasers, the students began to learn about extreme weather phenomena — they became virtual StormChasers. They viewed and compared YouTube clips, Discovery Channel videos, and online articles and reports of different storms. Using digital tools, they followed real storm chasers into danger and read accounts of families that had narrowly escaped recent tornadoes in Arkansas.

If we were targeting engagement, it was engagement we got. Pushing the limits further we read X-Men comics about the character Storm. The students created their own alter-ego superheroes to examine characters and how characteristics could change over time . . . and they provided evidence.

The kids were hooked. They were engaging in rich dialogues about online text, examining various media pieces, and starting to think critically and analytically about the information they were finding. We provided them with inquiry questions that motivated them to dig deeper into the resources, to form meaningful connections, and to constantly find evidence for their thinking through the texts. The kids were *using* reading as a way of accessing information that they found engaging and relevant.

How do we begin to measure the success of "StormChasers"? Did it achieve the goals that we set out to achieve? Judge for yourself. We assessed the students at seven stages throughout the tutoring, and we recorded the percentage of students who provided answers that were at or above the expectation for their grade (Level 3 or 4 answers). Here are the results:

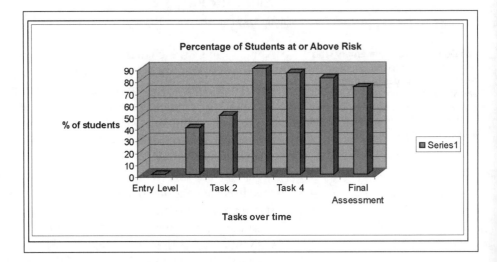

The data are one thing . . . but here is my highlight: On the day of our last session, a group of these students stopped me in the hall to ask if they could *please* sign up for StormChasers again because it was the "best club they'd ever been a part of"!

The students are reading much better, but that's only a part of our success. They now *enjoy* reading texts that matter to them!

Bringing the Black and White into Color: Active Reading

by Luke Coles

Luke Coles is Head of School at Blyth Academy in Lawrence Park in Toronto. He has extensive experience in working with literacy and boys in the middle years.

It's true: many boys will tell you that they don't love reading.

So, how to respond? There are two main ways. We can smile, shake our heads, make some comment about boys being boys, say isn't it too bad they're missing out on such a world of material — and wave the white flag of surrender. Or, we can ask questions: questions of them, questions of ourselves. Why *do* boys really think that reading isn't for them?

For 12 years, I taught English to Grade 8 boys at a single-gender, independent elementary school in Toronto. I conducted a small action research project over three years, and at the beginning of the year, only 35 percent of those students reported that they "enjoyed reading" as opposed to indicating either "reading is okay" (22 percent) or "I dislike reading" (43 percent).

But 92 percent reported that they enjoyed movies. Sure, we say — *of course*, they prefer movies to books! But do they really? Must it be an automatic? Are they hard wired to prefer the more passive medium of viewing over reading? In movies, they say, they are "excited". . . they can " identify with all the characters better". . . they "can *see* the characters and hear the characters' voices."

No Pictures in the Mind . . .

It was that last comment, in its many and varied forms, that came loudest off the page. They aren't seeing the characters when they read? They aren't hearing the voices? When asked this specific question — "When you read independently, do you create a picture in your mind of what each character looks like?" — 84 percent of the boys said no. So, in turn, I ask even the most fervent reader out there, could you imagine anything more painful and tedious than reading a novel with one tone, one voice, and no real settings or images in your mind? Is that really what our boys are doing, and if so, have we not stumbled upon one of our most pressing responsibilities in the teaching of reading?

It suddenly seemed so clear and significant.

Boys love to be read to. Eighty-eight percent of those surveyed here asked for "more" reading aloud to them in class (and 8 of the remaining 12 percent did not answer the question — perhaps the 21st was one too many for them). They enjoy reading when it is done by another and dramatic voices are used. Suddenly, the characters are distinct from one another, and the groundwork is laid for them to picture what they are listening to and act as directors of the stories they are reading.

We teach how to read for meaning, but do we teach how to read for pleasure? Is literacy about being able to understand what we read, or should it not entail an ability to appreciate as well — to make what we read relevant to ourselves?

And so the effort was made to isolate this theory in one hand-picked text. Three years' worth of students went home to read a challenging short story about a suspicious death of a man who has minimalized his wife for years. The husband is found dead in his own bed, and his wife claims no knowledge of what has transpired. She is, however, the only apparent suspect. The sheriff and several men from town come out to find the motive, but traditional detective work uncovers little. It is the women, thought to be silly and simple by the men, who look deeper into the clues of life around the home and see the widow's empty life and related motives.

Reading the story at home elicited little energy from the boys. They came in confused, and when asked if they would recommend that I teach this story to my future Grade 8 classes, only 11 percent felt it was worthy of repeat. Perfect. I wanted to know whether a text that boys had felt distant from could be brought to life and even enjoyed by adding color and character to the reading.

A Mock Trial as a Literacy Event

We tackle the work together. The story ends with a trial for the widow pending, but we undertake to see the story through further. The boys formally apply for roles within the story for a mock courtroom trial to take place a week later. Key roles are the county attorney, the defence attorney, the widow, and the men and women on scene, particularly the women who know a great deal but as yet haven't shared it with their dismissive men. Roles are posted early one morning, and I'm delighted to see that the list has generated the same kind of excitement among the boys as we typically see with the posting of teams.

Costumes are sought out, boys prepare for their parts in the trial, and the trial is a sight to behold. Boys play their roles magnificently, as law and order music plays in the background, and I try to keep things on time and authentic as judge. They love it, and student jurors depart the room, deliberate, and return several minutes later having found consensus and a verdict.

Judgment Time

Two weeks later, I have the boys fill out another survey. They aren't thinking about that earlier occasion when 11 percent thought the story was worth repeating. On this day, after they have chosen roles and thus indentified either themselves or their friends with those characters, no less than 87 of 90 surveyed determine the story worthy of repeat. It seems to have worked. Boys who did not enjoy reading a challenging story now connect with the material and want more.

Mock trials, travel logs, character analyses, improvisations, skits, voice recordings, directorial activities, storyboarding . . . we need to bring text to life.

Literacy is no longer about the antiquated canon. It is email, graphic fiction, the sports section, even horoscopes. To read is to do something *active* — we add our own connotations to words, we connect our own circles of people with characters, and we apply our own photo albums to settings. But we must teach our young charges to do this — to bring the black and white into color, and the monotone, into the charismatic.

Fantasy Fiction: An Interactive Genre Study

by David Willoughby

David Willoughby teaches Grade 7 Language Arts, Science, and Mathematics at Sam Sherratt Public School. He focuses on developing a trusting relationship with his students, engaging them by recognizing and honoring their interests.

A club I have started at my school gives students an opportunity to read interactive fantasy fiction novels. These game books are the very same books that I had read as an intermediate student back in the late 1980s. The idea to introduce them to my students came to me when I was looking through some old boxes of stuff and came across a collection of my old books. As I looked at the artwork on the front and read the description on the back, a flood of memories came pouring through my mind. I remembered treasuring these books and being really engaged in the plots — plots that I was able to choose.

As a teacher I thought that these might be a great way to engage some of the students in my classroom. I thought that they might consider the books "cool" just as I did. A friend of mine was able to supply me with some copies that he had kept safe, and I later found out that the books were back in print and sold at bookstores everywhere. I purchased some (the "new" covers were fancy with computer-generated artwork) and created the club. As I write this, we have two very keen girls and four very engaged boys.

A Typical Club Meeting

Here are some observations I made of their interactions during a typical gathering in our school library.

- Students are sitting close together around a table. They were invited to sit at different tables around the library to have more space, but they opted to sit together around a table (six students at one table during one of the meetings).
- Some students are paired up, adventuring through one book together. Other students are reading independently. Students who are paired up are either reading the same page quietly together, or one is reading out loud to the other student who is maintaining the character data sheet (a tracking outline to indicate traits in a character from their book).
- Students are making decisions collaboratively. They base their decisions on risk taking ("Let's just open the door and see what happens!"), on inventory they are carrying, according to the character data sheet ("We can't do that; we are not carrying the frost shield!"), and on students' morals ("That wouldn't be the right thing to do to that family of peasants").
- Socializing takes place. The students are talking about the books, about decisions made, and about monsters encountered, too, pointing out the illustrations.
- Students are discovering vocabulary unique to the fantasy genre. They are asking each other questions about what words mean, even about fantasy monsters ("What's a Hydra? . . . I just learned what Medusa is!").
- Arithmetic skills are practised during battles or even when testing luck.
- Students practise honesty by not peeking ahead to see how the story branches out. They engaged in discussions about this during moments where a student did look ahead.
- Organization is practised as the students maintain their character data sheets.
- Following instructions closely is a key part to success as the books can differ from one another in the way that stamina is determined, skill is calculated, luck is rolled, and so on.

Suggestions to Pass On to Students

1. Select a book you think you'll enjoy, and abandon books that aren't working for you after you've given them a good chance.
2. Read the book twice. During your second reading, take notes — this will affect your contribution to the conversation. The better the notes, the better the conversation will be.
3. Always have the book with you so you can refer back to it for support.
4. Focus on questions that do not have a right or wrong answer and can be useful for discussion.
5. Say what you believe, even if the rest of the group disagrees.
6. Give everyone a chance to talk, and listen to what each person says about the topic. Piggyback on ideas to develop them further.

7. Help group members understand words or situations that they are having trouble with.
8. Respect other people — no put-downs.

When Students Run the Book Club

by Robert Walters

Robert Walters is an elementary teacher who has just completed his Ph.D. His thesis examined the important role of literature circles in the literacy development of middle-years students.

In my summer school classroom, I was asked to use the picture book *Listen to the Wind: The Story of Dr. Greg and* Three Cups of Tea, as an anchor text. Since the text is deep and rich and linked well to the overall arching theme, global citizenship, I was really excited for this text on a personal level; however, I was uncertain how it would be received by the students. Since this short book was intended for a much younger audience than my underachieving Grades 7 and 8 students, I was not certain they would be interested.

Regardless, I shared the book and began the discussion. As predicted, the students did not immediately take to the text, raising many questions about the viability and believability of some of the events. Instead of wanting to discuss the theme of the book, the students seemed to be stuck on the plausibility of some of the events, causing a halt to the dialogue.

Since this was a class for underachieving students, I was reticent to offer them the text on which the picture book was based. I wanted just to give them the answers so that we could move on. Initially, I tried to do this but, as I had not read the text thoroughly and they had not read it at all, we wandered into what I considered to be more off-topic questions. Instead, I posed a solution: I asked the class if any students would like to start a book club. The book of choice would obviously be the original text to our picture book: *Three Cups of Tea* by Greg Mortenson and David Oliver Relin.

"A Brave, Excited Commitment"

In response to strong student interest, a small book club was initiated. Although it had been my suggestion to initiate the book club, the club was completely student driven. Thus, where and when we met was decided by the group as was the book and any activities or discussions that went with it. Instead of my taking charge and telling the students what to do in order to enrich their understanding of the text, we had conversations about how to approach the text and our meetings, and collectively agreed upon timelines and activities. The students thought it would be a good idea to "chunk" the book as it seemed overwhelming to them. They collectively decided to discuss the book and bring any outstanding questions they had about it to our weekly discussions.

Since none of the students knew one another before entering this class, the conversations were extremely bare initially; however, throughout the course of the book club, the members of the group became more familiar with one another and shared more and more ideas. By the final meeting, members laughed with one another, shared ideas freely, and were willing to challenge one another's ideas without hesitation.

In other words, to create an authentic dialogue within my classroom, I found a hook: a hook that included strong student interest balanced with academic learning in literacy and combined effective teacher effort. I provided students with whatever was needed to learn. I purchased a copy of the book for each student and gave them the space so that they could meet safely. I also facilitated their learning. I encouraged them to use each other as resources instead of looking towards me as their teacher for every answer, especially for opinion questions. Rarely would I share my opinion unless necessary to stimulate conversation.

Once student interest is high, if you provide a space that is easy and accessible for them to enter, student learning is both natural and easy. This is how I created an authentic learning opportunity for my students. Through this opportunity, authentic dialogue took place, and students made dramatic improvements both socially and academically.

As for my concern about the text being too difficult for these underachieving middle students, it turned out to be a non-issue. Since student interest was the number one priority, the students worked extremely hard to achieve their goals. Once I relinquished overt control and the students took ownership for their learning, they pushed forward with a brave, excited commitment.

Grappling with the Language of Shakespeare

by Marvin Karon

Marvin Karon, a well-known drama teacher, is, at present, the executive director of Shakespearience Performing Arts, a theatre in education company that works with students in the middle years to demystify the language in the Bard's plays and demonstrate why Shakespeare and his works are still held in such esteem.

When we work as guest instructors with middle-years students, we try to make sense of scenes from the Bard's plays the way an *actor* would prepare for a performance.

By so doing, we hope to make the language of Shakespeare accessible and understandable. Selected scenes from the drama being studied in class are brought to life by the students who are invited to participate in an interactive environment of exploration and discovery.

We always begin with a few direct questions: "Is there anyone in the room who has a problem with Shakespeare? Doesn't like Shakespeare? Wish they didn't have to study him? Wish he weren't on the curriculum?" At the high-school level, anywhere between one-half to two-thirds of the students in the room raise their hands. When asked why Shakespeare elicits such a negative response, the first thing that virtually all young people complain about is that "he's too hard to understand," a reference to the difficult, "archaic" language found in the plays. One student confessed that "Shakespeare makes me feel stupid."

Addressing the Fear Factor

We begin the task of removing the fear factor from the Bard's plays by first establishing that it's not necessary to understand every word in every scene. Some of the material in Shakespeare's plays, it is pointed out, has to do with specific, topical references that would resonate only with an Elizabethan audience. In Act II, Scene ii, of *Hamlet*, for instance, Rosencrantz and Guildenstern go on at some length in their conversation with the Danish prince about the "little eyases" and "aery of children," referring to the fad in the entertainment industry at the beginning of the 17th century when little boys' acting troupes, sponsored by churches such as St. Paul's and Blackfriars, were taking a big bite out of Shakespeare's box office. A chunk of text running some 20 lines is read aloud by the facilitator and the guest artist, and the references are explained.

Another tool used to minimize the fear of the seemingly inaccessible language in Shakespeare's plays is the always popular insult game. Readily available on the Internet, the game consists of three columns of words culled from the various plays in the canon — two columns of adjectives, one column of nouns. The students face a partner and by adding a "you" or a "thou" to the words on their papers, along with a dash of energy and a wallop of imagination, the air is soon filled with cries of "Peter, you Roguish pottle-deep moldwarp," "Susan, you Gorbellied fen-sucked *puttock* " and "Steve, thou yeasty unchin-snouted *skainsmate*."

After these preliminary warm-up exercises, by which students understand that the words being hurled at one another are not compliments but insults, students are reminded that the words in the plays were never written to be *read* by Shakespeare's predominantly illiterate audiences. The critical point is made that you can't approach *Romeo and Juliet* or *Hamlet* the way you do a short story or a novel; students are made privy to the "secret" that these scripts are written in a kind of code for actors.

Cracking the Code for Actors

So the work begins.

Romeo, for example, is loitering about somewhere with his friends, Mercutio and Benvolio. The Nurse enters with her servant, Peter, looking to pick up a message from the young man about the plans he has made for his marriage to Juliet. When they see the Nurse waddling on stage, one young man cries out, "Here's goodly gear," which prompts another to yell, "A sail, a sail," and another to join in with "Two, two; a shirt and a smock." With Shakespearience's guest star reading Mercutio, students assume the other roles of Benvolio, Romeo, the Nurse, and Peter. The lines are read — they seem utterly obscure and confusing.

But then the actor's work begins and questions — the artist's tools — are posed as a means of putting the scene in some sort of context. The Nurse is looking for Romeo in the piazza. What's the modern-day equivalent of a piazza? Someone from the audience yells it out: "A mall." Are Romeo, Benvolio, and Mercutio likely to be the only patrons of this mall? At the height of a business day, does one see only three or four people strolling among the shops of the Eaton Centre? Probably not — and so more students are called up to "dress" the scene.

The work continues and more questions are asked. What's the relationship between Romeo, Benvolio, and Mercutio? They're friends. And what do friends tend to do when they're hanging around with their buddies in a mall? Well, they "diss" people. They make fun of the way they dress. And if LA Gear can be identified as a kind of sportswear, then maybe the word *gear* used in this scene is used to refer to the same thing — to clothing — when it comes to describing what the Nurse is wearing. She thinks she is the height of fashion but is so frumpy she looks like she's wearing "a sail, a sail . . ."

In a short time, something has come into focus and language that was, on the surface, incomprehensible has been transformed into something accessible and easy to understand. At this point, the students come alive with suggestions, offering directions to the guest artist and their friends who are taking part in the scene; other basic acting exercises are introduced to demonstrate how a professional performer's approach to analyzing classical text can unlock and demystify it. The mystery surrounding Shakespeare's language begins to melt away, and young people begin to appreciate how seemingly insurmountable problems can be overcome with a little ingenuity, creativity, interactive hard work, and a sense of fun.

Shakespeare in the Classroom

What can teachers working on their own with Grades 7 and 8 students do to remove the fear factor so often associated with Shakespeare's language? How can they make the language come alive as a means of empowering their kids through language without access to the artistic community and with little experience with the kinds of tools, techniques, and skills used by actors to open up the language in Shakespeare's plays?

There are several strategies and exercises that teachers can employ to take away the fear so often associated with Shakespeare's Elizabethan language no matter what their background or comfort level with drama as a tool.

1. Choose brief scenes or excerpts for the students to explore. For example, *Macbeth* offers many opportunities for young people to find their way with the language and the meaning with a short scene. Students can do their lines in partners, with everyone involved at the same time, and then a few volunteers can read their lines aloud to the class. Using a variety of scenes, pairs of students can rehearse their lines, and then each scene can be read in sequential order. The students continue to deepen the understanding of the play as the scenes that precede theirs provide significant information in providing context for what each group will interpret.

2. With the technology available now, it is quite easy to have students do a You-Tube search and to compare, for example, Roman Polanski's assassination of Duncan in *Macbeth* with a version of the scene done by the BBC production of the play . . . or Franco Zefferelli's handling of the balcony scene in *Romeo and Juliet* with the way Baz Luhrman did it in his adaptation of the play.

3. A lot of the anxiety induced by Shakespeare's language can be minimized by turning it into a game. The teacher can cull lines from the 37 plays and write them down on strips of paper. Students are divided into two teams. One person stands at one end of the room and faces teammates at the opposite end of the room, who are all lined up, one behind the other. The leader calls out the line on the piece of paper, for example: "I am tied at the stake and I must stand the course." The line is recited slowly and clearly enough to be understood and the person standing opposite as far away as 5 m (depending on the size of the room) must repeat the line EXACTLY as it was delivered. "I am tied at the stake and I must stand the course." If *any* word is incorrect, the line must be repeated by the "leader" until the person who is being fed the words repeats them verbatim. Achieving this tends to be difficult with the distraction of the other team's players standing right beside them, yelling and screaming a different line to their teammates . . . and with the enthusiasm of the two teams yelling out encouragement and support, which also serves as a major barrier to quickly getting through the lines as written on the piece of paper. It does however turn Shakespeare's language into a competition and for those who are more inclined to that, doors to the learning objective that might otherwise be closed can open.

4. Students may be encouraged to learn that Shakespeare invented thousands of words in his plays. He turned nouns into adjectives, verbs into nouns, and so on. Very often, a word that might appear daunting and challenging on the page can become clear through context. So another language game that has proven effective is to ask the students to create a short scene in modern English, set against the backdrop of one of Shakespeare's stories, in which new words are invented to make a point. So, take, for example, this exchange in Act II, Scene iii, of *Othello*, where a drunken, angry Cassio pursues Roderigo into the presence of Montano:

MONTANO: What's the matter, lieutenant?
CASSIO: A knave teach me my duty! I'll beat the knave into a twiggen bottle.

The original lines can be adapted into something like this:

MONTANO: What's the matter, lieutenant?
CASSIO: A *kerplukt* teach me my duty! I'll beat the kerplukt into a *srcangy* bottle.

And the scene continues with students dropping in their own made-up words, made clear through context and body language.

5. A more challenging game pertaining to Shakespeare's language involves pulling lines from the canon, once again, and writing them on strips of paper. Three students are called up and might be handed "A horse, a horse . . . my kingdom for a horse," "O what a rogue and peasant slave am I," and "How happy some o'er others some may be." The participants are then instructed to construct a scene — using only the words on their slip of paper. They don't have to say the entire sentence and can extract phrases or individual words from their slip of paper. For example, the person with Hamlet's line can simply say: "What a rogue . . ." The student can repeat words: for example, the person with Richard's line might simply mutter, "A horse, a horse, a horse, a horse, a horse, a horse, a horse, a horse . . ." They don't have to go in any order. Lines spoken by one participant can overlap with lines spoken by another participant. But the objective is, through conflict and character, to make each of the three "actors" relate to one another and construct a new story — their own story — with Shakespeare's words.

6. Shakespeare wrote in iambic pentameter: five feet of *ba-BUM*. Students might be encouraged to say aloud some Shakespearean verse written in iambic pentameter: "But soft! What light through yonder window breaks?" — and then create their own. "I'd like a burger, French Fries and a Coke." Once some time has been spent on this, groups can be established to construct a whole scene written in modern iambic pentameter with a beginning, a middle, and an end — and then extended even further by writing a scene involving a prediction by some witches in modern English before moving on to an examination of the original text of *Macbeth*.

7. A thematic approach to the preoccupations of Shakespeare's writing — which remain so relevant and topical today — can be explored by, for example, dividing the students into two groups, perhaps one with all black hair and the other with any other colour, and establishing them as rival gangs. Using the Shakespearean insults described above, the two "families" must find reasons for "getting a hate on" for one another and, using the exercise described above, give voice to those reasons by expressing them in iambic pentameter.

8. A contextual approach to the language could be explored by setting the language against different backdrops: for example, *King Lear* set in Buckingham Palace.

9. Grades 7 and 8 students would likely find it easier to lose the fear factor associated with the language by physicalizing it — if the word *scut* was some kind of motion, what would that motion look like? If the words *barbarous Scythian* were a dance, what kind of dance would it be? If enough of these words are strung together in sequence to establish some sort of tableau, there are almost limitless possibilities in terms of what can be done to turn Shakespeare's language into a physical experience rooted more in the body than the mouth.

Teachers are encouraged to devise their own games, exercises, tools, and strategies in order to remove the fear factor associated with the Elizabethan language. The effort of removing the fear factor is well worth taking. This language all too often proves to be a major obstacle to a young person's enjoyment of these works of genius and, by so doing, compromises students' self-esteem. Shakespeare can offer students invaluable insights . . . a compass to open up their eyes, their hearts, and their minds as they navigate their way through life, and the sooner they come to be aware of these insights, the better.

Unlocking the Imagination: Linking the Head to the Heart

by Amah Harris

Amah Harris is a Grade 7 homeroom teacher in Toronto. With a wide background in educational theatre, Amah is well known for integrating drama, education, and the students' culture in her classroom curriculum.

How does a teacher nurture a sense of community, a sense of family in her core Grade 7 class? I was faced with that challenge this school year. With few exceptions, my core class, 7-B, presented themselves as shy students, needing self-confidence, not willing to take risks, afraid to be wrong in front of the other students, but when prompted, proving themselves to be a well of potential. I found them to be a group of exciting students, many of whom were not conscious of their level of ability, but so willing to learn, so willing to open themselves to receive from me — the core teacher — and my co-teacher, Nancy Watson-McCraken, the Special Education teacher, who also taught Mathematics. 7-B was an integrated Special Education and Regular Program class.

My approach to pedagogy is framed by the socio-cultural theory which defines human beings as socio-cultural by nature, the foundation for both practical and cognitive intelligences. The children's experiences, therefore, growing out of their family and societal cultures, are used as the initial source for learning. They are not "included" in the learning process; rather, they are the very threads used to weave the fabric that is the learning, and the learning process.

Drama is an integral element in the implementation of the socio-cultural framing of my pedagogy. Drama would be one of the most natural means to reach the children and couch them in a welcoming, nonthreatening community environment. It presents itself to me as an effective vehicle to initiate learning across the curriculum so that it is both relevant to the lives of the children and has an impact on the way they live their lives.

I had noticed that during Drama class, the original dramas the children shared were at an intellectual and concrete level. Even when drama games were used, it seemed difficult for them to move into the realm of the creative imagination so as to lift themselves into spheres not yet experienced, thus expanding their lived experience.

Into the Realm of Creative Imagination: Pictures

I would use artists with whom the students were unfamiliar. The *Mysteries of Harris Burdick* consists of a collection of black-and-white pictures. Each picture is fitted with a topic and short caption. Another portfolio of images by Austrian painter and architect Friedensreich Hundertwasser, the Hundertwasser, is a visual of spirals, irregular lines, and circles resplendent in the use of a wide range of color. Some of the pictures show no people at all, yet you get the feeling that the artist is trying to connect us deeply into human lives. Others portray humans in their habitat, yet interacting with color and their environment in out-of-the-usual ways.

7-B's homeroom space is relatively large. The desks were moved to the centre of the room. I then set up the room like an art gallery, the only difference being the chairs were set up facing the pictures. The students were invited to walk around the room, observing the pictures and deciding which ones they would like to write about. When at least 15 minutes had passed, I asked them to sit in front of their first picture of choice. I directed them to get their writing materials and observe their chosen picture. My statements and questions were paced with meaningful pauses to allow the children to reflect on them and then use them.

Some initial statements and questions used were as follows:
- Observe your picture simply to brainstorm what you see and jot notes down.
- What do you see? Try to give details.
- Who do you see? Give details.
- What is the location of this picture? What evidence causes you to think so?
- Is it happening now or long ago? What evidence makes you think so?

At this point, the students had been working for close to 40 minutes. There had been a still, gentle, but contemplative energy in the room. I was excited and amazed at how easily they were trusting this project, how genuinely engrossed they were in it. However, it was time to move from external, concrete observations to a different realm. I would allow them to explore for another 10 minutes, then call a break.

One question:
- How does your picture make you feel?

A different level of quietness began to circulate in the room. A few students raised their hands. One of them asked, "What do you mean, Ms. Harris?" The others lowered their hands. It seems as though they had the same question.

I answered: "What emotions does the picture stir up in you? What is the mood of the picture? Observe the colors. What are they? How are they interacting? Look at the shades? Do those colors and shades help you understand the mood? How do you think the author wants you to feel? What do you feel?"

These questions came slowly, but flowed one after the other; I then stopped speaking and allowed them to work.

I could sense the children wrestling with those questions: they were challenging them to dig below the surface, challenging them to organically involve themselves with the content of possibilities in the pictures. Slowly, they began to relax into the experience. They began to write energetically. Based on the writings they shared later, at that particular point, they seemed to have been finding freedom in their imagination and allowing past experiences to blend with the imagination to find answers. I had expected to let them work for only 10 minutes, but they seemed to be deeply into this section of the session, so I allowed them to continue on to the 60-minute mark. At that point, I called a 15-minute break where they could do as they pleased within reason, including listen to music.

After break, they went back to their seats and turned their chairs around so that they were sitting in a circle facing one another. One by one, each student stood and shared writings or experiences with the picture that had so engaged them. It seemed that their peers' sharings were triggering more thoughts. As the session came to a close, I promised them that we would return to the work within the same week.

Going further, going deeper

The classroom was set as it was during session 1. The students were handed their writing and allowed about 15 minutes with their ideas, their writing, and their pictures without me instructing them in any way. They had copied out the questions while I had been speaking in the previous session. They were using those, along with deeper observations and their involvement with the pictures, to expand on their writing.

So as to match the quietness in the room, I spoke softly and gently:

"Look at the interactions in the pictures. Are people interacting with people? Are there no people in the pictures? Are there animals in the pictures? What about lines? Are there any lines? Are they speaking to you? Observe the details. Are there spirals? Are there circles? What do they mean? What are the colors telling you? Relax with the ideas. Allow your imagination to take you . . . How does that make you feel? What is your picture saying to you?"

Again my pacing was slow, with questions punctuated by pauses.

They worked for 20 minutes more on their pictures and then I offered them the opportunity to change to a different picture. Few did so. For 50 minutes they chose to continue on the same picture that they had been working on.

At the end of session 2, I invited them to share their writing with their peers again. Their thoughts had deepened considerably. I then collected the pictures and writings again. I promised to return them quickly. My intent was simply to copy them and return the originals to the students. This I did, keeping the copies. My final instruction for this component was that they were to look over the writing, think of what they had heard their peers say, and see whether they had been influenced to make any adaptations on their writing.

Transposing Analyses into Tableaux

The students were allowed to choose their own groups for the purpose of transposing their analyses into tableaux. If five people were in a group, five different tableaux would be developed by the group. After the first student's frozen picture (tableau), she or he would step out of the tableau and either present a monologue based on an analysis of the picture or simply read the analysis aloud. A few chose the first option; most chose the latter.

The results were quite moving: full of imagination, emotion, creativity, and depth. The students had been able to get past the hurdle of sticking with the concrete and moving into the imagination, blending that experience with their emotions to visit worlds not yet experienced. They began to show differences in their everyday speech and began showing steps towards personal problem solving, which was quite exciting.

What carries my own excitement further is that my new schedule will allow me to interact with most of them in Drama class in Grade 8. I will be able to work with them on continuity.

A Student's Response to a Picture in *The Mysteries of Harris Burdick*

The mood to me feels like love and loss. It doesn't seem at all unhappy. It seems like someone you know that has passed is showing that they are there and showing their love. It's a warm mood because of all the doves, and one of them looks like it's landing on the wall. There are no actual people but the energy from the doves makes me think there's a presence.

The only lines the artist has drawn would be of the windowsill and what looks like a small dresser or bedside table. I think the artist is trying to show a bedroom or some sort of room with meaning to it. The picture is only black and white. It's what first drew me to the picture, even though it has no colour, it stood out!

I just realized that what really made me think about love and loss is that right outside the window are clouds. It reminds me of what I first thought of the movie *Up*, before I had seen it. In the movie, I thought that because his wife had passed away, he was trying to go up to heaven to be with her, and this particular setting/setup of room looks more old fashioned.

I see in my mind this picture being in one of my favourite movies, *Across the Universe*. If you know the movie and know that either Paul McCartney or John Lennon, or whoever wrote the song Dear Prudence, you would know that in the song they say "look around" over and over and they end up in the clouds. This picture made me think of that song — if I were to walk into this room in the picture, I would expect all the doves to start flying off the walls and I would hear the Beatles or Evan Rachel Wood and Joe Ferguson saying "Look around, round, round, round look around!" That does make you sound a little insane but, this picture is something my personality would come up with. This room would be a little bit more old fashioned and would only have the basic bed, bedside table, lamp, and dresser.

By Taryn

Reading Rocks! A Reading Mentoring Program

by Amy Robinson and Laura Miller

Amy Robinson is an itinerant literacy and numeracy teacher who works with teachers in Kindergarten through Grade 8. She also is an instructor for Literacy Additional Qualifications courses.

Laura Miller currently teaches Grade 3 students and enjoys opportunities where she can engage her class with older students. She continues to run this reading support program at her school.

Reading mentoring is a powerful tool that involves older students mentoring younger students in reading. It is based on relationships of trust between the younger and older students, so that they can work together towards improvements in reading.

An effective reading mentoring program not only supports student achievement in reading but also fosters a sense of community within a school. We have had a reading mentoring program running at an elementary school with Grades 2, 3, and 8 students for three years and have found it to be successful in creating better readers both at the primary and intermediate levels, establishing relationships among students, and supporting school improvement.

Our reading mentoring program meets once a week over recess and is supervised by teacher advisers. Intermediate students are partnered up to work one-on-one with primary students. In the past we ran our reading mentoring program during a 15-minute recess once a week; however, due to the student responses, we have switched to a 30-minute block over the lunch recess. The intermediate reading mentors requested more time with their partners in order to make a bigger impact — we feel that this speaks strongly to the ownership that they have with the program.

Our reading mentoring program runs for 10 weeks, allowing for an introductory session and a celebration at the end. We specifically chose the duration so that students are able to commit to attend each session — it isn't so long that students would want to drop out. Traditionally, we offer two 10-week sessions: one session for Grade 2 students and one for Grade 3 students. Reading mentors can sign up for one or both sessions.

How the Program Differs from Reading Buddies

The reading mentoring program differs significantly from a traditional reading buddies program. It is more formal, and there is a structure to it. Students in the program are called "mentors" and "partners," which creates a different tone than calling the pairs of students "reading buddies."

Intermediate students are trained by teacher advisers on how to mentor younger students in reading. The mentors are informed about the area(s) of focus for their partner (e.g., fluency, decoding, and comprehension), and they are supported by teacher advisers as they intentionally select strategies to target the identified area of concern. They understand the important role they are playing to help improve their partner's reading. The mentors are accountable for the work they do with their reading partners as they track their observations and ideas for future sessions.

There are three distinct roles involved in our reading mentoring program: teacher advisers, reading mentors, and reading partners.

Teacher advisers

Committed and knowledgeable teacher advisers are essential. At our school, teachers can sign up for the reading mentoring program as an extracurricular, similar to signing up for coaching an athletic sport. Teacher advisers commit to attending all reading mentoring sessions. They also attend the training session for the mentors and receive the same information so that a consistent message and approach is used. During the reading mentoring sessions, teacher advisers take attendance, quickly match up partners, help mentors in finding reading materials to use with their partners, and provide oral descriptive feedback to the mentors. Teacher advisers also model strategies that mentors could use with their partners. After each session they provide written descriptive feedback in each reading mentor's tracking sheets.

Reading mentors

The intermediate students selected to be part of the reading mentoring program must be responsible, dependable, and committed to the program's success. Reading mentors are typically successful readers who are willing to work with

Mentoring Program Components

- Formal structure
- Accountability
- Informed partnership
- Purposeful text selection (levelled text)
- Specific feedback provided by teacher advisers

Ownership of the Role

One year a reading mentor was quite concerned that he and his partner would not finish their text before the end of the reading mentoring program. He asked us several times how many sessions were left in the program so that he and his partner could plan out how to finish the book. The mentor would hold onto the book in his locker so that he always knew where the book was. He asked if he could continue reading with his partner outside of the program time if they did not finish their book.

Reading mentors treat the role seriously.

Sample 30-Minute Structure

5 minutes: Arrive, pair up mentors and partners, take attendance; mentors read teacher adviser's descriptive feedback of their tracking sheets; select reading material (if needed).

20 minutes: There is intense, focused reading work between mentors and partners based on identified area of need; teacher advisers monitor work and provide immediate descriptive feedback.

5 minutes: Mentors record in their tracking sheets; partners return reading materials; teacher advisers help mentors with tracking sheets (if necessary).

younger reading partners. However, there have been times when a weaker intermediate reader has been a mentor. The weak intermediate reader is still a more effective reader than the struggling primary student with whom he or she is partnered. We know that, no matter what the reading level of the mentors, they all benefit from being a part of this program. All students learn more about reading and become better readers.

Reading mentors receive training and are supported by teacher advisers throughout the program. They are expected to attend every session, be responsible for their work during the sessions, track their observations and strategies used for each session, and use their training manual to help guide their work. Teacher advisers give them a lot of control and authority over the work they do, which contributes to their sense of ownership and accountability.

Reading partners

The reading partners are the primary students who are struggling readers. These students come with a wide range of areas for improvement ranging from comprehension (including retells), fluency, word recognition, and confidence. Reading partners are each matched up with a reading mentor and develop a relationship with that student. They are expected to attend all reading mentoring sessions. Most often, the classroom teacher will send reading material for the reading partners to use with their mentors. We have witnessed how excited the reading partners are to work with their mentors and how enthusiastic they are about coming.

How We Set Up Our Program

We recommend having one teacher adviser from an intermediate class and one from a primary class. It is likely that the intermediate teacher will be recognizable to the reading mentors and the primary teacher adviser, recognizable to the partners, which helps in creating a comfort level within the program and establishes a safe, trusting environment. Furthermore, having a teacher adviser from each division assists with communication and reminders.

We try to partner up students one-on-one. In most cases, we have had up to 35 students. We use the library as our meeting location because it has enough space for pairs of students to work together without bothering others and reading material is accessible.

A set structure allows for a predictable routine and for mentors to efficiently use their time to focus on specific partner need(s). A sample structure appears at left.

We promote the program at staff meetings, divisional meetings, and through one-on-one conversations with teachers.

The primary classroom teachers are asked to select students in their class who are struggling readers and who are falling below the reading benchmarks for their grade. Classroom teachers use the data from oral running records as well as anecdotal observations to make decisions about selecting students. They are also asked to consider who would benefit most from the program and those that would be most likely to attend the sessions. They complete a Student Profile Summary on each of their selected students, providing information on the student's reading level, area(s) of focus, learning styles, and interests.

This information is used by the teacher advisers to match students with mentors. The reading mentors also have access to this information to inform the work that they do with their partner. Teacher advisers use a chart listing matches between reading mentors and partners and the areas that reading partners need to work on to stay organized and allow students to get to work quickly each session.

Reading mentors are recruited from Grades 7 and 8 through announcements to promote the program. The intermediate teachers are also asked to encourage students they think would be effective mentors to participate. When selecting reading mentors, teacher advisers look for students who like reading and who are enthusiastic, responsible, and willing to make a commitment to the program.

Mentor training

Our mentor training, called "Reading Mentor in an Hour Training Workshop," takes place over one full lunch hour. We deliver the training through a Power-Point presentation that has built-in direct instruction, whole-group discussion, small-group discussion, modelling, self-reflection, and questions and answers.

The training session provides an overview of the reading process and difficulties that the reading partners may encounter. Through a series of activities and discussions the students build an understanding of reading, reading mentoring, and how to select strategies to best meet the needs of their reading partner. We also highlight the importance of building relationships and trust with their partners. Finally, we provide an explicit outline of the reading mentoring role and our expectations, including the completion of the weekly tracking sheets.

At the training session, mentors receive a training manual, which we refer to during the training session. The manual has background information; specific strategies that mentors can use with their partners; reading comprehension questions that mentors can use for before, during, and after reading; a reading fluency checklist; and a simple reading diagnostic tool.

Monitoring Progress

In order to remain in touch with the struggling readers and support the mentors, teacher advisers monitor their progress. At each session, we move around the room, listen in to how partners are working together, and often join pairs to model strategies and help mentors to access resources in the manual.

Mentors track what they do. They make a note of what they were working on for that day, the texts that were read, and the strategies they tried. They also record ideas for the next session and any questions they have. They hand in this tracking form each week, and teacher advisers provide written descriptive feedback to each of them in order to assist them with their plans for the next session. This aspect of the program lets teacher advisers remain in touch with what each pair is working on.

Benefits of tracking forms

Since introducing the tracking form, we have noticed that our mentors are more engaged in their sessions and are more likely to remain committed to their partner throughout the 10 weeks. The mentors enjoy receiving feedback in their manuals every week as it validates the work they do. We strive to be specific and

---

Sample PowerPoint Slides

> **Your Partner May Have Difficulty With:**
> - Decoding
> - Oral language
> - Reading fluency
> - Written language
> - Comprehension (Summarize, Predict, Ask questions, Inferences, Connections)

> **Think/Pair/Share**
>
> **Think:** How did you learn to read? What have your experiences with reading been?
> **Pair:** Talk to your right elbow partner about your thoughts.
> **Share:** As a whole group share your thoughts.
> *Turn to the About Reading page in your Reading Rocks Duotang.*

"I learned that even some of the strategies I gave my partner I can use it on myself!"
— *Grade 8 participant*

"Good at sounding out words; needs to slow down his reading; can read quick but misses words. He reminds me of me!"
— *Comment from a Reading Mentor tracking sheet*

positive when writing descriptive feedback, making sure to point out the mentor's strengths as well as suggestions for next steps. This method of monitoring progress facilitates relationship building between the teacher advisers and the adolescents.

At the end of each 10-week session, the two student groups meet with the teacher advisers individually for debriefing. Students share their experience within the program and complete a survey. The comments we receive from our mentors are insightful, mature, and often amusing. Students will say that their partner reminds them of when they were that age or comment on what learning to read was like for them.

Celebrating Success

At the end of our 10-week sessions, we celebrate. Celebrating reiterates the important role that the mentors play in the reading development of their partners. Furthermore, acknowledging the mentors' work makes them feel valued and improves the likelihood that they will participate in the program again. Recognizing the improvements the partners have made motivates them as readers.

On this occasion, both reading mentors and partners write to each other. Reading mentors provide postcards, where they note their partner's improvements and provide motivating parting words. Reading partners make thank-you cards. The students exchange their items while enjoying some treats and a good chat.

The relationship created lasts well beyond the reading program. These students say hello in the halls and the little kids love that big kids know who they are.

We believe strongly in our reading mentoring program. We know that this type of program supports student self-confidence and reading development. We also know that this program builds community and relationships between primary and intermediate students. A reading mentoring program improves student reading not only in the primary grades but also the intermediate grades.

Entering the Forest of Reading
by Karen Upper

In 2007, the concept of the Forest of Reading was introduced to our library team at the annual Ontario Library conference. Once we learned about this Canadian "reading for fun" concept, around since 1994, we presented it to our schools.

Many of our teachers embraced the reading program; as for our students, the eagerness and enthusiasm of their responses caught many of us off guard. Those responses have been very gratifying. For many students, this program which focuses on all Canadian content and authors seems to have revitalized and reinvigorated reading in a way we had not foreseen. Reading programs of various types have always been in schools, but for many students, especially for the middle-school age, the books that were required reading often held little appeal. In the students' eyes, this tradition was now challenged. Here was a reading program that allowed them to make their own choices. Having the capability and opportunity to choose intrigued the students.

This program allows for students to show themselves in a different light. Working with vulnerable people, such as struggling readers, often brings out a softer side of people. We found this to be true in the adolescents that we have worked with.

Reading Survey Results

Ninety-five percent of Grade 2 participants consider themselves better readers because of Reading Rocks.

When asked, 100 percent of the reading mentors felt that they helped their younger reading partners.

Karen Upper, a teacher-librarian, serves staff and students in five elementary schools in the Near North District School Board. She served on the Red Maple Selection Committee in 2008–2009 and is a specialist in books written for middle-years students.

Choice, Competitive Spirit, and Pleasure

By reading five titles, students help determine the next winning author in a given category. They feel a sense of empowerment, which is reinforced by this student observation: "[The program] gives us, the students, a fun and competitive way of reading, because the more you read, the more you get to vote" (Fiona).

A budding anticipation and excitement, in turn, fosters a competitive spirit among many students, motivating them to become avid readers. A desire to surpass their peers creates a ripple effect. Students of all reading tastes and levels read voraciously in a variety of genres they would normally bypass.

Before being put on this prestigious list, the books that are nominated for the program are carefully read, scrutinized, and thoroughly discussed by a dedicated team of adult readers. These volunteers always keep the target audience (readers of middle school, Grades 7 and 8) in mind when taking any new titles under consideration. Students have remarked that they find this pre-selected list beneficial because not only does it allow them to keep focus, but as one student commented, "It opens your mind to new books and helps you choose things that you wouldn't pick up and try!" (Alex). Teens of both genders select titles equally from the non-fiction and fiction lists.

Over the past few years there have been many times where I've witnessed reluctant readers, even non-readers, pick up a book from this pre-selected list and become so immersed in a story that they have gone on to read everything else by that author. Once that link has been established, a student will often ask whether there are any similar books. This phenomenon was never better demonstrated to me than by the reaction of a former reluctant reader who began Philip Roy's Red Maple nominee *Submarine Outlaw* and was hooked! "I never would have read any of those books if it wasn't for the great program. I would recommend for all kids to participate in the program" (Keaton).

A mutual respect and confidence built between myself and the student will often allow me to suggest other possibilities (genres) that I think the student would like. I am often asked if what I'm recommending is something I have read. The answer most times is "yes." This acknowledgment has translated into a comfortable confidence that allows students to suggest books of their choosing to me.

Expressing What They Think

In 2011 a record number of students were so inspired by their selected book that they wanted to compliment the author. The overwhelmingly enthusiastic reactions prompted me to find a vehicle in which I could showcase these responses. I chose to explore the digital realm of technology and search for a Web 2.0 tool. Doing this would allow me to take their excitement for their book and express their reactions in a unique way. Voicethread was the Web tool I thought would enable me to expand on this idea; any student could verbally express an opinion on what he or she had read unhindered by the written word.

Once they heard of this idea, students from all levels wanted to lend their voices. A website was set up, and each student was given an avatar. Using first names only, they lined up to record their thoughts, feelings, and recommendations on the Internet. All students — whether avid readers, reluctant readers, or students with special needs — felt empowered by being able to lend their voices to the

Voicethread project (http://voicethread.com/?#q+grand+celebration.b1362152.i10480519).

At times, the trails opened by reading Forest books challenge both students and teachers. One teacher read aloud Sharon McKay's *War Brothers*, one of the nominated titles, to her Grade 7 class. At the end, she asked her students what they thought about the book. A student responded by saying he didn't like the book at all "'cause it made him *way* too uncomfortable." His comment led into a lively classroom discussion, touching on many human right issues. For many of the students in this teacher's class, *War Brothers* had opened their eyes to global social injustices and atrocities in the world.

The underlying philosophy of the Forest of Reading — of encouraging, promoting, and supporting Canadian books for teen readers — can be found coast to coast in many guises — from the Hackmatack Children's Choice Book Award in the Atlantic provinces to B.C.'s Red Cedar Award. For many students, the annual showcasing of authors and genres opens the pathway to imagination, adventure, and future creativity!

9

Helping Students Grow as Writers

How Am I Doing? Feedback for Improving Student Writing
by Shelley Stagg Peterson

Shelley Stagg Peterson is an associate professor at the Ontario Institute for Studies in Education, University of Toronto, where she teaches courses in children's literature, writing, and literacy. She has also written several books for teachers and conducted many research studies examining teaching practice.

Traditionally, teacher feedback has taken the form of written comments provided after the compositions were handed in to be marked. Received by students at the end of their writing process, the comments have not had as great an impact on students' writing development as teachers have intended. Students generally felt that they had finished working on the writing after they handed it in for a grade. Praise and high grades may have instilled greater confidence in some students' abilities as writers, but frequently students were not interested in further work to improve the writing.

Feedback During the Writing Process

Given that teachers spend much time providing written feedback to students on their writing, it is important that the feedback have a greater influence on students' development as writers. The verbal or written feedback can be a powerful teaching tool if it is given while students are writing drafts. Comments on drafts of writing provide students with timely information about the impact of their writing on readers and the clarity of their written communication. Because students receive the feedback while they are writing, they are more inclined to use it to revise and edit their drafts than they would be if they received the suggestions on a graded, polished copy. They also have an immediate opportunity to try out the suggestions in their writing, allowing for meaningful application of what they have learned from the feedback. Focusing on individual students' immediate writing needs, this ongoing feedback is a form of differentiated instruction that complements the teaching of mini-lessons to small groups or to the whole class.

The Content of Teacher Feedback

The content of the teacher's feedback should be both criterion based and reader based.

Criterion-based feedback indicates how well the writing meets the criteria on scoring guides or rubrics. Such feedback refers to the appropriateness of the ideas and information, the level of detail, and the chosen point of view. Criterion-based feedback also addresses the clarity of communication through the organization of ideas and use of writing conventions, together with the effectiveness of the language.

This type of feedback is most useful when students have previously been given the assessment criteria and clearly understand the expectations. Indeed, students have a deeper understanding of the expectations when they have an opportunity to participate in determining the assessment criteria.

Reader-based feedback reflects the reader's experience of the writing. Such feedback includes identifying images visualized, emotions evoked, particular words or phrases that stood out or had the greatest impact on the reader, as well as describing how the writing makes the reader feel, summarizing what the text says to the reader, or making connections to something else the reader has read.

Because writing is a form of communication, student writers benefit from reader-based feedback as they get a sense of how well their writing achieves the intended communicative purpose (e.g., to entertain, to inform, to persuade).

Teachers can determine the content of the feedback by considering the elements of the writing that stand out as being strong or needing more work. It is important to identify features of the writing or reader responses that are positive. Although students have indicated in research studies that they do not find positive comments helpful to improve their writing, they appreciate receiving support to nurture their confidence as writers and their motivation to write. Students say that they find direct, elaborated comments focusing on specific elements of their writing most helpful in guiding their revisions. They appreciate teachers getting involved with the subject of their writing, but do not like to have their ideas questioned or criticized.

Spelling, punctuation, and grammar may be the focus of criterion-based feedback, but they should not be the sole focus. When providing feedback on writing conventions, teachers should identify patterns of errors, rather than point out every error on the page (Haswell, 2006). Students then attend to and learn one or two types of spelling, punctuation, or grammar patterns as they edit and continue with their writing. It is also important to identify patterns that students have recently mastered, so that students get a sense of how much they already know and can use, as well as what they have yet to learn. Teachers may highlight students' correct use of apostrophes in contractions while identifying patterns in sentence fragments created when starting sentences with subordinating conjunctions, for example.

Students' sense of ownership of their writing needs to be considered when providing feedback (Graves, 2004). Revising and editing are difficult, time-consuming processes for many students. When students have the autonomy to decide how they will use their teachers' suggestions and observations, they are more likely to feel commitment to improving the writing and to becoming better writers (Bright, 2007).

Feedback from the Teacher and Student Peers

Student writers can benefit from feedback from both the teacher and their peers.

Verbal feedback from the teacher

Verbal feedback is given in a few different ways. It may be given on the spot as the teacher circulates around the room while students are writing. Students may request their teacher's input, or the teacher may offer a commendation or suggestion to consider as students draft and revise their writing. Verbal feedback may also be given in student–teacher conferences. Students may sign up to meet with their teacher when they feel ready for feedback or they may meet with the teacher on a regular basis. Effective as both teaching and assessment tools, student–teacher conferences provide individualized instruction for students and opportunities to gather information about students' thinking and writing processes.

Student–teacher conferences work best when there is a dialogue between student and teacher, with each learning something from the interaction. Both teacher and student can ask questions. The student may ask for help in a particular area or ask what effect the writing has on the teacher-as-reader. The teacher may ask about the student's goals for the writing and for self as writer, impressions of the strongest parts of the writing, and what the student has learned through writing a particular composition.

Scheduling one-on-one time with students is always difficult. However, the time spent with each student will pay off many times over in its impact on students' writing development. It is not necessary to read and respond to every student's writing every week. Reasonably, teachers should aim to provide feedback to each student in 5 to 10 minute student–teacher conferences every two to three weeks.

It is important to keep a record of the topics of student–teacher conferences to create an ongoing picture of students' writing development. Teachers can use the notes to acknowledge the improvements they see from one conference to the next. Students can use the notes to reflect on the challenges they have had in trying to achieve goals set in previous student–teacher conferences. Responsible for the students' writing development and for the final assessment, teachers provide valuable feedback to their students on their writing.

Peer feedback on student writing

Research has shown that peers can also make helpful contributions to students' writing development. They provide reader-based feedback that shows student writers the effect that the writing is having on a peer audience (often the intended audience for elementary students' writing).

Peer feedback helps to develop students' sense of audience — their recognition of the perspectives, language, sentence structure, voice, and other elements of writing that provoke, entertain, or satisfy their audience (among other reactions to the writing). In classrooms where students write at tables or with desks placed in blocks so that students can easily talk to each other, students may ask peers for feedback spontaneously as they feel it is needed.

Teachers may set up more formal opportunities for peer feedback by scheduling time for students to exchange their writing with one or two peers or to read their writing aloud to peers in a small-group setting. The reading of the writing is followed by a discussion of what the peers got out of the writing, what stands out about the writing, and what questions the writing raises for the peers. Many teachers use a "two stars and a wish" framework, asking peers to identify two elements of a student's writing that they thought were strong and one element that could be improved.

Teachers may model the dialogic type of interaction that works well when giving and receiving feedback on writing, showing how the student writers can ask questions, talk about their intentions, and identify parts they felt were strong or weak, in conversation with peers who talk about their impressions.

Four types of peer feedback have been shown to have the greatest influence on students' revisions:

- When the writer feels blocked, peers and the writer play with ideas to move the writing forward.
- Peers ask for clarification about what they find confusing or identify missing information.
- Peers give their emotional response to the writing, for example, that it makes them laugh.
- Peers question how plausible particular events or ideas are.

Peers may not be the best providers of criterion-based feedback regarding conventions, in particular, because they often lack the needed grasp of conventions. Their feedback should be valued for the information it provides about how readers respond to a piece of writing. Teacher feedback is generally more useful for moving students along in their use of writing conventions.

Issues in Effective Feedback Giving

Five issues are ranging from student autonomy to limited focus of feedback are outlined below.

Student autonomy in feedback use

To support students' sense of ownership of their writing, the feedback should

- be given in the spirit of showing student writers the positive effects their writing is having on readers
- identify potential areas where students could revise their writing to clarify meaning or more fully engage readers
- take the form of suggestions, observations, and open-ended questions, rather than instructions and criticism

Students should always feel that they can use the feedback in their own way — that the feedback is suggestive, rather than prescriptive.

Checking of understanding

Teachers need to ensure that student writers can process the feedback they receive. Student writers will not benefit from feedback that they do not fully understand. At the end of a student–teacher conference or after students receive written feedback, teachers could invite students to explain their interpretations of the feedback and speculate what they might do to use the feedback. Explaining their plans for using the feedback may strengthen students' commitment to improving their writing. Teachers could also invite students to submit a "revise-and-resubmit" letter explaining how the feedback has been addressed or providing a rationale for disregarding it. Writing this letter would enhance students' metacognitive awareness of their writing processes and intentions.

Timing of feedback

Providing feedback on student writing is most valuable to students in their writing development when it takes place at the beginning and middle stages of the writing process. This is the time when students can use the feedback to revise and edit their writing. Teachers could allot a small percentage of the final grade to handing in a draft by a certain date or at particular intervals (if there is time to provide feedback more than once on a piece of writing). Students would automatically be given the grade if they hand in the drafts, the teacher would write comments on the drafts, and then students would revise the drafts before handing in the final copies. Marking the final copies would involve assigning the grade and writing a few comments on how the students have improved their writing subsequent to handing in the initial drafts.

It is preferable to give feedback on the content, organization, and style features of the writing in early drafts and on the writing conventions when the writing is almost complete. If editing writing conventions is students' focus early on in their writing processes, students' flow of ideas may be curtailed. In addition, students may be editing sentences that will later be cut during revision.

Student writers learn about the power of writing when peers and their teacher provide reader-based feedback about what they have learned, what engaged them, and what evoked strong emotions in their writing. They come to recognize how closely specific features of their writing match the expectations for the writing when they receive criterion-based feedback, particularly from their teachers. Responsive to students' immediate needs, verbal and written feedback provided on drafts of students' writing is a powerful tool for differentiating instruction to support students' writing development.

References

Bright, R. (2007). *Write through the grades: Teaching writing in secondary schools.* Winnipeg, MB: Portage & Main Press.

Graves, D. (2004). What I've learned from teachers of writing. *Language Arts, 82*(20), 88–94.

Haswell, R. (2006). The complexities of responding to student writing; or, looking for shortcuts via the road of excess. *Across the disciplines,* 4. Retrieved from http://wac.colostate.edu/atd/articles/haswell2006.cfm

---

Going Graphic: Organizing Our Thoughts

by Flora Fung

Flora Fung teaches at Oshawa Central Collegiate. She was a finalist for the 2011 Governor General's Awards for Excellence in Teaching Canadian History, as selected by Canada's History Society. She promotes literacy through her excellent teaching that makes history come alive to her students.

Our students today live in a highly visual world. They are constantly bombarded with thousands of images and graphics. From the video games they play to the movies and television they watch, their world is brightly illuminated, often in HD.

I use graphic organizers consistently in all my classes and for all my students, from academic to high-risk. They not only help students organize their information but appeal to their need for graphic stimulation.

More than one student has remarked that using graphic organizers seems like doing "less work." Little do they realize that by organizing their thoughts and summarizing them in a diagram, they've done quite a bit of thinking even if there isn't a lot of writing: quality versus quantity.

Graphic organizers also serve as a memory cue. In regards to the *Identify and Significance* graphic organizer, on the next page, many of my students refer to it as the "triangle thingy." Whatever they choose to call it, they have had greater success with the concept of significance since I implemented this graphic organizer. In fact, once they have grasped the concept and must instead write "identify and significance" responses as a paragraph, many of my students bemoan the loss of the "triangle thingy."

In many of my handouts and graphic organizers, my secret goal is to appeal to the students' need for graphic gratification. Consider this: In the advertising world consumers are drawn usually to the brightly lit, visually appealing displays. Why should our handouts and graphic organizers be any different?

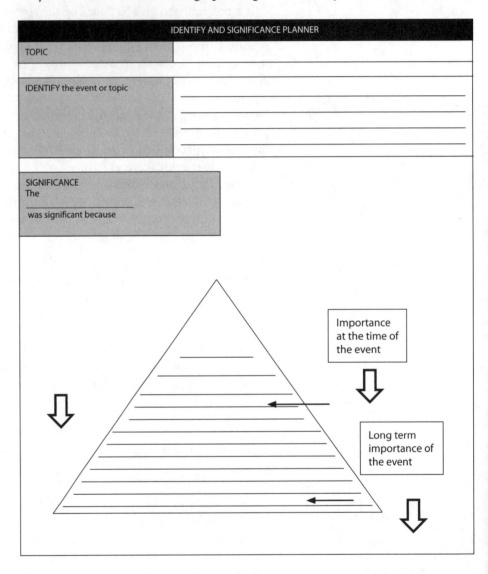

Graphic Organizer Choices

Which of the following popular graphs do you think has the greatest potential of helping students understanding the complex nature of causes for any historical event?

Is it the fishbone?

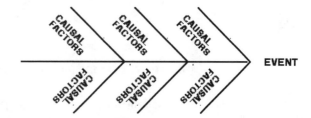

Is it this graphic ?

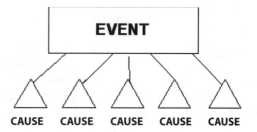

Is it this sequence ladder?

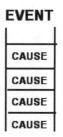

Or is it this one?

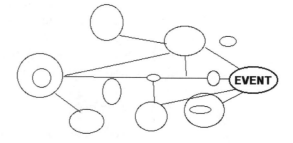

Any tool can be used appropriately or otherwise!

Teaching Grammar as a Subversive Activity

by Joan O'Callaghan

Joan O'Callaghan is a curriculum instructor in Secondary and Elementary Education at the Ontario Institute for Studies in Education, University of Toronto. As a drama and literacy specialist, Joan brings the power of interactive experience to her teaching of how language works.

Few things engender greater panic among teacher-candidates and young teachers than the possibility that they may be called upon to teach grammar. Many were not taught grammar, or if they were, the teaching of grammar was relegated to tedious worksheets.

Yet, with a little imagination, the teaching of grammar can be effective and engaging for both students and teachers.

How to Teach Grammar with Pizzazz

"The overriding aim of any good grammar program should be, through experience and knowledge, to enhance the students' control of language. The essence of style is choice, and choice entails a working knowledge of the available alternatives. Grammar is one means to that end, but not in isolation. Nor is it an end in itself. The process must not stop with, or be replaced by, arid analysis or a parroting of nomenclature. Students need to understand the concepts (and know the terms that represent them), but above all, they need to use this knowledge."
— Ian S. Fraser and Lynda Hodson, in "Twenty-one kicks at the grammar horse," *English Journal, 67*(9)

What follows are some activities, games, and strategies that will allow you to teach grammar effectively and engagingly. The activities may be modified — simplified or made more challenging — to meet the needs of the students.

Building sentences through interviews

Begin by showing students a video clip of a television reporter conducting an interview. Ask students to notice how the reporter uses questions to draw out more information. Alternatively, older students may work backwards by analyzing newspaper or magazine articles based on interviews: they can note what information is conveyed and determine what questions might have been asked.

Put students in pairs to interview one another. As the "reporters" pose questions, invite them to incorporate the new information into longer sentences.

If possible, for the use of younger students, obtain plastic microphones (from a dollar store or party supply store).

> *Reporter:* Where do you live?
> *Subject:* On Main Street.
> *Reporter:* What is Main Street like?
> *Subject:* It is nice. There are lots of houses with gardens and big trees.
> *Teacher:* Can we make one sentence from this information? Here's one: Johnny lives on Main Street which has lots of houses with gardens and big trees. Here's another: There are lots of houses with gardens and big trees on Main Street where Johnny lives. How are the two sentences different?

Depending on the sophistication of the students, you may encourage them to create more elegant sentences or to experiment with word order to demonstrate how order and structure affect emphasis or meaning. You could also have the reporters continue questioning subjects to draw out more information. The activity may even be integrated with literature study by having the interview subject assume the persona of a character from a literary selection. Finally, it may lead into a writing activity that both incorporates sentence structures and highlights how description makes writing more interesting to read.

Poetic grammar

Poetry may be used to enhance the study of grammar. One of my favorite poems is "The Job of an Apple" by Ronna Bloom.

The Job of an Apple

This poem lends itself wonderfully to study of the parts of speech.

The job of an apple is to be hard, to be
soft, to be crisp, to be red,
yellow and green. The job of an apple
is to be pie, to be given to the teacher,
to be rotten.
The job of an apple is to be bad
and good, to be peeled, cored, cut,
bitten and bruised. The job of an apple
is to pose for painters, roll behind
fridges, behind grocery aisles,
to be hidden, wrapped in paper, stored for months,
brought out in the dry heat of India and eaten like a treasure.
The job of an apple is to be handed over in orchards, to be wanted and forbidden.
The job of an apple is to be Golden
Delicious, Granny Smith and crab.
The job of an apple is to be imported,
banned and confiscated going through customs
from Montreal to New York.
The job of an apple is to be round. Grow.
Drop. Go black in the middle when cut.
To be thrown at politicians. To be carried around
for days, to change hands, to change hands,
to change hands. The job of an apple is
to be a different poem in the mouth of every eater.
The job of an apple is to be juice.

After reading the poem carefully, pass around different fruits and vegetables for students to examine; then, invite them to rewrite the poem, substituting words, phrases, and clauses that apply to the item they were given. Or, ask them to substitute the name of a character from whatever literary selection (play, novel, short story, or poem) they have been reading. This activity enhances awareness and appreciation of poetry, underscores how language works, and encourages students to generate rich descriptions of items or characters.

Formula poetry

Formula poetry — in particular, diamantes — is a useful means of encouraging students to understand and use parts of speech in creative ways:

Line 1: a *noun*, indicating the subject of the poem
Line 2: two *adjectives*
Line 3: *–ing* words, or *participles*
Line 4: a four-word *phrase*
Line 5: three *–ing* words, or *participles*
Line 6: two *adjectives*
Line 7: a *noun synonym* for the noun in line one

Benny
Funny, furry
Sleeping, prowling, cuddling
Guardian of my house
Meowing, purring, stretching
Soft, lovable
Cat

Pizza anyone?

Do Not Feed
Monkey's.

Neil Marr has devised a game that encourages students to review grammatical concepts. Neil, who loves to travel, photographs signs that contain errors in grammar and incorporates them into a PowerPoint presentation. Neil places students in permanent groups. He shows the PowerPoint images, and the teams take turns identifying and correcting the errors. He has a scoring system based on the complexity of the error. The team that amasses the most points by the end of the term is treated to a pizza lunch. Neil says that the students enjoy the game and that it encourages discussion and collaboration.

Madcap grammar

Mad Libs, a variation of a cloze activity, is another game that is lots of fun, yet reinforces grammatical concepts, as well as parts of speech and how they work. Pads of *Mad Libs* may be purchased in many stores, or teachers may create their own stories with blanks.

The teacher is the only person with a copy of a story from which many words have been blanked out. Without giving away any information, the teacher asks students to volunteer words, for example, nouns, verbs (past tense), and adjectives. All language contributed must be appropriate. When all the words have been collected, the teacher reads the story back to the students, inserting the words they have contributed, in the appropriate spots. The resulting story is usually very funny; however, for the game to work, students must know the required parts of speech. The activity may also be done in small groups.

Winter Vacation

At last! The _____ (adjective) day all teachers long for had arrived! _____. The _____(noun) arrived to take them to the airport.

Picture this!

Collect picture postcards, as well as newspaper and magazine photos. Remove any captions or text. Distribute the cards to students. Ask them what things or people they see. After they share their findings, explain that these are nouns (common). Then, have them describe the items (adjectives). Next, ask them what is happening (verbs). Students are generating parts of speech. This information may then be used in sentence construction or sentence-combining activities, and finally, in a piece of writing based on the image.

10

Sharing, Responding, Changing the World

Sharing Thoughts Through Blogging
by Royan Lee

Royan Lee is a teacher leader in the York Region District School Board, Ontario. Currently an Intermediate Literacy teacher, he has experience teaching all elementary grades. His professional preoccupations include contemporary literacy and assessment practice, social media in the classroom, and passion-based learning.

Some of the things we know about adolescents have always been truisms, while others are uncharted territory thanks, in part, to the ubiquity of certain technologies. We know that the beginning of the teen years is a time of massive, speedy, and sometimes exponential change. The changes that occur both mentally and physically are at times exhilarating, and at others overwhelming.

The Lure of Social Networking

We know that relationships mean everything to these kids and that many are completely preoccupied with — or, rather, reliant on — technology to maintain these connections. It's becoming normal for a 13-year-old to own a Smartphone, and not just in the upwardly mobile demographics. We also know that intermediate kids are avid readers and prolific writers, not necessarily in the traditional sense, but in the way that they read and write all the time to communicate and share their thoughts online with one another and the world.

It's interesting that the very thing these children gravitate towards — peer relationships and independence from parents — is the precise thing that is available for free and omnipresent in the form of Facebook and other technologies.

This is why social media — specifically, blogging — is such a powerful learning tool for adolescents in Grade 7. In the four classes I teach English to at our French immersion school, I try to leverage their seeming predisposition for social networking to enhance literacy instruction, assessment, and collaboration.

What We Blog About

Blogging, when used as a digital portfolio and network of thinking, is an immensely powerful tool. In our class, students use blogs to read, write, reflect, create, share, mentor, lead, and learn how to be a contemporary networked learner. They post assignments, reading responses, video, audio, slideshows, formal pieces of writing, informal and spontaneous thoughts, drawings, poetry, and even music.

I assign my students blogging tasks and open-ended, what-have-you-got-to-say tasks that encourage divergence of thought. In the former, one of "Mr. Lee's Posts" might be a reading response question, a writing prompt, or a thinking challenge. In the latter, the students' "Personal Posts" encourage free form thoughts and opinions. They are either sharing a reflection on a text I have assigned or making a comment about life in general.

If you were to ask which one of these results in the most spectacular thought and work, what would I say? The Personal Posts in a landslide.

My students are reading a diverse array of text genres and forms; in addition, they are writing or creating texts using paragraph writing, storyboarding for digital comics (Bitstrips) and multimedia slideshows (Animoto), visual art (iPad, Glogster), voice (podcasting), presentation tools (Prezi), and so on. In other words, they get to dabble in a lot in different media, as well as hone and craft their favorites and strengths. It's amazing to see what students will do if you let them flourish in the forms of communication they are really passionate about.

Why We Blog

Here is the rationale we developed as a class to elucidate the rationale for blogging as a high-yield avenue for thought expression and connection.

Blogging . . .
- provides a real audience for our work
- serves as a portfolio for our work and thinking
- allows us to see each other's work and provide feedback on it
- lets us practise how to post online and how to craft our digital footprint
- gives us teacher support and guidance on how to use the social media we are already using on our own
- teaches us to think critically about our online presence, and the importance of creating a positive one
- creates a community of learners
- lets us practise contemporary literacy skills
- lets us stay connected even away from class time
- makes all the Grade 7 kids feel like they are in one big class
- means handwriting has nothing to do with the quality of your work
- is really fun

A summary of specific benefits associated with blogging follows.

Networked Learning: The networked thinking and collaborating that the learners do is a sight to behold. Our blogs form a network. All 108 blogs (including my own) are linked together using RSS feeds and "following." In other words, when you enter one blog, you have immediate access to all the others — it is a web. To read one writer's blog is to enter the seemingly unending array of 107 others. A more authentic audience I have rarely been able to facilitate in all my years of teaching. What is more, I no longer have to preach the value of borrowing one another's ideas and genuinely taking heed of peer feedback. These things happen organically now.

Student Voice and Distributed Leadership: As an open classroom in our school board, we receive many visitors — stakeholders within our board and province, as well as international guests. One consistent bit of positive feedback concerns the extent to which student voice is valued in our class. In our English class, you do not need to be an extrovert or have a demonstrative personality to have your voice heard. As a digital portfolio of work, thoughts, and, thus, passions, blogs are one great way to get students' voices out to the crowd.

We never know whose piece of writing or artwork will inspire and lead a group of others. In the sometimes-brutal social melee that is middle school, our blogs allow my students to expand their influence and connection to peers, particularly those they may not consider their "friends."

Creative, Divergent Thinking: Our world has transformed into a complex place where innovation and divergent thinking are in high demand, and blogs allow students to follow paths of literacy not always opened by the teacher. Whether it's composing a love poem to Edward from *Twilight* as a synthesizing activity, or creating a Bitstrip about the absurdity of Silly Bandz, my students' innovative blog posts never fail to amaze me.

Broadened View of Reading and Writing: As the world changes, so does the meaning of literacy, and most certainly too the concepts of reading and writing. Instead of looking at it as a school-centric process, students in my class come to think of writing as a dynamic method of idea and message communication. Empowered to "write" using images and words in a variety of media, students learn to differentiate between the power of one medium over another depending on the context and audience. In the beginning, students are bewildered at the suggestion that they take initiative in choosing the best tool to communicate a particular message. Soon, however, they begin to flourish in a dynamic and differentiated literacy environment, where they assume responsibility for deciding which tool will do the right job.

Self-Publishing: One of the main *aha!* moments I see my students having in the early stages of blogging is when they realize what it means to self-publish. *Oh, you mean, I'm in control of everything? I write the content, decide on the layout, control permissions, and design the blog so it represents me . . .?*

Blogs as Building Blocks: Because the concept of blogging was so new to my students, I had to be patient with their comfort levels around posting for such a large audience on an ongoing basis. It didn't take long.

Around late September Erica wrote her famous (in our class) post about her brother Evan. I'll never forget the day we all read the post together. My favorite part was observing everyone's facial expressions when Erica's post, just by existing, did more to explain the purpose of blogging than I could ever have done in explicit instruction. From that day forward, it became normal for students' posts to begin in the following manner:

> *I just finished reading Erica's awesome post about her brother and it made me think about . . .*
>
> *Erica's post inspired me to write this about . . .*
>
> *I loved Erica's post and it made me want to write about . . .*

My students began to understand that blogging is about authenticity, purpose, and voice. Most of all, they learned what it means to be collaborative, not only in the sense that we do group projects together, but also in the way that *I need your ideas to fulfill my own potential.*

Sample Student Blogs

It was immensely difficult to choose samples from the array of sensational posts, so I decided to pare it down to two instances (of many) where one student's post gave inspiration to others.

First, I've chosen Erica's seminal post, as well as two others that directly and indirectly developed because of it. Interestingly, Jerry's piece, the last one of the three, is a transcribed version of a video recording he did. A reluctant writer, Jerry is most in his element when explaining or presenting ideas orally. The use of blogging and other technologies opens up the communication channels so that other text forms are not marginalized or devalued in class. A story told orally is, thus, as relevant as one written out using handwriting or typing.

This is one snapshot from an array of clustered thinking and creating that naturally occurs in a genuine personal learning network like ours.

My Brother Evan

Hey, this week I decided to do my weekly blog post on the person I admire the most in the ENTIRE universe, my brother Evan.

Evan, my brother, is the person I most admire in my life because he has the biggest impact on me. Whatever he does, I secretly want to do the same. I always try to impress him so that he can be proud to have me as a sister. I always want to try to be involved in his life because I feel that if I stop trying to get involved, he will stop caring as much about me. I like hanging out with him.

He teaches me how to play guitar (acoustic and electric) but only heavy death metal on electric guitar. The only song he taught me on acoustic is Blackbird. When he goes out with his friends I'm always begging to come with him, but only occasionally does he actually let me. The only reason that I want to come is so that I can be with Evan.

Without my brother, my life wouldn't be the same. I'd be lonely, sad, not very smart because he helps me with a lot of my work, and just . . . very bored. We used to play hockey a lot in the basement and on the road sometimes, but then he turned 13 and I was 9 or 10 and he became too cool for school.

When we were little my mom bought us a pair of "Sock 'em Boppers" which were basically huge foamy things that looked like marshmallows with straps on them that you'd put on your hands, and wrestle. But we went the extreme way. What we did was we put the Sock 'em Boppers on our feet and kicked each other! Our mom would yell at us like crazy, but we kept going.

Then he got me into wrestling. And he got me caught up in wanting to be the next girl version of the WWE superstar John Cena. Well, look how well that turned out?!?

He is an amazing brother and one thing that I will never forget is the time I was crossing a busy road. He stopped me with his arm and looked both ways, then "allowed" me to walk across, but only if I held his hand.

When I went to sleep away camp a few years back, I got a really nice letter from him saying how much he missed me and what they did while I was gone, and even though I had gotten a gazillion letters from my parents, and only that one from my brother, I only cried when I read his note.

He is my greatest role model in life and I hope to turn out as funny, as nice, and as compassionate as my older brother.

By Erica

Brittney and Brooke! My Two Favorite People in the World!

During English class, we were looking at different blogs and reading the various blog posts. One particular blog post that caught my eye was the post by Erica who wrote about her brother Evan. I thought that was an extraordinary idea and it made me immediately contemplate my sisters. I am so lucky to have two older sisters. Brooke is the middle girl. She just left to go to the University of Western [Ontario] this past September. My other sister, Brittney, just completed University. Both of my sisters mean the world to me and my life would not be the same if they weren't a part of my life.

First of all, I want to share that although my two sisters are older than me, one is 11 years older and one is 6 years older than me (I'm the baby of the family :)), we still spend a huge amount of time together. We shop, we talk, we eat, we see movies, we laugh and fight, and we go on vacations together. My sisters and I have such an amazing bond, you cannot tear us apart. When they're not home, they're usually with friends, studying at the library, at school, at dance or the gym. Even though both of my sisters have very busy lives and aren't always home, they're always there for me and they love me the way I am.

The younger of my two sisters, Brooke, is a role model to me. She really loves and nurtures me because I am me. She encourages me to do anything I set my mind to and she also helps me in every way she can. It is her first year in University, studying sciences. She is 18 years old and is an amazing dancer. Everyone says she should audition for *So You Think You Can Dance*. Brooke is also a straight A student and whenever I need help in absolutely any subject, she is there for me. She really knows how to teach me because she is also a tutor to younger kids. Brooke is a really funny and energetic person. She loves to make people laugh and loves to be herself. For such a young age Brooke has done so much with her life. She's traveled, she's volunteered, she's done incredible at school (many honour rolls, scholarships, etc.) and she is just a superb sister. All of these accomplishments have made me realize what a good role model she is. I could not ask for a better sister.

I remember the night before she left to University, I was looking at old pictures of the two of us and I was making her a good luck present. Suddenly I realized she wasn't going to live with us for more than 3 years. I ran to her room and started hugging her until she could not breathe. The next day I wouldn't let go of her! Now I know it will be fine because I talk to her all the time, she visits us as much as she can and we visit her too! I am so proud of her and I know she will do amazing and she will be successful in school and in life!

My older, amazing and incredible sister, Brittney, graduated University and is a social worker. She wants to help people solve their problems and gives advice to those in need. Brittney has traveled almost all around the world from Europe, to Israel, to Miami and much more! My sister Brittney means the world to me. Although she is older than me, 23 years old (but smaller than me!), we have an incredibly strong bond and we will never get bored of each other. Brittney is so much fun to be around and she is also my role model. She is sweet, beautiful (both of my sisters are), kind, caring, a great listener, and just a superb friend. She will put anything aside to come and help me if I am upset or hurt. She is a great secret keeper and gives good advice. Anytime of the day or night, I know I can knock on her door, if I am sad or lonely or just need company, and she will invite me in and give me just the right amount of hugs. Right now she is applying to different jobs, getting interviewed, helps my mom do chores around the house, looks after our dog and helps drive me places. She has her own way of doing things, and does not worry about what other people say. She's her own person and knows how to stick up for her family and friends. Brittney is fantastically helpful and she knows how to solve a problem. People say Brittney and I do not look alike at all, that we don't even look related, but I think we do! We both have very curly long light brown hair and we always have big smiles on our faces. Having her as a sister really makes my life different.

There was one time when I couldn't thank my sister enough! I was going through the horrible week of swine flu and Brittney stayed home with me the whole time and took care of me. I had to stay in my room for days and, finally, on the fourth day I finally came out of my room and went outside. I wanted somebody to come with me outside and I remember how she and I walked out into the fresh air with our dog Bailee. It meant so much to me that she cared for me during such a hard time. She really is an amazing sister. I wouldn't change one thing about her, because I love her the way she is!

The truth is, I'm lucky because my sisters are my best friends! I love them so much and my life would be completely different without them. Thank you for reading my post. I hope you enjoyed reading about my spectacular sisters.

By Tara

My Best Story Ever

One day, about three years ago, my dad did something really special for me. He told me that he had to work that Saturday, so I wasn't expecting to be woken up so early. But he did wake me up at 6:30 in the morning.

"Why are you waking me up, dad?" I asked.

"I wanna show you something," he said.

He then took me to the garage and showed me some fishing rods. We put them in the car and drove to Oshawa Creek, an amazing river.

The second we got to this pool, there were about a million humungous salmon just sitting there, waiting to be caught.

So I grabbed my rod and cast it out. The row bag was just sitting there, floating along the water. Suddenly, a big salmon just grabbed it and took off. My line started screaming ZZZZZZZSSSSSSSS! The salmon was taking it all the way down the river. I didn't know what to do. It was so strong I actually had to run after the fish in the river. I reached in, picked it up, and it was a beautiful, thirty-pound salmon. I was so proud of myself.

It was about ten-o-clock at the time. We kept on fishing 'til about one. We must have caught about 200 pounds of fish that day. But, don't worry, we let them go.

I looked at my dad and he asked me, "So Jerry, do you like salmon fishing?"

I said, "Dad, that was the best day ever."

By Jerry

Finally, you can see two satirical Bitstrips comics. Justin's comic, Uggs, was a poke at the fashion craze of Ugg boots. After students read this, Justin began to be looked upon as a lead blogger. Students frequently would read his blog to decide what they wanted to blog about.

I did not have to assign a "Satirical Comic Project" — Justin did it for us.

Once upon a Time: Relating to English Language Learners

by Burcu Yaman Ntelioglou

Burcu Yaman Ntelioglou is a drama educator with a wide range of teaching experience. At present, she is completing her Ph.D. at the Ontario Institute for Studies in Education in Drama and English Language Learning.

Bir varmis, bir yokmus, evvel zaman icinde, kalbur saman icinde, deve tellal iken, pire berber iken, ben annemin besigini tingir mingir sallar iken . . .
Once there was, once there was not, a long time ago when the camel was a town's crier, when the flea was a barber, when I was swinging my mother's cradle, tinger, minger . . . [translation by Burcu]

I have worked with a group of young adolescents in a multicultural school in Toronto, exploring drama that focused on language, literacy, and issues of English Language Learners.

Warming Up to the Ways of Language

To introduce these processes, I did a warm-up in Turkish because none of the students in this class spoke Turkish. In the scene a mother puts a child to sleep, reading a bedtime story. In role as the mother, I began the story with a traditional opening, similar to "once upon a time." The child tries to imitate some of the words the mother uses, and then falls asleep. The mother gives the child a kiss, covers the child with a blanket, and leaves the room.

I ask the students to share their feelings and thoughts about what happens when they watch or listen to this interaction, all in a language they do not understand. "What do you think the scene was about? Which clues helped you make those guesses? Can you guess the relationship between the two characters? What do you think the topic is? Where do you think the scene takes place? How do physical movements, gestures, intonation, and rhythm add meaning to what is said? Are there any words you thought you understood?" (I ask this question especially because, in the Turkish story I tell, I use onomatopoeic words, such as "knock, knock, knock." Later on we can discuss how different languages use similar sounds for the same meaning.)

I question further: "How did you feel watching a scene and listening to a language you didn't understand? Did you become frustrated? detached?"

But students do understand some things. Students always guess correctly that the scene is about a mother putting a child to sleep, reading a bedtime story. They are usually excited that they can understand this, without knowing any of the scene's language. They also quickly realize that no matter what language we speak, we are exposed to the rhythm of poetic language from our earliest childhood.

This warm-up achieves several goals.

Because students have not understood the words but have made some sense of what was going on, they begin to recognize that there is more to language than vocabulary and grammar. They become aware of the significance of body language. They also notice that the way we say something can be just as important as the words we use to say it.

We illustrate this latter point. Playwright George Bernard Shaw once said that there are 50 ways of saying "Yes" and 500 ways of saying "No," but only one way of writing them down. We experiment with the word "Oh." Inspired by the poem "Oh" by Sonnet L'Abbé, I ask them who can give me an "Oh" that shows shock, disbelief, lack of understanding, or frustration. This invitation brings a lot of understanding and laughter to the exercise.

Then, together we discuss that when we listen, we pay attention not only to the words but also to the non-verbal communication, such as gestures, facial expressions, and physical movements, as well as intonation and rhythm that give meaning to utterances.

We also discuss that contextual cues such as the props I use when doing this scene — a blanket, a pillow, and a storybook — give us cues about meaning.

By the end of this warm-up, students notice how learning a new language is complex.

Transitioning into Drama

We then discuss how more than 50 percent of the school population in urban centres such as Toronto has a first language other than English. These young adolescents are usually not surprised by this since in their school, more than 60 percent of the students are English Language Learners (ELLs).

In order to give these students a sense of the wide range of issues that ELLs struggle with, and to examine life stories and dilemmas of ELLs by working "as if" (applying material in a personal way), we move to the second phase of the session. Since moving to a new country is a physical and psychological transition, I use a transition phase to move from the warm-up to the main drama activity. In this transition, students are seated in rows on an "airplane," listening to a five-minute excerpt from one of the CBC's radio plays on immigration. As teacher-in-role, I interrupt with the following announcement:

This was a CBC radio immigration story. Sorry for interrupting, but we are about to land at Pearson International Airport. Please keep your seatbelt on until we come to a complete stop. The weather in Toronto is minus 15 degrees Celsius, but clear and sunny. Thank you for flying with Air Canada.

Students are usually surprised, but they begin to understand that I am in role. A few seconds later I tell them: "You can now leave the plane and proceed to Customs." As a flight attendant, I open the door and lead the students to a table with the sign Canadian Customs and Immigration. I say: "Bye. Have a nice day. Customs this way please." Students understand that they have to get up and go to the Customs and Immigration counter. They realize that they, too, are in role.

Students all line up in front of the Customs and Immigration table. In the role of a Customs officer, I ask them a couple of typical questions each and give them

Poem Resource

"Oh," by S. L'Abbé. In *Red Silk: An Anthology of South Asian Canadian Women Poets*, edited by Rishna Dunlop and Priscila Uppal (Toronto, ON: Mansfield Press, 2004).

Radio Play Resource

Where Is Here? The Drama of Immigration (Vol. 1), edited by P. Damiano (Winnipeg, MB: J. Gordon Shillingford Publishing, 2005).

an "official" piece of paper containing a number. I say: "Here are your landed immigrant documents. Please proceed to area number ___. You will find a package in each area with information about how to proceed." I find that this is not only a great way to break the students into groups, but it also gives them a small taste of the range of transitions — physical and psychological — that immigrants experience.

Responding to Real Issues Through Drama

I designate an area for each group within the room. Posted on the wall in each area are the group number and an envelope that contains that group's instructions for the drama activity. Students in groups listen to or read one of the following: an excerpt from a story, poem, play, novel, or student's first-hand account. All excerpts, written by newcomers and English Language Learners, deal with challenges that linguistically and culturally diverse people may face.

Students in groups present the problem outlined in their excerpt in one of several ways. They might create a tableau, or frozen image (crystallizing a key problem or conflict presented in the excerpt), use choral reading (conveying every word of the provided text to depict what the group decides is significant through spoken language and sound effects only), present an interview scene (acting in role), or mime to portray the problem.

After each group performs the scene it prepared, we discuss the moments that resonated with students, the experiences or memories they brought to them, or the aspects that troubled them. Within the context of these performances we identify some of the struggles that ELLs and newcomers to Canada face. Some of these are linguistic challenges (the difficulty of learning a new language; the loss of the first language; attitudes towards accents, dialects, and standards). Some of these are cultural challenges (adapting to a new culture; clashing with parents or children over conforming to the new culture; dealing with marginalization and stereotyping). Issues also pertain to how language use and language learning interact with dimensions such as class, race, ethnicity, sexuality, and gender in mediating power relations within Canadian society. Although they arise rarely, I sometimes have to discuss students' stereotypical or problematic representations or interpretations — I want to make sure that cultural stereotypes are not perpetuated mindlessly. Students often relate to these scenes by making connections with their own experiences or the experiences of people that they know.

I find that a good way to end this drama work is to ask students to each write a journal entry in-role, reflecting on the issues that they worked with. The use of text in different genres — for example, story, play, poem, and novel — in the voices of newcomers and English Language Learners as a springboard for drama activities helps students move between fictional and actual experiences. Students experience multiple drama strategies or conventions, such as tableau, mime, interview, choral reading, role play, improvisation, and teacher in-role. The drama activities that students engage in provide a space for them to read, listen, speak, and write as well as to use different modes of meaning making, including visual, audio, linguistic, performative, and spatial.

Promoting Literacy in Visual Arts: Banners on a Social Justice Theme

by David Mills

Keith Haring was an American artist who became to some extent a pop culture icon during the 1980s. The style of his art was simple and almost cartoon like. In many cases, he created huge banners and murals. Most of these murals made statements about social justice issues that were important to Haring. These included gay rights, AIDS education, and the ending of apartheid in South Africa. He always tried to support people who were at the fringes of society.

How We Do the Unit

David Mills teaches Grades 6, 7, and 8 Visual Arts at Hawthorne Village Public School. He selects important social issues and has his students connect emotionally to them through art, creating artistic pieces that illustrate their values and beliefs.

I start the unit with dozens of art cards of artworks by Haring. Students are asked to look for similarities among the pieces in terms of subject matter and visual arts elements (e.g., line, color, shape). Then, we watch a video about Haring that clearly discusses his art style as well as his passions for social justice issues. From there we move into a discussion about current social justice issues. Support materials for this discussion come from various sources, including Human Rights Watch, Free the Children, and Amnesty International. Invariably, the students connect to and have some interest in at least one current social justice issue.

We then look at and critique various exemplars. (There are dozens of donations from previous students; when I first taught this unit, I made a very careful exemplar myself.) The discussion focuses on style, content, artistic merit, as well as the connection of the art piece to the accompanying poem. I also have examples of poems and poetry types on hand for students to read. At this point we also connect the discussion to the evaluation rubric for the project.

Students go on to create large banners in the style of Keith Haring, on a social justice theme of their choice. The finished banner is displayed together with the student-composed poem on the theme. Students are permitted to work individually or with a partner (partner banners are much larger).

Comments on Engagement

I find this unit particularly successful because the kids are so engaged. I feel there are several reasons for this engagement. Some of these reasons are as follows:
- building in choice — allowing students to select a social justice theme as well as building in the choice to work individually or in pairs
- having several exemplars and establishing clear expectations connected to the evaluation
- knowing my students well and developing positive rapport: this is key to the general success and engagement in the room; it also allows students to feel safe and sometimes choose social justice issues that may be rather uncomfortable for some, for example, the stresses of growing up gay.
- sharing the banners and poems, and having a "Gallery Walk" at the end: these activities provide positive reinforcement for students' efforts and further affirm the importance of connecting literacy to visual arts.

Dramatic Deliberation: Conflicting Perspectives, Lingering Feelings, and Influencing Reality

by Antonino Giambrone

Antonino Giambrone is the Equitable and Inclusive Schools Instructional Leader for the Toronto District School Board. Antonino is also a doctoral candidate at the Ontario Institute of Studies in Education, University of Toronto, researching the role that the arts, particularly drama, might play in social and environmental justice–based teaching approaches.

"We're still feeling this. I mean, the drama is over, and those feelings we had while we were in role are still around!"

Sebastian had been in role as a single mother obliged to go to a food bank regularly in order to provide enough food for herself and her daughter. He exclaims these words after he has, in that role, deliberated with members of the community, including municipal officials, school board representatives, and food-bank workers. He has pleaded with them to address the fact that his daughter arrives to school without breakfast more often than not.

Had 12-year-old Sebastian been completely in role, or was the way he played the role a reflection of who he was?

I believe that Sebastian was not just in the single mother's shoes. My hope is that he was experiencing what can be referred to as "active empathy" — empathy that might reflect his own capacity for agency, his ability to interpret and create, and to bring his own life, social context, and perceptions into the drama.

Sebastian and his Grade 7 classmates were experiencing a dramatic deliberation to explore the issue of hunger and poverty in Toronto. A *dramatic deliberation* is a way of bringing together improvised drama with deliberation techniques associated with conflict resolution. It can be used to engage any issue deemed relevant in elementary or secondary classrooms.

Interestingly, deliberation techniques have been used as an alternative to debates; they usually involve goals of consensus building with attempts to minimize confrontation and manage conflict. My aim is to engage students in conflict, through the channel of deliberation, in a way that allows them to confront various perspectives and one another in a dramatic space. Generally, the process involves a pre-deliberation activity, the deliberation itself, and a post-deliberation engagement.

The Pre-deliberation Activity

In this stage, students explore the context of an issue from a variety of sources, whether from a newspaper or a food bank report. For example, the perspectives inherent in those sources mingle with the perspectives of the students. Such context building frames a discussion of stakeholders involved in particular issues; it also sets the stage for students to develop position statements based on chosen or assigned roles.

Sebastian and his classmates engaged in research, including informal telephone interviews (e.g., with food-bank managers), email exchanges (e.g., with city counsellors and community activists), and published testimonials of individuals deemed stakeholders in a particular issue. They then wrote in-role position statements based on their research. Prepared position statements were rehearsed and then performed as a kind of monologue in preparation for engaging in the deliberation in-role. Performing this position statement is how the students would begin the dramatic deliberation.

The Deliberation

Students (assuming their roles) sit in a circle with the teacher or assigned facilitator as part of the circle. The teacher explains the following guidelines, while the students consider all steps in role.

Part 1
1. One person presents a position statement.
2. Others listen actively and take notes on the presentation. They also write down questions.
3. Once the presentation is finished, the listeners can ask the presenter three questions for clarification. The presenter is to respond in role.
4. The next person presents a position statement, and the process is repeated.

Part 2
1. Go around the circle once more. Each presenter comments on a peer's position with respect to her or his own, with the goal of reaching a common understanding.
2. The person whose position is commented upon may respond.
3. The next person comments on a different position. Repeat the process until everyone has had a chance to comment and respond.
4. This process should be repeated until a common understanding is achieved, or until time is up.

While the above guidelines seem like an attempt to predetermine outcomes and manage the multiple perspectives, the dramatic deliberation, beyond the initial position statement, is improvised and unpredictable. After the first round, for example, some students find it difficult to contain themselves in their aim to challenge and offer conflicting perspectives to the ones they hear. Emotions may run high, students may become emboldened and impassioned, and the complexity of various issues may come to light. Potential also exists in bringing to light the various power relationships in our society, and the raising of questions such as these: Who has voice? Are some voices listened to more than others? What happens when some voices say things that others do not wish to hear?

Sebastian was but one student who, both in role and out of role, began expressing indignation at injustice in ways that made those in the room listen — particularly as he realized that his in-role voice was less listened to than other voices. So, sometimes, Sebastian spoke out of turn. Nonetheless, the ways in which he articulated indignation towards his in-role situation, and the connection (or realization of a lack of connection) he and others who heard him made to the situation of his character, was something that might have potential to foster something beyond the classroom. Perhaps, these were the beginnings of what Augusto Boal might see as a desire to *influence* reality, not merely reflect it.

Post-deliberation Engagement

One goal of post-deliberation debriefing, out of role, is to engage in discussions around possible ways to influence the reality of the issues that arise from such dramatic deliberation around real-life issues. Those discussions usually involve this question: "So, now what?" Many times, they also involve making plans to do something about the issues at hand, to ask more questions, to challenge injustices.

Notions of power are explored in debriefing, both within the roles students take on and through their thinking about their personal power when confronted with the situations presented. Such explorations of power embedded in real-life (and often sensitive) issues might allow us to realize that, in many cases, even when we ask students to empathize and "see what it's like to be in someone else's shoes," the shoes either don't fit — or perhaps fit too well.

Sebastian and many of his classmates worked through these complexities as they engaged the question "So, now what?" They wondered what their responsibilities were when the shoes didn't fit — when students did not share experiences of particular injustices — or what they could do when the shoes did fit, when students knew all too well hunger and poverty, for example. They engaged these questions further by helping to plan school-wide foodshares (donations for food banks), by holding a community hunger banquet, and by participating in community service with organizations that address hunger and poverty issues. These are all attempts to influence reality.

A dramatic exploration of hunger in the local context of Toronto meets curriculum expectations in various subject areas and provides a springboard for various literacy opportunities; it also becomes the impetus for social action. But it is more. It is an exploration of the multiple identities and conflictual perspectives of the various individuals and groups involved in issues of hunger and poverty in a city. It is an exploration of how issues of class, gender, race, sexuality, and ability might come into play and intersect in the reality of hunger and poverty. It is also an exploration of how students' identities and experiences play a part in how they interpret, react to, wish to engage, and even do something about particular issues.

Discovering Their Voices:
Critical Literacy on the Web

by Lisa Hascal

Lisa Hascal teaches middle-years students at York Region's Westminster Public School, where she is also the literacy coach and librarian. She and her Grade 7 students completed an educational film for Ontario's Numeracy and Literacy Secretariat.

"When the subjects are interconnected, you use your school time wisely."
— *Student speaking in support of cross-curricular activities*

My Grades 7 and 8 students participated in Missing Voices, a unit which embraces a cross-curricular approach to teaching. My purpose in creating the unit was to investigate the missing voices in the historical events outlined in the curriculum for our history unit. I planned to cover British North America with the Grade 7 students and the development of Western Canada with the Grade 8 students. I also intended to extend this unit into Language Arts and Drama. Our curricular focuses were point of view, voice, and extending understanding; we would use recount writing as the vehicle for exploration and discovery.

To achieve my goal, I recognized that the preteens had to find the tasks engaging. History, in particular, had a reputation among the students in the Intermediate division for being "boring." My job was to make it relevant and authentic. I wanted the activities to allow the students to extend their thinking from the curriculum to their own lives, and then beyond their immediate circle in order to understand global events. Under the umbrella of a Big Idea — Missing Voices — I believed that a cross-curricular inquiry approach, incorporating writing, drama, and technology, would enable me to make the activities authentic and meaningful.

Wondering About the Voiceless

As our unit unfolded, the students identified several missing voices in their history texts. For each event we read about, I had the students identify all the "players," whether they were mentioned in the text or not. They recognized that had an event been recounted from another point of view, it could seem different. The author could use personal relevance as the gauge for including or excluding certain details. The students began to wonder how those who remained voiceless in our texts (Métis, First Nations, women, children, and minorities) would have recounted the same events. What would they want us to know? Would these missing details change the way we viewed how Canada was established?

To build on the students' curiosity, we added these questions to our inquiry and explored the possibilities through writing and drama. The students developed their own recounts from the point of view of one missing voice in history to share what they believed the historical character would want us to know. In role, they could begin to understand the raw emotions of the various groups of people. They experienced the same kinds of universal emotions, suddenly able to recognize their connections to the history curriculum — humanity.

Writing from the Perspective of a Historical Role

Excerpt from the Journal of Arthur Seferin, an American Soldier

Dear Journal,   *June 3, 1812*

The time had come to banish the British from North America forever. Our family, our loved ones, risked their lives fighting in the war of independence and those spoiled brats thought that they could boss us around like slaves! It has come time to show the British what we are made of! We shall show them our strength and we shall prove our independence once and for all. The British were being egotistical to the point where they thought it was acceptable to board our ships and carry off our men like savages! Those British thought that we would not take action, even after they have blocked our trading with Europe and hurt our economy. Well, I tell you they are mistaken! They think they are so much better than us, well, we will show them! We shall indeed defeat the British. I certainly believe that we have a greater lead on the British because we have the population and we can defeat their weak farmers easily! The British militia are off fighting Napoleon, so they won't have enough troops to spare. We should use this opportunity and claim our rights to this continent.

"Using something we're familiar with makes it enjoyable and we can be successful."
— *History student*

The students began to discover inequities and the power of voice, namely, that those who use their voices dictate the course of events. This revelation led them to look at their own lives. They wondered whether they had used their voices effectively or whether they had allowed others to speak for them. We chose to recount times in our lives when we could have used our voices differently, in order to improve the outcome of an event. Once again, we expanded our thinking through written recounts. Often, the students recounted times when they stood by and watched a friend get hurt or bullied. Through the writing process, they recognized that they had the power to change events for the better: all they had to do was use their voice. They claimed that while some people may seem "voiceless," we all have voice and must learn how to use it effectively.

Example of Student Recounts

Choking Fear

In the early morning glow I gradually awakened from my slumber and reflected on the year. As I prepared for the day I thought to myself,

"If you could ever define a picture perfect school year that year was well on its way." The year was almost half over and there was nothing I could have grumbled about. Through hard work I achieved a lot and settled myself very well that year. Like a dog with a bone I walked in utter content as I came to school. Sadly I was oblivious to my journey ahead that year.

Soon after just as any routine morning I had met up with my good friends George and Victor. Today though, my friends did not seem to be in their usual comical moods but in moods of burning rage. They were aggravated as Ian once again started goading George and Victor into fighting with him. Ian was a classmate of mine as well as George and Victor but we three never chose to hang out with him much. I was amused with the situation recited to me by my friends as if it was a cat and mouse cartoon. There was not one reason I could have seen that this was my predicament as well.

An hour of learning had passed and it was lunch, the time I gave my mind a rest from working; to just relax. My two good friends were in a deep discussion as they prepared for how they could get back at Ian. I had kept myself quiet so I would stay out of this dilemma. A little prank couldn't be something I should have worried about. I felt innocent, like a child and unaware of what end result would come.

In a moment's time I reached outside and the winter cold refreshed me as I braced it with layers of clothing. Sadly I felt a bit edgy, trying to hide what I knew would happen. It was all a flash when I saw George and Victor pelting snowballs at Ian. When I saw it was getting of hand I said in a weak little worried voice,

"Guys, quit it."

Not only was I feeling helpless, I felt like it was my time to make a change but I had done nothing at all. Ian left screaming away and I felt sick to my stomach with shame.

In a little less than an hour I had reached home. As today wasn't at all a normal day I called some of my friends to see what happened with them. To my shock I had learned that my friends would get serious penalties involving the team. Shame loomed over me because I couldn't stand that if only I used my voice Mrs. K would have a better opinion and there would never have been an issue in the first place! Now I have truly learned that you have to give your voice every chance you think you should and to always question how a situation will end because not only will you regret it, people will share the pain with you. It may not be easy but it was the right thing that should have been done.

If only . . .

By Dan

The students began to ask, "How can we help those with seemingly weaker voices gain theirs?" As their teacher, I took this as an opportunity to shift our inquiry once again. The students no longer needed to identify the missing voices or consider how point of view alters the way we view events. Now, they wondered, "How do we give voice to the voiceless?" We had established relevancy; we were now ready for authentic tasks.

Striving to Be Heard

Through a series of class discussions, we recognized that the Web is a powerful tool to give voice to the voiceless. At my prompting, the students posted personal recounts about a time they could have used their voice differently. They used Glogster, where they knew other preteens might find their writings. This website allows students to post their written pieces and it lets them manipulate the layout, imagery, and text to support the writing and strengthen the message.

This activity enabled me to further enhance the media literacy component of our unit. Students were required to think critically about how to make their voices heard on the Web. To explore the elements that cause preteens to read websites, we had to engage in website deconstruction. In order to be heard, we had to discover the most effective images and layout to grab audience attention.

The students hoped their recounts would be read by other preteens to help them understand the importance of using their own voice. They hoped that perhaps upon reading their Glogs, others would be wiser and use their voice differently in similar circumstances. Recently, a student of mine wondered whether any students across the world had read their recounts and whether doing so had changed their thinking. The students were beginning to recognize that they had a voice and could use it to educate others and help them to act responsibly.

Social Networking for Change

While we used the Web to share our stories, we also recognized that the Web, in general, greatly influences our thinking. The students told me that most of the information they are receiving today comes from the Web. Having explored how missing voices can alter the way we view the truth, the students realized that they have a responsibility to uncover *whose* story is being told on the Web. Throughout our unit, we recognized that if some groups of people were silenced in history, then likely some groups of people are silenced now. The students continued to wonder if they could use the Web as a tool to give voice to the voiceless.

At this point, I was offered a wonderfully authentic opportunity for my students to assess how the Web can do just that.

We gained the chance to review a pilot educational website on the rights and responsibilities of humans. The website editor requested our students to review the website and provide written feedback about the site. This task was engaging to the students because it was an authentic learning opportunity. One student said, "I can't believe a professional editor is actually going to take our voice into account!" For me as a teacher, I could use this opportunity to discover what my students had really learned about voice.

As a class, we developed criteria by which to assess the website's effectiveness. Through this process, we would discover why some websites have greater voice than others.

In order to develop these criteria, we initially identified the purpose of the website. It was clear to us that the goal of this website was to give voice to the voiceless and to cause preteen readers to make a difference in the world. The students agreed that the comics, navigational ease, short articles, and strong imagery were all effective in helping preteens understand a wide variety of global issues pertaining to the oppression of groups of people.

Recognizing the importance of voice, however, most students felt that the website should have allowed for more student interactivity. They believed that while becoming aware of the voiceless was important, being able to plan action to cause change was equally important. The website did not offer a place for students to respond to the articles in forums, where perhaps, they could create an action plan.

The students explained that most of them use forums regularly to voice their opinions. What amazed me was how they are so adept at utilizing social networking to initiate change. Of course, this led into a natural discussion about the recent revolutions in the Middle East which were sparked by social networking — the students could now relate to this.

After deconstructing the site thoroughly, the students were prepared to provide their feedback to the editor. First, we used a social networking site called Moodle, provided by our Board, to share our thoughts with our peers and seek descriptive feedback. Students posted their letters to the editor on the site, and their peers reviewed them immediately and suggested modifications. The editing process became transparent; not only could students read feedback from their peers, but they could also view the feedback of others simultaneously.

Perhaps the most powerful part of the unit occurred when we received a letter back from the editor of the website. The students were thrilled that their voices were acknowledged by a professional! One student marvelled: "Not only did she write back, but she addressed most of our individual letters. It means she actually read and considered each one. It made me feel 'Big.'"

What began as expectations from the curriculum had led into an in-depth inquiry about voice. Clearly, the investigation of their history unit allowed the students first to reflect on their own lives and now, the world today. The students understand that they are global citizens with a responsibility towards one another. They now wonder, if past Canadian leaders had engaged in the type of thinking they had, would Canada be different today? Would they have First Nations classmates? Would First Nations worldviews be part of our education?

During our first history class of the year, I had the students analyze the following statement by George Orwell:

Who controls the past controls the future;
who controls the present controls the past.

This unit allowed the students to see that their understanding and interpretation of the past ensures that the future truly is in their hands.

Appendix: Resources for Middle-Years Students

Poetry

A Nest Full of Stars: Poems
by James Berry
I Am Raven and
The Secret of Your Name
by David Bouchard
Long Powwow Nights
by David Bouchard and Pam Aleekuk
Joyful Noise: Poems for Two Voices
by Paul Fleischman
Technically, It's Not My Fault: Concrete Poems and *Blue Lipstick: Concrete Poems*
by John Grandits
Requiem: Poems of the Terezin Ghetto and *Worlds Afire*
by Paul Janeczko
Here in Harlem: Poems in Many Voices
by Walter Dean Myers
A Wreath for Emmett Till
by Marilyn Nelson

19 Varieties of Gazelle: Poems of the Middle East and *Words Under the Words: Selected Poems*
by Naomi Shihab Nye
Guyku: A Year of Haiku for Boys
by Bob Raczka
BookSpeak! Poems About Books
by Laura Salas
Mirror Mirror: A Book of Reversible Verse and *Footprints on the Roof*
by Marilyn Singer
Hoop Kings and *Hoop Queens*
by Charles R. Smith Jr.
Fearless Fernie: Hanging Out with Fernie & Me
by Gary Soto

Picture Books

Gleam and Glow
Riding the Tiger
Smoky Night and
Your Move
by Eve Bunting
Voices in the Park
by Anthony Browne
The Watertower
by Gary Crew (illus. Steven Woolma)
14 Cows for America
by Carmen Agra Deedy
Way Home
by Libby Hathorn (illus. Greg Rogers)
Goal!
by Mina Javaherbin
Rose Blanche
by Roberto Innocenti

At Gleason's Gym
by Ted Lewin
The Rabbits
by John Marsden (illus. Shaun Tan)
Schnorky the Wave Puncher
by Jeff Raglus
The Singing Hat
by Tohby Riddle
Grandfather's Journey
by Allen Say
The Wall: Growing Up Behind the Iron Curtain
by Peter Sis
The Arrival
by Shaun Tan
The Last Alchemist
by Colin Thompson

Faithful Elephants
by Yukio Tsuchiya
The Widow's Broom and
The Chronicles of Harris Burdick
by Chris Van Allsburg
Why War Is Never a Good Idea
by Alice Walker
Tuesday
by David Wiesner

Fox
by Margaret Wild (illus. Ron Brook)
The Librarian of Basra
by Jeanette Winter
Muhammad Ali: Champion of the World
by Jonah Winter

Novels

Chains, Forge, and *Ashes*
by Laurie Halse Anderson
Home of the Brave
by Katherine Applegate
Nothing but the Truth and
City of Orphans
by Avi
Trouble on the Voyage
by Bob Barton
Skeleton Creek
by Patrick Carman
The Hunger Games and
Catching Fire
by Suzanne Collins
Bloomability
by Sharon Creech
Tilt and *The Secret Life of Owen Skye*
by Alan Cumyn
Bucking the Sarge
by Christopher Paul Curtis
The Breadwinner and
Parvana's Journey
by Deborah Ellis
Bifocal
by Deborah Ellis and Eric Walters
The Skin I'm In
by Sharon G. Flake
Coraline and
The Graveyard Book
by Neil Gaiman
Missing 01 Found and
Always War
by Margaret Haddix

Raven's Gate (The Gatekeepers #1) and
Stormbreaker (Alex Ryder series)
by Anthony Horowitz
Dragon Seer's Gift
by Janet McNaughton
Slam!
by Walter Dean Myers
Midnight for Charlie Bone
by Jenny Nimmo
Big Mouth & Ugly Girl
by Joyce Carol Oates
Half Brother and
Silverwing
by Kenneth Oppel
The Whole Truth
by Kit Pearson
I'll Be Watching and
The Crazy Man
by Pamela Porter
Heroes of Olympus and
Percy Jackson
by Rick Riordan
Divergent
by Veronica Roth
Taking Sides
by Gary Soto
Maniac Magee
by Jerry Spinelli
Shattered We All Fall Down and
Branded
by Eric Walters

Novels as Poems

After the Death of Anna Gonzales
by Terri Fields
Jump Ball: A Basketball Season in Poems
by Mel Glenn

Bronx Masquerade
by Nikki Grimes
Things Left Unsaid: A Novel in Poems
by Stephanie Hemphill

Witness
by Karen Hesse
The Brimstone Journals
by Ronald Koertge
Ann and Seamus
by Kevin Major

Girl Coming in for a Landing
by April Halprin Wayland
Escaping Tornado Season: A Story in Poems
by Julie Williams

Novels of Global Issues

Zora and Me
by Victoria Bond and T. R. Simon
Stir It Up
by Ramin Ganeshram
Five Flavors of Dumb
by Antony John
A Million Shades of Gray
by Cynthia Kadohata
Thunder over Kandahar
by Sharon E. McKay
Akata Witch
by Nnedi Okorafor

A Long Walk to Water
by Linda Sue Park
Bamboo People
by Mitali Perkins
Heart of a Samurai
by Margi Preus
Ninth Ward
by Jewell Parker Rhodes
The Last Summer of the Death Warriors
by Francisco X. Stork
Lost Boy, Lost Girl
by Peter Straub

Graphic Novels

Tower of Treasure
by Scott Chantler
Artemis Fowl
by Eoin Colfer
Coraline: The Graphic Novel
by Neil Gaiman
Skeleton Key and
Stormbreaker
by Anthony Horowitz
Popularity Papers
by Amy Ignatow
The Stonekeeper (Amulet #1)
by Kazu Kibuishi
Excalibur: Legend of King Arthur
by Tony Lee

Zeus: King of the Gods
by George O'Connor
Daniel X: Alien Hunter
by James Patterson
Sidekicks
by Dan Santat
Smile
by Raina Telgemeier
Bad Island and
Ghostopolis
by Doug Tennapel
Percy Jackson and the Olympians: Lightning Thief
by Robert Venditti

Non-Fiction

I Shall Not Hate: A Gaza Doctor's Journey
by Izzeldin Abuelaish
A Gift of Days: The Greatest Words to Live By
by Stephen Alcorn
We Are All Born Free
by Amnesty International

The Hive Detectives: Chronicle of a Honey Bee Catastrophe
by Loree Griffin Burns (illus. Ellen Harasimowicz)
The Bat Scientists
by Mary Kay Carson (illus. Tom Uhlman)

Gaia Warriors
by Nicola Davies and James Lovelock
Dave the Potter: Artist, Poet, Slave
by Laban Carrick Hill (illus. Bryan Collier)
Three Cups of Tea
by Greg Mortenson and David Oliver Relin

Of Thee I Sing
by Barack Obama
Earth Matters
by David Rothschild
If the World Were a Village
by David J. Smith
Peaceful Heroes
by Jonah Winter (illus. Sean Addy)

Index